FORUM BOOKS

General Editor Martin E. Marty

Other Forum Books published by SCM Press

CONTEMPORARY RELIGIOUS THINKERS
From Idealist Metaphysicians to Existential Theologians
edited by John Macquarrie

ON BEING RESPONSIBLE
Issues in Personal Ethics
edited by James M. Gustafson and James T. Laney

SCIENCE AND RELIGION
New Perspectives on the Dialogue
edited by Ian G. Barbour

SOCIAL ETHICS
Issues in Ethics and Society
edited by Gibson Winter

THE THEOLOGIAN AT WORK
A Common Search for Understanding
edited by A. Roy Eckardt

ATTITUDES TOWARD OTHER RELIGIONS
Some Christian Interpretations
edited by Owen C. Thomas

PHENOMENOLOGY OF RELIGION
edited by Joseph D. Bettis

OLD TESTAMENT ISSUES
edited by Samuel Sandmel

NEW TESTAMENT ISSUES
edited by Richard Batey

PERSONALITY AND RELIGION
The Role of Religion in Personality Development
edited by William A. Sadler, Jr.

LITERATURE AND RELIGION
edited by Giles B. Gunn

Words about God

The Philosophy of Religion

edited by

Ian T. Ramsey

SCM PRESS LTD

LONDON

334 01383 6

First British edition 1971
published by SCM Press Ltd
56 Bloomsbury Street London WC1

Printed in Great Britain by
Billing & Sons Limited
Guildford and London

CONTENTS

IV. Recent Empiricism: its later Broadening

V. The Logical Character of Religious Language

FORUM BOOKS

The editors of this series recognize the need for books of a convenient size on religion and related topics. Laymen and clergymen, students, and the interested general reader can use *Forum Books* for personal study, or as a basis for group discussion. At a time when religious institutions are experiencing dramatic change, when religious ideas are being debated with new intensity, and when religious elements in culture are being called into question, the books in the series gather together examples of important writings which reproduce both historical and contemporary reflections on these subjects. Each editor has taken pains to provide helpful background comment as a context for the readings, but for the most part the selections speak for themselves with clarity and force.

MARTIN E. MARTY, *General Editor*
Divinity School
University of Chicago

The reader will notice that the authors represented in this volume sometimes vary in their spellings and systems of reference. This is because the extracts are taken from previously published works, and we have not attempted to impose a consistency which could conceivably be distasteful to an individual author or publisher.

EDITOR'S FOREWORD

I would like to acknowledge my great indebtedness to my Secretary and Chaplain at Auckland Castle, and to the Staff of the SCM Press for the assistance they have given me in the production of this book, which has not been without its vicissitudes.

The project had to survive a move from Oxford to Durham; to recover from what has proved to be the permanent loss of the original manuscript, and to endure the discovery that the original selection of extracts was far too long for the series. I only hope that, on reading this book, no one will feel bound to conclude that, for those with eyes to see, these vicissitudes meant that the book was never really intended to come to the light of day. On the other hand, it is perhaps too much to expect them to think of this book on a Pauline parallel as the outcome of a modern missionary journey not without its hazards in a territory where there is still much pioneering work to be done. However, if the book encourages others to pioneer I shall be well content.

IAN DUNELM:

PART ONE

EDITOR'S INTRODUCTION

THESE READINGS have not been collected together with a view to giving a general panorama of the philosophy of religion over a thousand years and more. For there are already a number of volumes which admirably fulfil that function. The purpose of this volume is rather to provide in a convenient way a collection of readings many of which are not always easily accessible, and all of which are of special interest to those concerned with problems arising around the language of theology and religious discourse generally.

While the recent interest in language goes back philosophically to the turn of the century, and in religious language for nearly twenty years, the problems have been with us for centuries and are in no wise new. From one point of view we may locate some of the earliest of them in the Hebrew disinclination – to express it no more strongly – ever to utter the divine name; other problems are implied in the doctrine of the *deus absconditus* ("Verily, thou art a God that hidest thyself" – Isa. 45.15) who is quite consistently spoken of as beyond good and evil (cf. also "I make peace and create evil" – Isa. 45.7). There is Augustine's well-known remark that when we speak of the Three Persons of the Trinity it is "not because the phrases are adequate – they are only an alternative to silence" (*non ut illud diceretur, sed ne taceretur*, Augustine, *de Trin.* v. 9). There are also the equally important but perhaps less well-known admissions of St Thomas Aquinas: "This is what is ultimate in the human knowledge of God: to know that we do not know God" (*Quaestiones Disputatae de Potentia Dei*, 7, 5 ad 14).

Included in the first group of extracts are some examples which are expressive of these classical attitudes to religious language, which exemplify historically the problem of how to speak meaningfully about God, and they illustrate how philosophers down the years have grappled with the problem of understanding the language which is used about God, especially its use of words more obviously appropriate to human beings, e.g. in discourse about God which talks in terms of wisdom, not to say wrath, let alone hand and voice. The first section concludes with a particular problem in this field, and it is a problem which has emerged again in recent controversy viz., whether, and how far, God can be spoken of as personal.

It is when we turn to the second group of extracts that we are reminded of the current interest in language which began in England at the turn of the century with the logical and empirical concerns of Bertrand Russell and G. E. Moore. I think it may be helpful to the reader if I now give a broad background survey of the development of empiricism over the last half-century and more. Set against such a background, the extracts which are to be found in the second and third sections of the book will be all the more significant. Along with his mathematical, scientific and logical interests, Russell brought a critical mind, accustomed to clarity and precision, to bear on traditional metaphysics, not least the absolute idealism of his day. Moore, too, though he had not the same kind of scientific background, shared in the same critical quest for clarity. They protested against what seemed to them extravagant language, but they did not take up an extreme position which rejected all metaphysics of every possible brand. Meanwhile, they were joined by Ludwig Wittgenstein, whose logical and philosophical interests had a background of science and engineering, and who once belonged to the Vienna Circle of empiricists of which Moritz Schlick and Rudolf Carnap were notable members. I have not included an extract from the Vienna Circle, but it is relevant to recall a distinction which Carnap introduced between the "material" and the "formal" mode. Suppose we have an assertion, like "Five is a number", which would be an assertion in the *material* mode. The verbal form of this assertion is parallel to "Helsinki is a city", and in this latter case we are obviously interested in what the noun describes, viz., the city of Helsinki, where it is and what it is like. Now by being cast in the *material* mode, the first assertion tempts us to ask similarly what sort of things numbers are, to look for things like numbers, and to suppose that somewhere they "subsist", though admittedly not near the Gulf of Bothnia. Now, says Carnap, and to put it no more strongly, let us avoid these misleading and bogus metaphysical questions by translating the original assertion into the *formal* mode: " 'Five' is a number word"[1] which brings us much closer to the concrete situation of enumeration. It may seem a far cry from this to theology, but as I suggest in an extract later in the book,[2] a good deal of the doctrinal controversy of the early church might have been avoided had the Christological problem, for example, been seen to be one of how to use language reliably about Jesus Christ, rather than supposed to be a problem of anthropology or psychology or ontology which asked how two "natures" could be combined into something which, while being completely both, yet was a single homogeneous unity. To phrase the problem in this way is virtually to preclude any intelligible solution.

But to mention the Vienna Circle is to be reminded of an empiricism far more stereotyped and monolithic than Russell, and especially Moore, ever contemplated. This more rigid viewpoint is associated with those empiricists called "logical positivists" who in their Verification Principle expressed an inflexible criterion for meaningful language. The view was first popularized in England some thirty-five years ago,[3] by A. J. Ayer in his *Language, Truth and Logic*. These logical positivists believed that there were only two brands of reliable assertion. First there were those assertions which occurred in logic and pure mathematics. These were merely verbal and said nothing; the only question to raise about them was whether they conformed to certain agreed conventions concerning symbols, transformation rules and so on. Those assertions in logic and pure mathematics aside, all meaningful assertions conformed to the so-called Verification Principle – they were, in other words, such that they could be verified, at least in principle, by sense-experience – "at least in principle" because in a pre-rocket age there seemed to be no chance of anyone ever seeing the other side of the moon, while nevertheless (it was claimed) meaningful assertions could be made about it. Whatever other assertions there might seem to be were considered to be meaningless, and styled as nonsense – a word which was attractively ambiguous, since it could either be technical and inoffensive, when "non-sense" was taken to be "not verifiable by sense-experience" and so used by the philosopher in his cool hour; or it could be popular and perjorative when taken to be synonym for rubbish and trash – and so used by the philosopher who had warmed up in debate. Here then was a logical positivism flourishing a rigid prescription for a clear, precise, unambiguous, significant language – and proclaiming a veto on all deviationists – and that meant a veto on most of ethics, almost all metaphysics and certainly all theology – for in various ways their assertions claimed to go beyond sense experience.

It is at this point that mention must be made again of Wittgenstein who, at this period when the word "nonsense" was so often in the air, insisted on a distinction between "useless" and "useful" nonsense, and pointed the way forward to a much more sensitive and open empiricism. The Verification Principle itself was admittedly nonsense – it was neither an assertion in logic nor something verifiable by sense-experience. It was a rule for meaning which could not apply to itself. So it was nonsense – but useful nonsense. In this way, we see Wittgenstein refusing to be bound within the narrow confines of the Verification Principle and so becoming the father of all those who now deprecate any narrow, restricted view of meaningful language, though at the first, like Russell, he had sponsored "atomic facts" of the sense-data variety.

This wider thinking characteristic of Wittgenstein, can be illustrated from some earlier pages in the *Philosophical Investigations* where he shows himself conscious of the limitations of the earlier view. He quotes from Augustine:

> When they (my elders) named some object, and accordingly moved towards something, I saw this and I grasped that the thing was called by the sound they uttered when they meant to point it out. Their intention was shewn by their bodily movements, as it were the natural language of all peoples: the expression of the face, the play of the eyes, the movement of other parts of the body, the tone of the voice which expresses our state of mind in seeking, having, rejecting, or avoiding something. Thus, as I heard the words repeatedly used in their proper places in various sentences, I gradually learnt to understand what objects they signified; and after I had trained my mouth to form these signs, I used them to express my own desires.[4]

Here, as Wittgenstein recognizes, is one particular view of human language, the view that "the individual words in language name objects – sentences are combinations of such names". He continues:

> In this picture of language we find the roots of the following idea: Every word has a meaning. This meaning is correlated with the word. It is the object for which the word stands. Augustine does not speak of there being any difference between kinds of word. If you describe the learning of language in this way you are, I believe, thinking primarily of nouns like "table", "chair", "bread", and of people's names, and only secondarily of the names of certain actions and

properties; and of the remaining kinds of word as something that will take care of itself.[5]

We could hardly have a more succinct account and appraisal of Russell's object language, that "primitive", protocol language where words name sense-data, the view indeed which Wittgenstein himself sponsored in the *Tractatus*. But now there is no suggestion that this is the only, still less the only reliable, view of language. On the contrary, he remarks later:

> Augustine, we might say, does describe a system of communication; only not everything that we call language is this system. And one has to say this in many cases where the question arises, "Is this an appropriate description or not?" The answer is: "Yes, it is appropriate, but only for this narrowly circumscribed region, not for the whole of what we were claiming to describe."
>
> It is as if someone were to say: "A game consists in moving objects about on a surface according to certain rules..." – and we replied: You seem to be thinking of board games, but there are others. You can make your definition correct by expressly restricting it to those games.[6]

The concept of a multiplicity of language-games implied in that quotation is characteristic of the later Wittgenstein and the broader view. Each language-game, he says, is a "whole, consisting of language, and the actions into which it is woven".[7] This multiple interweaving of words and action is also implied in Wittgenstein's illuminating comparison between words and tools:

> Think of the tools in a tool-box: there is a hammer, pliers, a saw, a screw-driver, a rule, a glue-pot, glue, nails and screws. The functions of words are as diverse as the functions of these objects (and in both cases there are similarities).[8]

Here again we are pointed to the variegation and diversity which language displays. Indeed, the transition in Wittgenstein between the *Tractatus Logico-Philosophicus* of 1922 and the *Philosophical Investigations*, whose translation first appeared in 1953, is a clue to the broadening which came to British empiricism in the post-war years, a broadening and a mellowing which can be discerned in all the varied strands of contemporary empiricism, and which the extracts in section four of this book illustrate.

I think we can see in the later Wittgenstein two features by reference to which these varied strands of later empiricism can be placed in a clearer perspective.

Firstly, and obviously, there is an interest in language – words, sentences, discourse. But there is also, as we have seen, a sense of its variegation and richness. With this goes a caution and circumspection in approaching every assertion, whether it is at first sight puzzling, or whether it seems only too clear. In particular, we must make sure we have not misread or misconstrued assertions, or wrongly assimilated one way of talking to another. So there arises on this view a suspicion of all reductionisms which tell us that "X is *really only* Y", e.g. "Tables are *really only* electrons", or "Physical objects are *really only* sense-data"; "Men are *really only* machines" or "Human beings are *really only* electronic computers". Such reductionisms are self-condemned, for they make use of the very distinctions they deny. Thus there arises a sense of the rich variety of language, a refusal to be bound by restrictive rules, and a generous view of what is taken to be reliable reasoning, a view which does not restrict it to the deductive inference of pure mathematics. For instance, says Wittgenstein, "the symbolism of chemistry and the notation of the infinitesimal calculus are, so to speak, suburbs of our language" which is no uniform stereotype, no ribbon development along the highway of human experience. Rather, says Wittgenstein, "Our language can be seen as an ancient city: a maze of little streets and squares, of old and new houses, and of houses with additions from various periods; and this surrounded by a multitude of new boroughs with straight regular streets and uniform houses."[9]

Language is a rich variegation – there are, he says, "*countless* kinds" (italics original) of sentences and language is constantly changing its variegated pattern. As he remarks:

> . . . this multiplicity is not something fixed, given once for all; but new types of language, new language-games, as we may say, come into existence, and others become obsolete and get forgotten. (We can get a *rough picture* of this from the changes in mathematics.)
>
> Here the term "language-*game*" is meant to bring into prominence the fact that the *speaking* of language is part of an activity, or of a form of life.
>
> Review the multiplicity of language-games in the following examples, and in others:
>
> Giving orders, and obeying them
> Describing the appearance of an object, or giving its measurements
> Constructing an object from a description (a drawing)
> Reporting an event
> Speculating about an event
> Forming and testing a hypothesis
> Presenting the results of an experiment in tables and diagrams
> Making up a story; and reading it
> Play-acting
> Singing catches

Guessing riddles
Making a joke; telling it
Solving a problem in practical arithmetic
Translating from one language into another
Asking, thanking, cursing, greeting, praying.

It is interesting to compare the multiplicity of the tools in language and of the ways they are used, the multiplicity of kinds of word and sentence, with what logicians have said about the structure of language.[10]

and then in a frank self-criticism he adds, in parenthesis, "including the author of the *Tractatus Logico-Philosophicus*".

Nor in this multiplicity of language-games must we look for the "essence" of language, as though there is some basic framework called "language", a supposedly "pure" or "real" or "essential" language which can be distilled from them all. Once again it is the variegation and richness of language to which Wittgenstein would call our attention, and so he tries to stop, once and for all, cravings for a stereotype that would think of it as somehow or other lying in all its purity below the level of the variety. It is in this context that he develops the illustration of games:

Consider for example the proceedings that we call "games". I mean board-games, card-games, ball-games, Olympic games, and so on. What is common to them all? – Don't say: "There *must* be something common, or they would not be called 'games' " – but *look* and *see* whether there is anything common to all. For if you look at them you will not see something that is common to *all*, but similarities, relationships, and a whole series of them at that. To repeat: don't think, but look! Look for example at board-games, with their multifarious relationships. Now pass to card-games; here you find many correspondences with the first group, but many common features drop out, and others appear. When we pass next to ball-games, much that is common is retained, but much is lost. – Are they all "amusing"? Compare chess with noughts and crosses. Or is there always winning and losing, or competition between players? Think of patience. In ball games there is winning and losing; but when a child throws his ball at the wall and catches it again, this feature has disappeared. Look at the parts played by skill and luck; and at the difference between skill in chess and skill in tennis. Think now of games like ring-a-ring-a-roses; here is the element of amusement, but how many other characteristic features have disappeared! And we can go through the many, many other groups of games in the same way; can see how similarities crop up and disappear.

And the result of this examination is: we see a complicated network of similarities overlapping and criss-crossing: sometimes overall similarities, sometimes similarities of detail.[11]

He speaks of languages being characterized by "family resemblances" rather than by some "essence" common to them all:

I can think of no better expression to characterize these similarities than "family resemblances"; for the various resemblances between members of a family: build, features, colour of eyes, gait, temperament, etc. etc. overlap and criss-cross in the same way. - And I shall say: "games" form a family.[12]

These various quotations and examples, all of which show Wittgenstein pointing to the variegation and richness which language displays, a feature of language well recognized by later empiricism, can be high-lighted by the well-known slogan: "Every assertion has its own logic", a slogan reminding us to treat every assertion with due logical caution, to eschew all restrictive vetos on meanings, and not to be over-confident about understanding or dismissing any assertion. It is in this tradition that I would set Russell's earlier distinction between *logical form* and *verbal form*, as well as his notion of *logical completeness*, for both help us to have a much better insight into the logic of our assertions. Let me give an example in each case. As an instance of the first distinction, it would be said that the sentences "Lions are real" and "Lions are yellow" conceal, because of their similar *verbal form*, the logical difference between "existential" and "characterizing" assertions. The *verbal form* is misleading as a guide to the *logical form*, as a guide to how the sentence is to be logically construed. To illustrate Russell's notion of logical completeness, let us consider "God is loving" which may seem *prima facie* to be a "complete" and clear assertion. So, in certain circumstances, may "Newcastle is north". But the theist would rightly point out that since "God" is not a proper name in the sense that "Jill" or "John" are proper names (and there is of course in principle no problem of meaning about "Jill (or John) is loving"), the assertion about God needs some qualifier to make it logically "complete" so that, as examples of complete, and therefore more reliable, assertions, we might give: "God is infinitely loving" or "God is perfectly loving" where "infinitely" and "perfectly" are qualifiers. Similarly, to say "Newcastle is north of London" is to speak more reliably than just to say "Newcastle is north".

More generally, contemporary empiricism encourages a broader approach to logic. No longer do we think of Aristotelian logic, and the syllogism in particular, as giving the pattern of all reliable argument; we recognize that reliable argument may take on many different patterns as to whether, for instance, the discourse is mathematical, scientific, historical, legal, poetical and so on.

It may be worthwhile remarking explicitly at this point that to speak of the "logic" of an assertion is to talk of the kind of argument or discourse in which it may be found – whether, for instance, it occurs in poetry, in a legal judgment, in a scientific investigation, in a company report, in a political speech or in a prayer. Alternatively, we may say that it is a compact way of referring to the distinctive kinds of reason which might be given for it; the distinctive kinds of evidence which might be given in support of it.

The second feature by reference to which more recent empiricism can be better understood, and of which the later Wittgenstein again reminds us, is an emphasis on context and use. This is a feature of language which is highlighted by Wittgenstein's concept of language-games and of words as tools, to which we have already made reference above. But it is also implied in what Wittgenstein says about "understanding" a sentence – "much more akin to understanding a theme of music than one may think":

> I mean that understanding a linguistic phrase lies nearer than one thinks to what is ordinarily called understanding a musical theme. Why is just *this* the pattern of variation in loudness and tempo? One would like to say "Because I know what it's all about". But what is it all about? I should not be able to say. In order to "explain" I could only compare it with something else which has the same rhythm (I mean the same pattern). (One says "Don't you see, this is as if a conclusion were being drawn" or "This is as it were a parenthesis", etc. How does one justify such comparisons? – There are very different kinds of justification here.)[13]

I believe that Wittgenstein's well-known duck-rabbit example and less well-known box example point in the same direction, suggesting that understanding a sentence involves much more than the understanding of a string of words:

> You could imagine the illustration

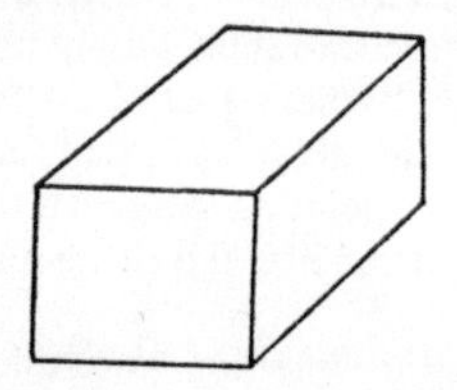

> appearing in several places in a book, a text-book for instance. In the relevant text something different is in question every time: here a glass cube, there an inverted open box, there a wire frame of that shape, there three boards forming a solid angle. Each time the text supplies the interpretation of the illustration.
>
> But we can also *see* the illustration now as one thing now as another. – So we interpret it, and *see* it as we *interpret* it.

Here perhaps we should like to reply: The description of what is got immediately, i.e. of the visual experience, by means of an interpretation – is an indirect description. "I see the figure as a box" means: I have a particular visual experience which I have found that I always have when I interpret the figure as a box or when I look at a box. But if it meant this I ought to know it. I ought to be able to refer to the experience directly, and not only indirectly. (As I can speak of red without calling it the colour of blood.)

I shall call the following figure, derived from Jastrow, the duck-rabbit. It can be seen as a rabbit's head or as a duck's.

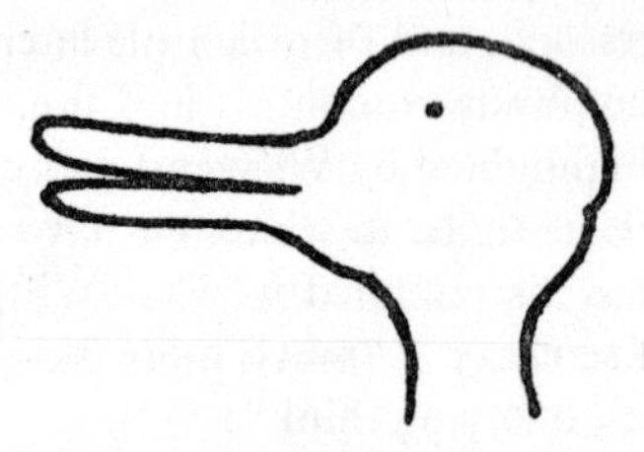

And I must distinguish between the "continuous seeing" of an aspect and the "dawning" of an aspect.

The picture might have been shewn me, and I never have seen anything but a rabbit in it.

Here it is useful to introduce the idea of a picture-object. For instance

would be a "picture-face".

In some respects I stand towards it as I do towards a human face. I can study its expression, can react to it as to the expression of the human face. A child can talk to picture-men or picture-animals, can treat them as it treats dolls.

I may, then, have seen the duck-rabbit simply as a picture-rabbit from the first. That is to say, if asked "What's that?" or "What do you see here?" I should have replied: "A picture-rabbit". If I had further been asked what that was, I should have explained by pointing to all sorts of pictures of rabbits, should perhaps have pointed to real rabbits, talked about their habits, or given an imitation of them.

I should not have answered the question "What do you see here?" by saying: "Now I am seeing it as a picture-rabbit". I should simply have described my perception: just as if I had said "I see a red circle over there." –

Nevertheless someone else could have said of me: "He is seeing the figure as a picture-rabbit."

It would have made as little sense for me to say "Now I am seeing it as . . ." as to say at the sight of a knife and fork "Now I am seeing this as a knife and fork." This expression would not be understood. – Any more than: "Now it's a fork" or "It can be a fork too."

One doesn't "*take*" what one knows as the cutlery at a meal *for* cutlery; any more than one ordinarily tries to move one's mouth as one eats, or aims at moving it.[14]

We use our words significantly and naturally only in a particular context, and then we do it just as naturally as we move the mouth when eating, or use cutlery at a meal. It is the context in which words are used, which in all its richness and complexity gives to those words all that is involved in "understanding" them, and part of this is what Wittgenstein calls later – "the flashing of an aspect on us" which "seems half visual experience, half thought".[15] Here are suggestions which may recall for the reader the epistemological place I give to "disclosure", claiming that the understanding, e.g. of many assertions in morality or religion depends on their having a disclosure basis. Be that as it may, the later Wittgenstein certainly leads us away from the segregated, clear cut, unambiguous picture-meanings supposed to hover behind every word or sentence like ghostly pictures, to contextual settings – and for Wittgenstein this meant not only the verbal context, the wider discourse, but the whole context, the concrete circumstances, to which the utterance would be appropriate. This was the point of Wittgenstein's own slogan: "Don't look for meanings, look for use."

It is in this context – where language is related closely to its use, that we may set J. L. Austin who was concerned to show how philosophers, and even some of the most empirically minded like A. J. Ayer, had overlooked diversities in language, had obliterated important distinctions which language, as used, enshrines, had ignored how language actually works. But for our present purpose there is another point to make. With great analytical skill and insight, and rich imagination, Austin introduced us in particular, as the relevant extracts in section three will show to one feature of language which had been hitherto unnoticed, viz., that *some* assertions are peculiar in having performative force, or what he called later "illocutionary force". In *saying some* sentences we *do* something more than saying the words. As examples, we may take such assertions as "I appoint you as Secretary of State for Foreign Affairs", or "I pronounce that they be man and wife together". Now with insights like this, which in their own way point to the significance of some first person assertions, and which highlight self-involvement, Austin cannot fairly be accused of mere verbalism; though this meticulous concern with language has led to many cries of pedantry, and perhaps of all Oxford philosophers he has seemed to the outside world the most linguistic.

From another direction J. L. Austin can be seen, I believe, as pointing us towards that element of commitment and involvement in which recent epistomology, not least in R. M. Hare's stress on the evaluative, prescriptive character of the language of morals, has shown an increasing interest. This is Austin's notion of assertions as "speech-acts", activities on our part whose focal point is the utterance of words, rather than (say) the use of a paint brush, violin bow, or football. Commitment may be of course at a minimum with some "descriptive" scientific assertions such as "Water boils at 100°C under normal pressure", and at a maximum with a religious utterance like that of St Thomas, "My Lord and my God". But probably every assertion has some degree of descriptive force, and some self-involvement. In other words, it incorporates both some descriptive ingredients and some degree of commitment. In this way we begin to see possibilities of understanding better not only the distinctive character of religious assertions, but also their kinship with other segments of our discourse.

The third and fourth sections of the book give extracts illustrative respectively of those earlier and later developments in empiricism in Great Britain, developments which, as I have hinted already, have, I believe, an important bearing on our better understanding of religious discourse. The last group of extracts then gives more explicitly specimens of the kind of discussion, argument and conclusions that emerge when these empirical insights are used in the understanding of an appraisal of theological assertions, in the clarification of theological puzzles, and in the elucidation of religious discourse. Broadly speaking, the dominant themes and suggestions which arise when empirical insights are brought to bear in this way on religious discourse are these:

1. The need to relate religious discourse to some concrete situation called variously a "vision", "a sense of mystery", a "disclosure".

2. The need to make clear the logic of religious assertions, which may be misleading to believer and unbeliever alike.

3. The need to make clear, if genuine belief in God is being claimed, that the commitment involved must be more than the taking up of

an attitude to the world. It must arise as a response, in a situation where we are aware of an objective referent. Belief in God thus occurs as one way of styling and being articulate about what we are then encountering.

It is hoped that these extracts taken from a panorama of wide historical range, and exhibiting many insights into the language of religion, may help the reader to develop his own empirical approach to religious themes, and to the language and problems of the Christian faith in particular. In that way he will be continuing in his own day, but with some new tools, specific work on one of the frontiers of faith and philosophy, which has a distinguished historical tradition behind it. He will be encouraged in this work by remembering that without such "under-labouring" (as Locke called it) – albeit critical, careful, sensitive, knowledgeable – doctrine may become the basest superstition, faith but a synonym for irrationality, and worship supposed to be nothing more than the satisfying of the emotions of the conventional and credulous. It is such considerations as these that give this book and its extracts a significance not only for the philosopher of religion, but for the pastor; and some of us try to be both.

NOTES

1. Logical Syntax of Language, Routledge & Kegan Paul 1937, p. 238.
2. See pp. 218–22.
3. In the next few paragraphs I incorporate, with the permission of the editor, material from an article I wrote in *Religious Studies* Vol. I, No. I, October 1965, pp. 47–61, entitled, *Contemporary Philosophy and the Christian Faith.*
4. Ludwig Wittgenstein, *Philosophical Investigations*, trs. G. E. Anscombe, Blackwells 1953, Pt I, p. 2e 1.
5. *Ibid.*, p. 2e 1
6. *Ibid.*, p. 3e 3.
7. *Ibid.*, p. 5e 7.
8. *Ibid.*, p. 6e 11
9. *Ibid.*, p. 8e 18.
10. *Ibid.*, pp. 11e–12e 23.
11. *Ibid.*, pp. 31e–32e 66.
12. *Ibid.*, pp. 32e 67.
13. *Ibid.*, p. 143e 527.
14. *Philosophical Investigations*, Pt II xi, pp. 193e, 194e, 195e.
15. *Ibid.*, p. 197e.

PART TWO: THE LANGUAGE OF RELIGIOUS BELIEF: SOME CLASSICAL DISCUSSIONS

I

EARLY CHRISTIAN FATHERS

Theological Reticence. *In his book* The Doctrine of the Trinity, *J. R. Illingworth gives examples from the Fathers to illustrate their caution in speaking of God. The inadequacy of human language points to the religious awe and reverence from which it arises, and to which it constantly points us back. Words are "helpful to man, rather than descriptive of God". They suggest rather than exhaust their topic. But unless we would keep silence, we must use them with all their limitations. We know God "not what he is, but what he is not". For some philosophers, this made "the things which have been divinely revealed to us" all the more significant. At the same time, we must not suppose that what is revealed to us is free from the limitations there must always be on our talking of God.*

CLEMENT OF ALEXANDRIA quotes with approval the saying of Plato: "It is a difficult task to discover the Father and Maker of this universe; and when we have found Him, it is impossible to declare Him to all; since expression, such as we use in other instruction, is here impossible." He then himself continues, "No one can rightly express Him wholly. For on account of His greatness He is ranked as the All, and is the Father of the Universe. Nor are any parts to be predicated of Him. For the One is indivisible – without form and

Reprinted from J. R. Illingworth, *The Doctrine of the Trinity*, Macmillan & Co. 1907, pp. 102–110.

name. And if we name it, we do not do so properly, terming it either the One, or the Good, or Mind, or Absolute Being, or Father, or God, or Creator, or Lord. We speak not as supplying His name; but for want we use good names, in order that the mind may have these as points of support. . . . It remains then that we understand the Unknown by divine grace, and by the word alone that proceeds from Him." While, even in union with Christ, "we only reach in a measure to the conception of God, knowing not what He is, but what He is not."[1]

To the same effect Origen writes: "According to strict truth God is incomprehensible and inestimable. . . . For among all intelligent, that is incorporeal beings, what is so superior to all others – so unspeakably and incalculably superior – as God, whose nature cannot be grasped or seen by the power of any human understanding, even the purest and brightest?"[2]

And again, commenting on the above passage from Plato:

"For ourselves, we maintain that human nature is in no way able to seek after God, or to attain a clear knowledge of Him, without the help of Him whom it seeks. He makes Himself known to those who after doing all that their powers will allow, confess that they need help from Him, who discovers Himself to those whom He approves, in so far as it is possible for man and the soul still dwelling in the body to know God."[3]

Such is the language of the two first great philosophical theologians of the Church; and it is echoed a century later by Athanasius, who is popularly credited rather with confidence than diffidence of thought: "God, Maker of all and King of all, that has His being beyond our substance and human discovery . . . made through His own Word . . . the human race after His own image."[4]

"For God . . . since He is by nature invisible and incomprehensible, having His being beyond all created existence, . . . by His own Word gave the universe the order that it has, in order that since He is by nature invisible, men might be able to know Him at any rate by His works."[5]

"God . . . when He was making the race of man through His own Word, seeing the weakness of their nature, that it was not sufficient of itself to know its Maker, nor to attain to any idea at all of God, . . . gives them a share in His own image, . . . and makes them after His own image, and after His likeness; so that perceiving the image that is the Word of the Father they may be able through Him to attain to an idea of the Father."[6]

"Although it be impossible to comprehend what God is, yet it is possible to say what He is not."[7]

He is followed, again, by the great Cappadocian group – Basil and the two Gregories, – who all speak to the same effect.

"That God is, I know," says Basil; "but what His essence is, I hold to be above reason, . . . faith is competent to know that God is, not what He is."[8] "With regard to the Creator of the world," says Gregory of Nyssa, "we know that He is, but deny not that we are ignorant of the definition of His essence."[9]

And again, Gregory Nazianzen: "A theologian among the Greeks has said in his philosophy that to conceive God is difficult, to express Him is impossible. . . . But I say that it is impossible to express Him, and more impossible to conceive Him."[10]

And if we turn from the Greek to the Latin fathers, we find similar language used; notably by Hilary of Poictiers, and Augustine, who both wrote special treatises upon the Trinity.

Hilary writes: "There can be no comparison between God and earthly things. . . . We must, therefore, regard any comparison as helpful to man rather than as descriptive of God, since it suggests rather than exhausts the sense we seek. . . . Neither the speech of man, nor the analogy of human nature can give us a full insight into the things of God. The ineffable cannot submit to the bounds and limitations of definition. . . . God is a simple Being: we must understand Him by devotion, and confess Him by reverence. He is to be worshipped, not pursued by our senses, for a conditioned and weak nature cannot grasp with the guesses of its imagination the mystery of an infinite and omnipotent nature. . . . What presumption to suppose that words can adequately describe His nature, when thought is often too deep for words, and His nature transcends even the conception of thought."[11]

The same thought continually recurs in Augustine; who repeatedly speaks of the inadequacy of human language. "God must not," he says, "even be described as unspeakable (*inaffabilis*), since by the very use of this term, something is spoken. . . . Yet God, since nothing can be worthily spoken of Him, accepts the service of the human voice, and wills us to rejoice in praising Him with words of our own".[12]

And again: "Our thoughts of God are truer than our words, and

His existence is truer than our thoughts." (*Veritas cogitatur Deus, quam dicitur, et verius est quam cogitatur.*)[13]

And again: "We say three persons, not as being satisfied with this expression, but because we must use some expression." (*Non ut illud diceretur, sed ne taceretur.*)[14]

And again: "God is erroneously called substance, as a familiar synonym for essence, which is the truer and more proper term to use."[15]

These quotations are all, it will be seen, from leading thinkers of their day; and they might be multiplied indefinitely from others of less note. But we will merely conclude them with a reference to John of Damascus, who, at the end of the patristic age gave a general summary of what was commonly held to be the orthodox belief of the Church. He writes as follows: "Neither do we know, nor can we tell what the essence of God is. . . . It is not, therefore, within our capacity to say anything about God, or even to think of Him, beyond the things which have been divinely revealed to us. It is plain that there is a God. But what He is in His essence and nature is absolutely incomprehensible and unknowable."[16]

Now the view thus described is not analogous to the modern agnostic position, as some of the language in which it is expressed might seem at first sight to imply. For the fathers attach the fullest value to the various arguments of natural theology for God's existence, and for our ability to know something of His character from the beauty and harmony and purpose in the world; while Augustine, in especial, elaborates the ontological argument in various ways. But, further, and this is still more important, they were all profoundly religious men. Their religion was their life. They lived in the full conviction of their personal dependence upon God, and of their need for conscious communion with Him. And the same Augustine who says that God cannot even be named, says also: "Thou hast made us, O God, for Thyself, and our souls are restless till they rest in Thee."

The language, therefore, that we have been quoting, is not that of intellectual agnosticism, but of religious awe – awe intensified not by the thought of God's remoteness, but by the conviction and experience of His intimate nearness to men. It is thus much more akin to the reverential abstinence from the use of God's name, which characterised later Judaism, than to any sympathy with the Neo-Platonic exaggeration of His transcendence – His aloofness from the world.

NOTES

1. Clem. Alex. *Strom.* v.12; v.11.
2. Orig. *De Prin.* 1.
3. Orig. *Contr. Cel.* vii.42.
4. Athan. *Contr. Gent.* 2.
5. Athan. *Contr. Gent.* 2.35.
6. *De Incar.* 11.
7. *Ep. ad Monachos*, i.2.
8. Basil *Adv. Eun.* i.12.
9. Greg. Nys. *Adv. Eun. orat.* 12.
10. Greg. Naz. *Orat.* 34.
11. Hil. *De Trin.* i.19; iv.2; ix.72; xi.44.
12. Aug. *De Doct. Christ.* i.6.
13. Id. *De Trin.* vii.7.
14. Aug. *De Trin.* v.9.
15. *Ibid.* vii.10.
16. John Damas. *De F. O.* i.2, 4.

2

PLOTINUS

Here, in Plotinus, who was a neo-Platonist and a mystic, is one of the classical examples of "negative" theology, though experts differ as to how far his outlook which is prima facie *pantheistic can bear a theistic interpretation. For Plotinus ideas of the inadequacy of religious language matched the mystical contemplation which for him was the highest human activity and in which all else was transcended. Indirectly, he had considerable influence on Christian thought, and through Augustine and Dionysius the Pseudo-Areopagite influenced the theologians and mystics of the Middle Ages.*

VI 8.13

But if we must introduce these names for what we are seeking, though it is not accurate to do so, let us say again that, speaking accurately, we must not admit even a logical duality in the One but we are using this present language in order to persuade our opponents, though it involves some deviation from accurate thought. . . . We must be forgiven for the terms we use, if in speaking about Him in order to explain what we mean, we have to use language which we, in strict accuracy, do not admit to be applicable. *As if* must be understood with every term.

VI 9.6

What then do we mean by "One", and how do we fit this Unity into our thought? "One" is used in more senses than that of the unity of a numerical unit or a point: in this sense the soul, taking away magnitude and numerical plurality, arrives at the smallest possible and rests on something which is certainly without parts, but belongs to the divisble and exists in something else. But the One is not in something else or in the divisible, nor is It without parts in the sense of the smallest possible. For It is the greatest of all things, not in size but in power – that which is without magnitude can be great in power, for the things which come after It are indivisible and without parts in their powers, not in their bulk. It must be considered as infinite, not by unlimited extension of size or number but by the unboundedness of Its power.

When you think of Him as Mind or God, He is still more: and when you unify Him in your thought, the degree of unity by which He transcends your thought is still greater than you imagine it to be. For He exists in and by Himself without any attributes. One might conceive of His unity in terms of His self-sufficiency. For He must be the most sufficient of all things, the most independent, and the most without wants. Everything which is multiple and not one is defective, since it is composed of many parts. Substance needs Him in order to be one: but He does not need Himself; for He is Himself. A thing which is multiple needs its full number of parts and each of its parts, since it exists with the others and not independently, is in need of the others; so a thing of this kind shows itself defective as a whole and in each individual part. If then, as is in fact true, there must be something supremely self-sufficing, it must be the One, Which is the only Thing of such a kind as not to be defective either in relation to Itself or to anything else.

It seeks nothing towards Its being or Its well-being or Its establishment in Its place. It does not derive Its being from others, for It is the Cause of the others; and what from outside Itself could conduce to Its well-being? To be in a good state is not something accidental to It, for It is the Good. And It has no place: It needs no establishing as if It could not support Itself; that which has to be established is a lifeless mass which falls till it is set in place. All other things are established through It. Through It they at once exist and receive the place ordained for each. That which seeks place is defective. But a principle has no need of what comes after it; and the Principle of all things needs none of them; for that which is defective is defective because it is in quest of a principle. Then again, if the One is defective, it is clear that It is seeking not to be one; that is, It is in need of something to destroy It. But everything which is said to be in need is in need of well-being and something to preserve it: so there is nothing which is good for the One, nor does It wish for anything.

It transcends good, and is Good not for Itself, but for the others, if any of them can participate in It. It is not thought, for there is no otherness in It. It is not movement, but prior to movement and thought. For what would It think about? Itself? But then It would be ignorant before Its thought, and would need thought to know Itself, It which is self-sufficient! There is no ignorance in It because It does not know or think Itself, because ignorance is always of something else, when one of two things does not know the other. But That Which is One Alone neither knows nor has anything of which to be ignorant; being One, present to Itself, It needs no thought of Itself. We ought not in fact even to speak of "self-presence", in order to preserve the unity. We should leave out thought and self-presence, and thinking about Itself and other things. We ought not to class It as a thinking being but rather as thought; for thought does not think, but is cause of thinking to something else; and the cause is not the same as its effect. So the Cause of all things is none of them. We should not even speak of It as Good, in the sense of the good which It gives to others. It is the Good in a different sense, transcending all other goods.

3

MOSES MAIMONIDES

The Place of Figurative Language in Theory: The Necessity of Caution in speaking about God. *The language used of God is figurative, says Maimonides, and in particular the attribution of physical organs to God is primarily to make a claim for his existence and activity, viz.: that they are somewhat parallel to that existence and activity which these organs express in ourselves.*

The second extract asks why hearing, sight and smell, while being human attributes, are also predicated of God, while taste and touch are not. The answer is that taste and touch have their defects, like those of the imagination compared with thought – so that their limitations are more obvious. But the author readily grants that in the last resort this is only a matter of degree.

As for the emotions ascribed to God, these are meant, again by an appeal to ourselves, to portray an activity rather than describe some divine emotion. It is in this context that the author asserts "That all attributes ascribed to God are attributes of his acts and do not imply that God has any qualities". Even terms like "thirst" and "lust" are "metaphorical", and are but popular ways, "borrowed from the language commonly used among the people" of expressing the point that God "is not subject to any change or innovation whatever".

Singers and preachers are often "extravagant in praise, fluent and prolix in the prayers they compose, and in the hymns they make in the desire to approach the Creator". In short, they treat the Creator too familiarly. Let no one have too much "looseness of tongue" in reference to God.

The last extract is an example of how we think in terms of negative attributes, and concludes with a warning that certain ways of talking about God can begin to erode belief until eventually it is entirely lost. For this reason, the language of religion is not only of philosophical interest, but of high importance for our faith and religious conviction.

On the attribution of senses and sensations to God

We have already stated, in one of the chapters of this treatise, that there is a great difference between bringing to view the existence of a thing and demonstrating its true essence. We can lead others to notice the existence of an object by pointing to its accidents, actions, or even most remote relations to other objects: e.g. if you wish to describe the king of a country to one of his subjects who does not know him, you can give a description and an account of his existence in many ways. You will either say to him, the tall man with a fair complexion and grey hair is the king, thus describing him by his accidents; or you will say, the king is the person round whom are seen a great multitude of men on horse and on foot, and soldiers with drawn swords, over whose head banners are waving, and before whom trumpets are sounded; or it is the person living in the palace in a particular region of a certain country; or it is the person who ordered the building of that wall, or the construction of that bridge; or by some other similar acts and things relating to him. His existence can be demonstrated in a still more indirect way, e.g. if you are asked whether this land has a king, you will undoubtedly answer in the affirmative. "What proof have you?" "The fact that this banker here, a weak and little person, stands before this large mass of gold pieces, and that poor man, tall and strong, who stands before him asking in vain for alms of the weight of a carob-grain, is rebuked and is compelled to go away by the mere force of words; for had he not feared the king, he would, without hesitation, have killed the banker, or pushed him away and taken as much of the money as he could." Consequently, this is a proof that this country has a ruler and his existence is proved by the well-regulated affairs of the country, on account of which the king is respected and the punishments decreed by him are feared. In this whole example nothing is mentioned

Moses Maimonides, *The Guide for the Perplexed*, trs. from the Arabic text by M. Friedlander, 2nd, 1951, pp. 59–62, 63–64, 76–77, 81, 86, 87–88. Reprinted by permission of Routledge & Kegan Paul, London and Dover Publications Inc., New York.

that indicated his characteristics, and his essential properties, by virtue of which he is king. The same is the case with the information concerning the Creator given to the ordinary classes of men in all prophetical books and in the Law. For it was found necessary to teach all of them that God exists, and that He is in every respect the most perfect Being, that is to say, He exists not only in the sense in which the earth and the heavens exist, but He exists and possesses life, wisdom, power, activity, and all other properties which our belief in His existence must include, as will be shown below. That God exists was therefore shown to ordinary men by means of similes taken from physical bodies; that He is living, by a simile taken from motion, because ordinary men consider only the body as fully, truly, and undoubtedly existing; that which is connected with a body but is itself not a body, although believed to exist, has a lower degree of existence on account of its dependence on the body for existence. That, however, which is neither itself a body, or a force within a body, is not existent according to man's first notions, and is above all excluded from the range of imagination. In the same manner motion is considered by the ordinary man as identical with life; what cannot move voluntarily from place to place has no life, although motion is not part of the definition of life, but an accident connected with it. The perception by the senses, especially by hearing and seeing, is best known to us; we have no idea or notion of any other mode of communication between the soul of one person and that of another than by means of speaking, i.e. by the sound produced by lips, tongue, and the other organs of speech. When, therefore, we are to be informed that God has a knowledge of things, and that communication is made by Him to the Prophets who convey it to us, they represent Him to us as seeing and hearing, i.e. as perceiving and knowing those things which can be seen and heard. They represent Him to us as speaking, i.e. that communications from Him reach the Prophets; that is to be understood by the term "prophecy", as will be fully explained. God is described as working, because we do not know any other mode of producing a thing except by direct touch. He is said to have a soul in the sense that He is living, because all living beings are generally supposed to have a soul; although the term soul is, as has been shown, a homonym.

Again, since we perform all these actions only by means of corporeal organs, we figuratively ascribe to God the organs of locomotion, as feet, and their soles; organs of hearing, seeing and smelling, as ear, eye, and nose; organs and substance of speech, as mouth, tongue, and sound; organs for the performance of work, as hand, its fingers, its palm, and the arm. In short, these organs of the body are figuratively ascribed to God, who is above all imperfection, to express that He performs certain acts; and these acts are figuratively ascribed to Him to express that He possesses certain perfections different from those acts themselves. E.g., we say that He has eyes, ears, hands, a mouth, a tongue, to express that He sees, hears, acts, and speaks; but seeing and hearing are attributed to Him to indicate simply that He perceives. You thus find in Hebrew instances in which the perception of the one sense is named instead of the other; thus, "See the word of the Lord" (Jer. ii. 31), in the same meaning as "Hear the word of the Lord", for the sense of the phrase is, "Perceive what he says"; similarly the phrase, "See the smell of my son" (Gen. xxvii. 27) has the same meaning as "Smell the smell of my son," for it relates to the perception of the smell. In the same way are used the words, "And all the people saw the thunders and the lightnings" (Exod. xx. 15), although the passage also contains the description of a prophetical vision, as is well known and understood among our people. Action and speech are likewise figuratively applied to God, to express that a certain influence has emanated from Him, as will be explained (chap. lxv. and chap. lxvi.). The physical organs which are attributed to God in the writings of the Prophets are either organs of locomotion, indicating life; organs of sensation, indicating perception; organs of touch, indicating action; or organs of speech, indicating the divine inspiration of the Prophets, as will be explained.

The object of all these indications is to establish in our minds the notion of the existence of a living being, the Maker of everything, who also possesses a knowledge of the things which He has made. We shall explain, when we come to speak of the inadmissibility of Divine attributes, that all these various attributes convey but one notion, viz., that of the essence of God. The sole object of this chapter is to explain in what sense physical organs are ascribed to the Most Perfect Being, namely, that they are mere indications of the actions generally performed by means of these organs. Such actions being perfections respecting themselves, are predicated of God, because we wish to express that He is most perfect in every respect, as we remarked above in explaining the Rabbinical phrase, "The language of the Torah is like the language of man." Instances of organs of locomotion being applied to the Creator occur as follows: "My footstool" (Isa. lxvi. 1); "the place of the soles of my feet" (Ezek. xliii. 7). For examples of organs of touch applied to God, comp. "the hand of the Lord" (Exod. ix. 3); "with the finger of God" (ib. xxxi. 18); "the work of thy fingers" (Ps. viii. 4), "And thou hast laid thine hand upon me" (ib. cxxxix. 5); "The arm of the Lord" (Isa. liii. 1); "Thy right hand, O Lord" (Exod. xv. 6). In instances like the following, organs of speech are attributed to God: "The mouth of the Lord has spoken" (Isa. i. 20); "And He would open His lips against thee" (Job xi. 5); "The voice of the Lord is powerful" (Ps. xxix. 4); "And his tongue as a devouring fire" (Isa. xxx. 27). Organs of sensation are attributed to God in instances like the following: "His eyes behold, His eyelids try" (Ps. xi. 4); "The eyes of the Lord which run to and fro" (Zech. iv. 10); "Bow down thine ear unto me, and hear" (2 Kings xix. 16); "You have kindled a fire in my nostril" (Jer. xvii. 5). Of the inner parts of the human body only the heart is figuratively applied to God, because "heart" is a homonym, and denotes also "intellect"; it is besides the source of animal life. In phrases like "my bowels are troubled for him" (Jer. xxxi. 20); "The sounding of thy bowels" (Isa. lxiii. 15), the term "bowels" is used in the sense of "heart"; for the term "bowels" is used both in a general and in a specific meaning; it denotes specifically "bowels", but more generally it can be used as the name of any inner organ, including "heart". The correctness of this argument can be proved by the phrase "And thy law is within my bowels" (Ps. xl. 9), which is identical with "And thy law is within my heart". For that reason the prophet employed in this verse the phrase "my bowels are troubled" (and "the sounding of thy bowels"); the verb hamah is in fact used more frequently in connection with "heart" than with any other organ; comp. "My heart maketh a noise (homeh) in me" (Jer. iv. 19). Similarly, the shoulder is never used as a figure in reference to God, because it is known as a mere instrument of transport, and also comes into close contact with the thing which it carries. With far greater reason the organs of nutrition are never attributed to God; they are at once recognized as signs of imperfection. In fact all organs, both the external and the internal, are employed in the various actions of the soul; some, e.g. all inner organs, are the means of preserving the individual for a certain time; others, as the organs of generation, are the means of preserving the species; others are the means of improving the condition of man and bringing his actions to perfection, as the hands, the feet, and the eyes, all of which tend to render motion, action, and perception more perfect. Animate beings require motion in order to be able to approach that which is conducive to their welfare, and to move away from the opposite; they require the senses in order to be able to discern what is injurious to them and what is beneficial. In addition, man requires various kinds of handiwork, to prepare his food, clothing, and dwelling; and he is compelled by his physical constitution to perform such work, namely, to prepare what is good for him. Some kinds of work also occur among certain animals, as far as such work is required by those animals. I do not believe that any man can doubt the correctness of the assertion that the Creator is not in need of anything for the continuance of His existence, or for the improvement of His condition. Therefore, God has no organs, or, what is the same, He is not corporeal; His actions are accomplished by His Essence, not by any organ, and as undoubtedly physical forces are connected with the organs, He does not possess any such forces, that is to say, He has, besides His Essence, nothing that could be the cause of His action, His knowledge, or His will, for attributes are nothing but forces under a different name. It is not my intention to discuss the question in this chapter. Our Sages laid down a general principle, by which the literal sense of the physical attributes of God mentioned by the prophets is rejected; a principle which evidently shows that our Sages were far from the belief in the corporeality of God, and that they did not think any person capable of misunderstanding it, or entertaining any doubt about it. For that reason they employ in the Talmud and the Midrashim phrases similar to those contained in the prophecies, without any circumlocution; they knew that there could not be any doubt about their metaphorical character, or any danger whatever of their being misunderstood; and that all such expressions would be understood as figurative (language), employed to communicate to the intellect the notion of His existence. Now, it is well known that in figurative language God is compared to a king who commands, cautions, punishes, and rewards, his subjects, and whose servants and attendants publish his orders, so that they might be acted upon, and they also execute whatever he wishes. Thus the Sages adopted that figure, used it frequently, and introduced such speech, consent, and refusal of a king, and other usual acts of kings, as became necessary by that figure.

We have already stated several times that the prophetic books never attribute to God anything which ordinary men consider a defect, or which they cannot in their imagination combine with the idea of the Almighty, although such terms may not otherwise be different from those which were employed as metaphors in relation to God. Indeed all things which are attributed to God are considered in some ways to be perfection, or can at least be imagined (as pertaining to Him).

We must now show why, according to this principle, the senses of hearing, sight and smell, are attributed to God, but not those of taste and touch. He is equally elevated above the use of all the five senses; they are all defective as regards perception, even for those who have no other source of knowledge; because they are passive, receive impressions from without, and are subject to interruptions and sufferings, as much as the other organs of the body. By saying that God sees, we mean to state that He perceives visible things; "He hears" as identical with saying "He perceives audible things"; in the same way we might say, "He tastes and He touches", in the sense of "He perceives objects which man perceives by means of taste and touch". For, as regards perception, the senses are identical; if we deny the existence of one sensation in God, we must deny that of all other sensations, i.e. the perceptions of the five senses; and if we attribute the existence of one sensation to Him, i.e. the perception appertaining to one of the senses, we must attribute all the five sensations. Nevertheless, we find in Holy Writ, "And God saw" (Gen. vi. 5); "And God heard" (Num. xi. 1); "And God smelt" (Gen. vi. 21); but we do not meet with the expressions, "And God tasted", "And God touched". According to our opinion the reason of this is to be found in the idea, which has a firm hold in the minds of all men, that God does not come into contact with a body in the same manner as one body comes into contact with another, since He is not even seen by the eye. While these two senses, namely, taste and touch, only act when in close contact with the object, by sight, hearing, and smell, even distant objects are perceived. These, therefore, were considered by the multitude appropriate expressions (to be figuratively applied to God). Besides, the object in figuratively applying the sensations to Him, could only have been to express that He perceives our actions; but hearing and sight are sufficient for that, namely, for the perception of what a man does or says. Thus our Sages, among other admonitions, gave the following advice and warning: "Know what is above thee, a seeing eye, and a hearing ear." (Mishnah Abot, ii. 1.)

You, however, know that, strictly speaking, the condition of all the sensations is the same, that the same argument which is employed against the existence of touch and taste in God, may be used against sight, hearing, and smell; for they all are material perceptions and impressions which are subject to change. There is only this difference, that the former, touch and taste, are at once recognized as deficiencies, while the others are considered as perfections. In a similar manner the defect of the imagination is easily seen, less easily that of thinking and reasoning. Imagination (ra'ayon) therefore, was never employed as a figure in speaking of God, while thought and reason are figuratively ascribed to Him. Comp. "The thoughts which the Lord thought" (Jer. xlix. 20); "And with his understanding he stretched out the heavens" (ib. x. 12). The inner senses were thus treated in the same way as the external; some are figuratively applied to God, some not. All this is according to the language of man; he ascribes to God what he considers a perfection, and does not ascribe to Him that he considers a defect. In truth, however, no real attribute, implying an addition to His essence, can be applied to Him, as will be proved.

On the attributes of God

Whenever any one of His actions is perceived by us, we ascribe to God that emotion which is the source of the act when performed by ourselves, and call Him by an epithet which is formed from the verb expressing that emotion. We see, e.g. how well He provides for the life of the embryo of living beings; how He endows with certain faculties both the embryo itself and those who have to rear it after its birth, in order that it may be protected from death and destruction, guarded against all harm, and assisted in the performance of all that is required (for its development). Similar acts, when performed by us, are due to a certain emotion and tenderness called mercy and pity. God is, therefore, said to be merciful; e.g. "Like as a father is merciful to his children, so the Lord is merciful to them that fear Him" (Ps. ciii. 13); "And I will spare them, as a man spareth (yaḥamol) his own son that serveth him" (Mal. iii. 17). Such instances do not imply that God is influenced by a feeling of mercy, but that acts similar to those which a father performs for his son, out of pity, mercy and real affection, emanate from God solely for the benefit of His pious men, and are by no means the result of any impression or change (produced in God).

When we give something to a person who has no claim upon us, we perform an act of grace; e.g. "Grant them graciously unto us" (Judges xxi. 22). The same term is used in reference to God, e.g. "which God hath graciously given" (Gen. xxxiii. 5); "Because God hath dealt graciously with me" (ib. 11). Instances of this kind are numerous. God creates and guides beings who have no claim upon Him to be created and guided by Him; He is therefore called gracious (ḥannum).

His actions towards mankind also include great calamities, which overtake individuals and bring death to them, or affect whole families and even entire regions, spread death, destroy generation after generation, and spare nothing whatsoever. Hence there occur inundations, earthquakes, destructive storms, expeditions of one nation against the other for the sake of destroying it with the sword and blotting out its memory, and many other evils of the same kind. Whenever such evils are caused by us to any person, they originate in great anger, violent jealousy, or a desire for revenge. God is therefore called, because of these acts, "jealous", "revengeful", "wrathful", and "keeping anger" (Nah. i. 2); that is to say, He performs acts similar to those which, when performed by us, originate in certain psychical dispositions, in jealousy, desire for retaliation, revenge, or anger; they are in accordance with the guilt of those who are to be punished, and not the result of any emotion; for He is above all defect! The same is the case with all divine acts; though resembling those acts which emanate from our passions and psychical dispositions, they are not due to anything superadded to His essence.

The principal object of this chapter was to show that all attributes ascribed to God were attributes of His acts, and do not imply that God has any qualities.

On the identity of the essence of God and his attributes

The same is the case when we say God is the First (Kadmon), to express that He has not been created; the term "First" is decidedly inaccurate, for it can in its true sense only be applied to a being that is subject to the relation of time; the latter, however, is an accident to motion which again is connected with a body. Besides the attribute "first" is a relative term, being in regard to time the same as the terms "long" and "short" are in regard to a line. Both expressions "first" and "created", are equally inadmissible in reference to any being to which the attribute of time is not applicable, just as we do not say "crooked" or "straight" in reference to taste, "salted" or "insipid" in reference to the voice. These subjects are not unknown to those who have accustomed themselves to seek a true understanding of the things, and to establish their properties in accordance with the abstract notions which the mind has formed of them, and who are not misled by the inaccuracy of the words employed. All attributes, such as "the First", "the Last", occurring in the Scriptures in reference to God, are as metaphorical as the expressions "ear" and "eye". They simply signify that God is not subject to any change or innovation whatever; they do not imply that God can be described by time, or that there is any comparison between Him and any other being as regards time, and that He is called on that account "the first" and "the last". In short, all similar expressions are borrowed from the language commonly used among the people.

On the character of the knowledge of God consisting of negations

We cannot approve of what those foolish persons do who are extravagant in praise, fluent and prolix in the prayers they compose, and in the hymns they make in the desire to approach the Creator. They describe God in attributes which would be an offence if applied to a human being; for those persons have no knowledge of these great and important principles, which are not accessible to the ordinary intelligence of man. Treating the Creator as a familiar object, they describe Him and speak of Him in any expressions they think proper; they eloquently continue to praise Him in that manner, and believe that they can thereby influence Him and produce an effect on Him. If they find some phrase suited to their object in the words of the Prophets they are still more inclined to consider that they are free to make use of such texts – which should at least be explained – to employ them in their literal sense, to derive new expressions from them, to form from them numerous variations, and to found whole compositions on them. This license is frequently met with in the compositions of the singers, preachers, and others who imagine themselves to be able to compose a poem. Such authors write things which partly are real heresy, partly contain such folly and absurdity that they naturally cause those who hear them to laugh, but also to feel grieved at the thought that such things can be uttered in reference to God. Were it not that I pitied the authors for their defects, and did not wish to injure them, I should have cited some passages to show you their mistakes; besides, the fault of their compositions is obvious to all intelligent persons. You must consider it, and think thus: If slander and libel is a great sin, how much greater is the sin of those who speak with looseness of tongue in reference to God, and describe Him by attributes which are far below Him; and I declare that they not only commit an ordinary sin, but unconsciously at least incur the guilt of profanity and blasphemy. This applies both to the multitude that listens to such prayers, and to the foolish man that recites them. Men, however, who understand the fault of such compositions, and, nevertheless, recite them, may be classed, according to my opinion, among those to whom the following words are applied: "And the children of Israel used words that were not right against the Lord their God" (2 Kings xvii. 9); and "utter error against the Lord" (Isa. xxxii. 6). If you are of those who regard the honour of their Creator, do not listen in any way to them, much less utter what they say, and still less compose such prayers, knowing how great is the offence of one who hurls aspersions against the Supreme Being. There is no necessity at all for you to use positive attributes of God with the view of magnifying Him in your thoughts, or to go beyond the limits which the men of the Great Synagogue have introduced in the prayers and in the blessings, for this is sufficient for all purposes, and even more than sufficient, as Rabbi Haninah said.

On the difference between positive and negative attributes

I will give you in this chapter some illustrations, in order that you may better understand the propriety of forming as many negative attributes as possible, and the impropriety of ascribing to God any positive attributes. A person may know for certain that a "ship" is in existence, but he may not know to what object that name is applied, whether to a substance or to an accident; a second person then learns that the ship is not an accident; a third, that it is not a mineral; a fourth, that it is not a plant growing in the earth; a fifth, that it is not a body whose parts are joined together by nature; a sixth, that it is not a flat object like boards or doors; a seventh, that it is not a sphere; an eighth, that it is not pointed; a ninth, that it is not round-shaped; nor equilateral; a tenth, that it is not solid. It is clear that this tenth person has almost arrived at the correct notion of a "ship" by the foregoing negative attributes, as if he had exactly the same notion as those have who imagine it to be a wooden substance which is hollow, long, and composed of many pieces of wood, that is to say, who knows it by positive attributes. Of the other persons in our illustration, each one is more remote from the correct notion of a ship than the next mentioned, so that the first knows nothing about it but the name. In the same manner you will come nearer to the knowledge and comprehension of God by the negative attributes. But you must be careful, in what you negative, to negative by proof, not by mere words, for each time you ascertain by proof that a certain thing, believed to exist in the Creator, must be negatived, you have undoubtedly come one step nearer to the knowledge of God.

It is in this sense that some men come very near to God, and others remain exceedingly remote from Him, not in the sense of those who are deprived of vision, and believe that God occupies a place, which man can physically approach or from which he can recede. Examine this well, know it, and be content with it. The way which will bring you nearer to God has been clearly shown to you; walk in it, if you have the desire. On the other hand, there is a great danger in applying positive attributes to God. For it has been shown that every perfection we could imagine, even if existing in God in accordance with the opinion of those who assert the existence of attributes, would in reality not be of the same kind as that imagined by us, but would only be called by the same name, according to our explanation; it would in fact amount to a negation. Suppose, e.g. you say He has knowledge, and that knowledge, which admits of no change and of no plurality, embraces many changeable things; His knowledge remains unaltered, while new things are constantly formed, and His knowledge of a thing before it exists, while it exists, and when it has ceased to exist, is the same without the least change: you would thereby declare that His knowledge is not like ours; and similarly that His existence is not like ours. You thus necessarily arrive at some negation, without obtaining a true conception of an essential attribute; on the contrary, you are led to assume that there is a plurality in God, and to believe that He, though one essence, has several unknown attributes. For if you intend to affirm them, you cannot compare them with those attributes known by us, and they are consequently not of the same kind. You are, as it were, brought by the belief in the reality of the attributes, to say that God is one subject of which several things are predicated; though the subject is not like ordinary subjects, and the predicates are not like ordinary predicates. This belief would ultimately lead us to associate other things with God, and not to believe that He is One. For of every subject certain things can undoubtedly be predicated, and although in reality subject and predicate are combined in one thing, by the actual definition they consist of two elements, the notion contained in the subject not being the same as that contained in the predicate. In the course of this treatise it will be proved to you that God cannot be a compound, and that He is simple in the strictest sense of the word.

I do not merely declare that he who affirms attributes of God has not sufficient knowledge concerning the Creator, admits some associations with God, or conceives Him to be different from what He is; but I say that he unconsciously loses his belief in God.

4

ST THOMAS AQUINAS

No book of extracts on the language of religion could fail to include one from St Thomas, whose work on the subject has for long been definitive, and will always be classical. In this section of major importance St Thomas faces squarely the question: how do we speak of God?

QUESTION 13. THEOLOGICAL LANGUAGE

Article 1. *Can we use any words to refer to God?*

THE FIRST POINT: 1. It seems that we can use no words at all to refer to God. For Dionysius says, *Of him there is no naming nor any opinion,*[1] and we read in *Proverbs, What is his name or the name of his son if thou knowest?* [30.4].

2. Nouns are either abstract or concrete. The concrete noun is inappropriate to God because he is altogether simple; and the abstract noun is also ruled out because it does not signify a complete subsistent thing. Hence no noun can be used to refer to God.

3. A noun signifies a thing as coming under some description, verbs and participles signify it as enduring in time, pronouns signify it as being pointed out or as in some relationship. None of these is appropriate to God: we have no definition of him nor has he any accidental attributes by which he might be described; he is non-temporal and cannot be pointed to because he is not available to the senses; moreover he cannot be referred to by relative pronouns

St Thomas Aquinas, *Summa Theologica*, ed. Thomas Gilbey, 1964 ff., pp 47–85. Reprinted by permission of Eyre & Spottiswoode, London and McGraw-Hill Book Company, New York.

since the use of these depends on the previous use of some other referring term such as a noun, particle or demonstrative pronoun. Hence there is no way of referring to God.

ON THE OTHER HAND we read in *Exodus*, *The Lord is a great warrior; Almighty is his name* [15.3].

REPLY: Aristotle says that words are signs for thoughts and thoughts are likenesses of things,[2] so words refer to things indirectly through thoughts. How we refer to a thing depends on how we understand it. We have seen already that in this life we do not see the essence of God, we only know him from creatures; we think of him as their source, and then as surpassing them all and as lacking anything that is merely creaturely. It is the knowledge we have of creatures that enables us to use words to refer to God, and so these words do not express the divine essence as it is in itself. In this they differ from a word like "man" which is intended to express by its meaning the essence of man as he is – for the meaning of "man" is given by the definition of a man which expresses his essence; what a word means is the definition.

Hence: 1. God is said to have no name, or to be beyond naming because his essence is beyond what we understand of him and the meaning of the names we use.

2. Since we come to know God from creatures and since this is how we come to refer to him, the expressions we use to name him signify in a way appropriate to the material creatures we ordinarily know. Amongst such creatures the complete subsistent thing is always a concrete union of form and matter; for the form itself is not a subsistent thing, but that by which something subsists. Because of this the words we use to signify complete subsistent things are concrete nouns which are appropriate to composite subjects. When, on the other hand, we want to speak of the form itself we use abstract nouns which do not signify something as subsistent, but as that by which something is: "whiteness", for example, signifies the form as that by which something is white.

Now God is both simple, like the form, and subsistent, like the concrete thing, and so we sometimes refer to him by abstract nouns to indicate his simplicity and sometimes by concrete nouns to indicate his subsistence and completeness; though neither way of speaking measures up to his way of being, for in this life we do not know him as he is in himself.

3. To signify a thing as coming under some description is to signify it as subsisting in a certain nature or definite form. We have already said that the reason we use concrete nouns for God is to indicate his subsistence and completeness, it is for the same reason that we use nouns signifying a thing under some description. Verbs and participles can be used of him although they imply temporal succession because his eternity includes all time. Just as we can understand what is both simple and subsistent only as though it were composite, so we can understand and speak of the simplicity of eternity only after the manner of temporal things: it is composite and temporal things that we ordinarily and naturally understand. Demonstrative pronouns can be used of God in so far as they point, not to something seen, but to something understood, for so long as we know something, in whatever way, we can point it out. And thus according as nouns and participles and demonstrative pronouns can signify God, so in the same way relative pronouns can be used.

Article 2. Do any of the words we use of God express something of what he is?

THE SECOND POINT: 1. It seems that no word is used of God to express what he is. For John Damascene says, *The words used of God signify not what he is but what he is not, or his relationship to something else, or something that follows from his nature or operations.*[3]

2. Dionysius says, *You will find a chorus of holy teachers seeking to distinguish clearly and laudably the divine processions in the naming of God.*[4] This means that the names which the holy teachers use in praising God differ according to his different causal acts. However, to speak of the causal activity of a thing is not to speak of its essence, hence such words are not used to express what he is.

3. We speak of things as we understand them. But in this life we do not understand what God is, and so we can use no words to say what he is.

ON THE OTHER HAND Augustine says, *The being of God is to be strong, to be wise or whatever else we say of his simplicity in order to signify his essence.*[5] All such names then signify what God is.

REPLY: It is clear that the problem does not arise for negative terms or for words which express the relationship of God to creatures; these obviously do not express what he is but rather what he is not or how he is related to something else – or, better, how something else is related to him. The question is concerned with words like "good" and "wise" which are neither negative nor relational terms, and about these there are several opinions.

Some have said that sentences like "God is good", although they sound like affirmations are in fact used to deny something of God rather than to assert anything. Thus for example when we say that God is living we mean that God is not like an inanimate thing, and likewise for all such propositions. This was the view of the Rabbi Moses.

Others said that such sentences were used to signify the relation of God to creatures, so that when we say "God is good" we mean that God is the cause of goodness in things, and likewise in other such propositions.

Neither of these views seem plausible, and for three reasons. Firstly, on neither view can there be any reason why we should use some words about God rather than others. God is just as much the cause of bodies as he is of goodness in things; so if "God is good" means no more than that God is the cause of goodness in things, why not say "God is a body" on the grounds that he is the cause of bodies? So also we could say "God is a body" because we want to deny that he is merely potential being like primary matter.

Secondly it would follow that everything we said of God would be true only in a secondary sense, as when we say that a diet is "healthy", meaning merely that it causes health in the one who takes it, while it is the living body which is said to be healthy in a primary sense.

Thirdly, this is not what people want to say when they talk about God. When a man speaks of the "living God" he does not simply want to say that God is the cause of our life, or that he differs from a lifeless body.

So we must find some other solution to the problem. We shall suggest that such words do say what God is; they are predicated of him in the category of substance, but fail to represent adequately what he is. The reason for this is that we speak of God as we know him, and since we know him from creatures we can only speak of him as they represent him. Any creature, in so far as it possesses any perfection, represents God and is like to him, for he, being simply and universally perfect, has pre-existing in himself the perfections of all his creatures, as noted above. But a creature is not like to God as it is like to another member of its species or genus, but resembles him as an effect may in some way resemble a transcendent cause although failing to reproduce perfectly the form of the cause – as in a certain way the forms of inferior bodies imitate the power of the sun. This was explained earlier when we were dealing with the perfection of God. Thus words like "good" and "wise" when used of God do signify something that God really is, but they signify it imperfectly because creatures represent God imperfectly.

"God is good" therefore does not mean the same as "God is the cause of goodness" or "God is not evil"; it means that what we call "goodness" in creatures pre-exists in God in a higher way. Thus God is not good because he causes goodness, but rather goodness flows from him because he is good. As Augustine says, *Because he is good, we exist.*[6]

Hence: 1. John Damascene says that these words do not signify what God is, because none of them express completely what he is; but each signifies imperfectly something that he is, just as creatures represent him imperfectly.

2. Sometimes the reason why a word comes to be used is quite different from the meaning of the word. Thus the word "hydrogen" derives from what produces water, but it does not mean something that produces water, it means a particular chemical element, otherwise everything that produced water would be hydrogen. In the case of words used of God we may say that the reason they came to be used derives from his causal activity, for our understanding of him and our language about him depends on the different perfections in creatures which represent him, however imperfectly, in his various causal acts. Nevertheless these words are not used to *mean* his causal acts. "Living" in "God is living" does not mean the same as "causes life"; the sentence is used to say that life does pre-exist in the source of all things, although in a higher way than we can understand or signify.

3. In this life we cannot understand the essence of God as he is in himself, we can however understand it as it is represented by the perfections of his creatures; and this is how the words we use can signify it.

Article 3. *Can we say anything literally about God?*

THE THIRD POINT: 1. It seems that no word can be used literally of God. For we have already said that every word used of God is taken from our speech about creatures, as already noted, but such words are used metaphorically of God, as when we call him a "rock" or a "lion". Thus words are used of God metaphorically.

2. A word is not used literally of something if it would be more accurate not to use it than to use it. Now according to Dionysius it would be truer to say that God is not good or wise or any such thing than to say that he is.[7] Hence no such thing is said literally of God.

3. Words for bodily things can only be used metaphorically of God because he is incorporeal. All our words, however, belong to a bodily context, for all imply such conditions as temporal succession and composition of matter and form which belong to the material world. Therefore such words can only be used metaphorically.

ON THE OTHER HAND Ambrose says, *There are some ways of referring to God which show forth clearly what is proper to divinity, and some which express the luminous truth of the divine majesty, but there are others which are used of God metaphorically and through a certain likeness.*[8] Hence not all words are used of God metaphorically; some are used literally.

REPLY: As we have said, God is known from the perfections that flow from him and are to be found in creatures, yet which exist in him in a transcendent way. We understand such perfections, however, as we find them in creatures, and as we understand them so we use words to speak of them. We have to consider two things, therefore, in the words we use to attribute perfections to God, first the perfections themselves that are signified – goodness, life and the like – and secondly the way in which they are signified. So far as the perfections signified are concerned the words are used literally of God, and in fact more appropriately than they are used of creatures, for these perfections belong primarily to God and only secondarily to others. But so far the way of signifying these perfections is concerned the words are used inappropriately, for they have a way of signifying that is appropriate to creatures.

Hence: 1. Some words that signify what has come forth from God to creatures do so in such a way that part of the meaning of the word is the imperfect way in which the creature shares in the divine perfection. Thus it is part of the meaning of "rock" that it has its being in a merely material way. Such words can be used of God only metaphorically. There are other words, however, that simply mean certain perfections without any indication of how these perfections are possessed – words, for example, like "being", "good", "living" and so on. These words can be used literally of God.

2. The reason why Dionysius says that such words are better denied of God is that what they signify does not belong to God in the way that they signify it, but in a higher way; thus in the same passage he says that God *is beyond all substance and life.*[9]

3. These words have a bodily context not in what they mean but in the way in which they signify it; the ones that are used metaphorically have bodily conditions as part of what they mean.

. . . .

Article 5. *Are words used univocally or equivocally of God and creatures?*

THE FIFTH POINT: 1. It seems that words used both of God and of creatures are used univocally: the equivocal is based on the univocal as the many is based on the one. A word such as "dog" may be used equivocally of a hound and a fish, but only because it is first used univocally – of hounds – otherwise there would be nowhere to start from and we should go back for ever. Now there are some causes that are called univocal because their effects have the same name and description as themselves – what is generated by a man, for example, is also a man. Some causes, however, are called equivocal, as is the sun when it causes heat, for the sun itself is only equivocally said to be hot. Since, therefore, the equivocal is based on the univocal it seems that the first cause upon which all others are based must be an univocal cause, hence what is said of God and of his creatures must be said univocally.

2. There is no resemblance between things that are only equivocally the same, but according to *Genesis* there is a resemblance between creatures and God; *Let us make man in our own image and likeness* [1.26]. So it seems that something can be said univocally of God and creatures.

3. Aristotle says that the measure must be of the same order as the thing measured,[10] and he also describes God as the first measure of all beings. God, therefore, is of the same order as creatures; and so something can be said univocally of both.

ON THE OTHER HAND for two reasons it seems that such words must be used equivocally. First, the same word when used with different meanings is used equivocally, but no word when used of God means the same as when it is used of a creature. "Wisdom", for example, means a quality when it is used of creatures, but not when it is applied to God. So then it must have a different meaning, for we have here a difference in the genus which is part of the definition. The same applies to other words; so all must be used equivocally.

And second, God is more distant from any creature than any two creatures are from each other. Now there are some creatures so different that nothing can be said univocally of them – for example when they differ in genus. Much less, therefore, could there be anything said univocally of creatures and God.

REPLY: It is impossible to predicate anything univocally of God and creatures. Every effect that falls short of what is typical of the power of its cause represents it inadequately, for it is not the same kind of thing as the cause. Thus what exists simply and in a unified way in the cause will be divided up and take various different forms in such effects – as the simple power of the sun produces many different kinds of lesser things. In the same way, as we said earlier, the perfections which in creatures are many and various pre-exist in God as one.

The perfection words that we use in speaking of creatures all differ in meaning and each one signifies a perfection as something distinct from all others. Thus when we say that a man is wise, we signify his wisdom as something distinct from the other things about him – his essence, for example, his powers or his existence. But when we use this word about God we do not intend to signify something distinct from his essence, power or existence. When "wise" is used of a man, it so to speak contains and delimits the aspect of man that it signifies, but this is not so when it is used of God; what it signifies in God is not confined by the meaning of our word but goes beyond it. Hence it is clear that the word "wise" is not used in the same sense of God and man, and the same is true of all other words, so they cannot be used univocally of God and creatures.

Yet although we never use words in exactly the same sense of creatures and God we are not merely equivocating when we use the same word, as some have said, for if this were so we could never argue from statements about creatures to statements about God – any such argument would be invalidated by the Fallacy of Equivocation. That this does not happen we know not merely from the teachings of the philosophers who prove many things about God but also from the teaching of St Paul, for he says, *The invisible things of God are made known by those things that are made* [Rom. 1.20].

We must say, therefore, that words are used of God and creatures in an analogical way, that is in accordance with a certain order between them. We can distinguish two kinds of analogical or "proportional" uses of language. Firstly there is the case of one word being used of two things because each of them has some order or relation to a third thing. Thus we use the word "healthy" of both a diet and a complexion because each of these has some relation to health in a man, the former as a cause, the latter as a symptom of it. Secondly there is the case of the same word used of two things because of some relation that one has to the other – as "healthy" is used of the diet and the man because the diet is the cause of the health in the man.

In this way some words are used neither univocally nor purely equivocally of God and creatures, but analogically, for we cannot speak of God at all except in the language we use of creatures, and so whatever is said both of God and creatures is said in virtue of the order that creatures have to God as to their source and cause in which all the perfections of things pre-exist transcendently.

This way of using words lies somewhere between pure equivocation and simple univocity, for the word is neither used in the same sense, as with univocal usage, nor in totally different senses, as with equivocation. The several senses of a word used analogically signify different relations to some one thing, as "health" in a complexion means a symptom of health in a man, and in a diet means a cause of that health.

Hence: 1. Even if it were the case that in speech the equivocal were based on the univocal, the same is not true of causality. A non-univocal cause is causal by reference to an entire species – as the sun is the cause that there are men. An univocal cause, on the other hand, cannot be the universal cause of the whole species (otherwise it would be the cause of itself, since it is a member of that same species), but is the particular cause that this or that individual should be a member of the species. Thus the universal cause which must be prior to the individual cause, is non-univocal. Such a cause, however, is not wholly equivocal, for then there would be no resemblance in any sense between it and its effects. We could call it an analogical cause, and this would be parallel to the case of speech, for all univocal predications are based on one non-univocal, analogical predicate, that of being.

2. The resemblance of creatures to God is an imperfect one, for as we have said, they do not even share a common genus.

3. God is not a measure that is proportionate to what is measured; so it does not follow that he and his creatures belong to the same order.

The two arguments in the contrary sense do show that words are not used univocally of God and creatures but they do not show that they are used equivocally.

Article 6. *Are words predicated primarily of God or of creatures?*

THE SIXTH POINT: 1. It seems that the words we use of God apply primarily to creatures. For we speak of things as we know them since, as Aristotle says, words are signs for things as understood. But we know creatures before we know God, hence our words apply to creatures before they apply to God.

2. Dionysius says that *the language we use about God is derived from what we say about creatures*[12]. But when a word such as "lion" or "rock" is transferred from a creature to God it is used first of the creature. Hence such words apply primarily to the creature.

3. Words used of both God and creatures are used of him in that he is the cause of all things, as Dionysius says.[13] But what is said of something in a causal sense applies to it only secondarily – as "healthy" applies primarily to a living body and only secondarily to the diet that causes its health. Hence such words are applied primarily to creatures.

ON THE OTHER HAND we read in *Ephesians, I bow my knees to the Father of our Lord Jesus, from whom all fatherhood in heaven and on earth is named* [3.14 f.]; and the same seems to apply to other words used of God and creatures. These words, then, are used primarily of God.

REPLY: Whenever a word is used analogically of many things, it is used of them because of some order or relation they have to some central thing. In order to explain an extended or analogical use of a word it is necessary to mention this central thing. Thus you cannot explain what you mean by a "healthy" diet without mentioning the health of the man of which it is the cause; similarly you must understand "healthy" as applied to a man before you can understand what is meant by a "healthy complexion" which is the symptom of that health. The primary application of the word is to the central thing that has to be understood first; other applications will be more or less secondary in so far as they approximate to this use.

Thus all words used metaphorically of God apply primarily to creatures and secondarily to God. When used of God they signify merely a certain parallelism between God and the creature. When we speak metaphorically of a meadow as "smiling" we only mean that it shows at its best when it flowers, just as a man shows at his best when he smiles: there is a parallel between them. In the same way, if we speak of God as a "lion" we only mean that, like a lion, he is mighty in his deeds. It is obvious that the meaning of such a word as applied to God depends on and is secondary to the meaning it has when used of creatures.

This would be the case for non-metaphorical words too if they were simply used, as some have supposed, to express God's causality. If, for example, "God is good" meant the same as "God is the cause of goodness in creatures" the word "good" as applied to God would have contained within its meaning the goodness of the creature; and hence "good" would apply primarily to creatures and secondarily to God.

But we have already shown that words of this sort do not only say how God is a cause, they also say what he is. When we say he is good or wise we do not simply mean that he causes wisdom or goodness, but that he possesses these perfections transcendently. We conclude, therefore, that from the point of view of what the word means it is used primarily of God and derivatively of creatures, for what the word means – the perfection it signifies – flows from God to the creature. But from the point of view of our use of the word we apply it first to creatures because we know them first. That, as we have mentioned already, is why it has a way of signifying that is appropriate to creatures.

Hence: 1. This is valid so far as our first application of the words is concerned.

2. Words used of God metaphorically are not in the same case as the others, as we have said.

3. This objection would be valid if all words were used to express the causality of God and not to say what he is, as "healthy" expresses the causality of a diet and not what it consists in.

. . . .

Article 9. *Is the name "God" peculiar to God alone?*

THE NINTH POINT: 1. It seems that "God" is not peculiar to God, but can be used of other things. For whatever shares in what a name signifies can share in the name, but we have just said that "God" signifies the divine nature and this is something that can be communicated to others, according to *II Peter*, *He has bestowed upon us precious and very great promises . . . that by this we may become partakers of the divine nature* [1.4]. Hence "God" may be applied to others besides God.

2. Only proper names are altogether incommunicable. But "God" is not a proper name as is clear from the fact that it can be used in the plural, as in the *Psalm*, *I say you shall be gods* [82.6]. Hence the word "God" is applicable to many things.

3. The name "God" is applied to God, as we have just seen, because of his operations. But other words that are used of God because of his operations such as "good", "wise" and such-like, are all applicable to many things. So "God" is as well.

ON THE OTHER HAND we read in *Wisdom*, *They gave the incommunicable name to sticks and stones* [14.21], and the reference is to the name of the Godhead. Hence the name "God" is incommunicable.

REPLY: A noun may be used of many things in two ways, either properly or by metaphor. It is properly used of many when the whole of what it means belongs to each of them; it is used metaphorically when some part of what it means belongs to each. The word "lion", for example, properly speaking applies only to the things that have the nature it signifies, but it is also applied metaphorically to other things that have something of the lion about them. The courageous or the strong can be spoken of in this way as "lions".

To understand which nouns properly speaking apply to many things we must first recognize that every form that is instantiated by an individual either is or at least can be thought of as being common to many; human nature can be thought of, and in fact is, common to many in this way; the nature of the sun, on the other hand, can be thought of as being, but in fact is not, common to many. The reason for this is that the mind understands such natures in abstraction from the individual instances, hence whether it be in one individual or in many is irrelevant to our understanding of the nature itself; given that we understand the nature we can always think of it as being in many instances.

The individual, however, from the very fact of being individual, is divided from all others. Hence a word that is used precisely to signify an individual cannot be applicable to many in fact, nor can it be thought of as applicable to many. It is impossible to think that there could be many of this individual. Hence no proper name is properly speaking communicable to many, though it may be communicable through some resemblance – as a man may metaphorically be called "an Achilles" because he has the bravery of Achilles.

But consider the case of forms which are not instantiated by being the form of an individual, but by themselves (inasmuch as they are subsistent forms). If we understood these as they are in themselves it would be clear that they are not common to many in fact and also cannot be thought of as being common to many – except perhaps by some sort of resemblance as with individuals. In fact, however, we do not understand such simple self-subsistent forms as they are in themselves, but have to think of them on the model of the composite things that have their forms in matter. For this reason, as we said earlier, we apply to them concrete nouns that signify a nature as instantiated in an individual. Thus the nouns we use to signify simple subsistent natures are grammatically the same as those we use to signify the natures of composite things.

Now "God" is used, as we saw, to signify the divine nature, and since this nature cannot have more than one instance, it follows that from the point of view of what is in fact signified, the word cannot be used of many, although it can mistakenly be thought of as applying to many – rather as a man who mistakenly thought there were many suns would think of "sun" as applying to many things. Thus we read in *Galatians*, *You were slaves to gods who by nature were not gods* [4.8], and a gloss says, *not gods by nature but according to the opinion of men.*

Nevertheless the word "God" does have several applications, though not in its full meaning. It is applied metaphorically to things that share something of what it means. Thus "gods" can mean those who by resembling God share in some way in the divine, as in the *Psalm*, *I say you shall be gods* [82.6].

If, however, a name were given to God, not as signifying his nature but referring to him as this thing, regarding him as an individual, such a proper name would be altogether incommunicable and in no way applicable to others – perhaps the Hebrew name of God, the Tetragrammaton was used in this way: it would be as though someone were to use the word "Sun" as a proper name designating this individual.

Hence: 1. The divine nature can be communicated to others only in the sense that they can share in the likeness of God.

2. "God" is a common noun and not a proper name because it signifies in the concrete the divine nature, although God himself is neither universal nor particular. We do not, however, name things as they are in themselves but as they are to our minds. In actual fact the name "God" is incommunicable rather as we said of the word "Sun".

3. Words like "good" and "wise" are applied to God because of the perfections that flow from God to creatures. They do not mean the divine nature, they mean these perfections; and so not only can they be thought of as applicable to many things but they actually are in fact. But the word "God" is applied to him because of the operation peculiar to him which we constantly experience, and it is used to signify the divine nature.

NOTES

1. *De div. nom.* I. PG 3, 593.
2. *De Interpretatione* I, 1. 16a3.
3. *De Fide orthodoxa* I, 9. PG 94, 835.
4. *De div. nom.* I, PG 3, 589.
5. *De Trinitate* VI, 4. PL 42, 927.
6. *De doctrina Christiana* I, 32. PL 34, 32.
7. *De cœlesti hierarchia.* II PG 3, 41.
8. *De Fide* II, *prol.* PL 16, 583.
9. *Loc. cit.*
10. *Metaphysics* X, 1. 1053a24.
11. *De Interpretatione* I, 1, 163a3.
12. *De div. nom.* I. PG 3, 596.
13. *De mystica theologia* I. PG 3, 1000.

5

GEORGE BERKELEY

God and Persons. *Berkeley is here arguing for a close parallel between our awareness of God and our awareness of the activity and presence of a person ("soul, spirit or thinking principle") which suggests a parallel between the logic of God and that of first person language. His view blossoms out into a theory of the world as divine visual language. As he says through the mouth of Euphranor: "In consequence . . . you have as much reason to think the Universal Agent or God speaks to your eyes, as you can have for thinking any particular person speaks to your ears", and Crito contends that "this Visual Language proves, not a Creator merely, but a provident Governor."*

ALCIPHRON Do you pretend you can have the same assurance of the being of a God that you can have of mine, whom you actually see stand before you and talk to you?

EUPHRANOR The very same, if not greater.

ALCIPHRON How do you make this appear?

EUPHRANOR By the person Alciphron is meant an individual thinking thing, and not the hair, skin, or visible surface, or any part of the outward form, colour, or shape, of Alciphron.

ALCIPHRON This I grant.

EUPHRANOR. And, in granting this, you grant that, in a strict sense, I do not see Alciphron, i.e. that individual thinking thing, but only such visible signs and tokens as suggest and infer the being of that

The Works of George Berkeley, ed. A. A. Luce and T. E. Jessop, Thomas Nelson 1950. Vol. III, *Alciphron* or *The Minute Philosopher*, ed. T. E. Jessop, pp. 147, 289–90, 291–93 (Seventh Dialogue, 3rd ed. version).

invisible thinking principle or soul. Even so, in the self-same manner, it seems to me that, though I cannot with eyes of flesh behold the invisible God, yet I do in the strictest sense behold and perceive by all my senses such signs and tokens, such effects and operations, as suggest, indicate and demonstrate an invisible God, as certainly, and with the same evidence, at least, as any other signs perceived by sense do suggest to me the existence of your soul, spirit, or thinking principle; which I am convinced of only by a few signs or effects, and the motions of one small organized body: whereas I do at all times and in all places perceive sensible signs which evince the being of God.

The Logic of Christian Doctrine. *Theological words like grace are not to be supposed purely descriptive ("Standing for ideas"). Indeed their descriptive criteria may be highly problematical. But their function is to direct us how to act, and in this way they have affinities with the logic of person words, which speak of myself as an agent who is active about ideas.*

ALCIPHRON *Grace* is the main point in the Christian dispensation; nothing is oftener mentioned or more considered throughout the New Testament, where in it is represented as somewhat of a very particular kind, distinct from anything revealed to the Jews, or known by the light of nature. This same grace is spoken of as the gift of God, as coming by Jesus Christ, as reigning, as abounding, as operating. Men are said to speak through grace, to believe through grace. Mention is made of the glory of grace, the riches of grace, the stewards of grace. Christians are said to be heirs of grace, to receive grace, grow in grace, be strong in grace, to stand in grace, and to fall from grace. And lastly, grace is said to justify and to save them. Hence Christianity is styled the covenant or dispensation of grace. And it is well known that no point hath created more controversy in the church than this doctrine of grace. What disputes about its nature, extent and effects, about universal, efficacious, sufficient, preventing, irresistible grace, have employed the pens of Protestant as well as Popish divines, of Jansenists and Molinists, of Lutherans, Calvinists, and Arminians, as I have not the least curiosity to know, so I need not say. It sufficeth to observe that there have been and are still subsisting great contests upon these points. Only one thing I should desire to be informed of, to wit, What is the clear and distinct idea marked by the word *grace*? I presume a man may know the bare meaning of a term, without going into the depth of all those learned inquiries. This surely is an easy matter, provided there is an idea annexed to such a term. And if there is not, it can be neither the subject of a rational dispute, nor the object of real faith. Men may indeed impose upon themselves or others, and pretend to argue and believe, when at bottom there is no argument or belief, farther than mere verbal trifling. Grace taken in the vulgar sense, either for beauty, or favour, I can easily understand. But when it denotes an active, vital, ruling principle, influencing and operating on the mind of man, distinct from every natural power or motive, I profess myself altogether unable to understand it, or frame any distinct idea of it; and therefore I cannot assent to any proposition concerning it, nor, consequently have any faith about it: and it is a self-evident truth, that God obligeth no man to impossibilities. At the request of a philosophical friend, I did cast an eye on the writings he shewed me of some divines, and talked with others on this subject, but after all I had read or heard could make nothing of it, having always found, whenever I laid aside the word *grace*, and looked into my own mind, a perfect vacuity or privation of all ideas. And, as I am apt to think other men's minds and faculties are made much alike, I suspect that other men, if they examined what they call grace with the same exactness and indifference, would agree with me that there was nothing in it but an empty name.

EUPHRANOR Be the use of words or names what it will, I can never think it is to do things impossible. Let us then inquire what it is, and see if we can make sense of our daily practice. Words, it is agreed, are signs: it may not therefore be amiss to examine the use of other signs, in order to know that of words. Counters, for instance, at a card-table are used, not for their own sake, but only as signs substituted for money, as words are for ideas. Say now, Alciphron, is it necessary every time these counters are used throughout the progress of a game, to frame an idea of the distinct sum or value that each represents.

ALCIPHRON By no means: it is sufficient the players at first agree on their respective values, and at last substitute those values in their stead.

EUPHRANOR And in casting up a sum, where the figures stand for pounds, shillings and pence, do you think it necessary, throughout the whole progress of the operation, in each step to form ideas of pounds, shillings and pence?

ALCIPHRON I do not; it will suffice if in the conclusion those figures direct our actions with respect to things.

EUPHRANOR From hence it seems to follow, that words may not be insignificant, although they should not, every time they are used, excite the ideas they signify in our minds; it being sufficient that we have it in our power to substitute things or ideas for their signs when there is occasion. It seems also to follow that there may be another use of words besides that of marking and suggesting distinct ideas, to wit, the influencing our conduct and actions, which may be done either by forming rules for us to act by, or by raising certain passions, dispositions and emotions in our minds. A discourse, therefore, that directs how to act or excites to the doing or forbearance of an action may, it seems, be useful and significant, although the words whereof it is composed should not bring each a distinct idea into our minds.

ALCIPHRON It seems so.

EUPHRANOR Pray tell me, Alciphron, is not an idea altogether inactive?

ALCIPHRON It is.

EUPHRANOR An agent therefore, an active mind or spirit, cannot be an idea, or like an idea. Whence it should seem to follow that those words which denote an active principle, soul, or spirit do not, in a strict and proper sense, stand for ideas. And yet they are not insignificant neither; since I understand what is signified by the term *I*, or *myself*, or know what it means, although it be no idea, nor like an idea, but that which thinks, and wills, and apprehends ideas, and operates about them. Certainly it must be allowed that we have some notion that we understand, or know what is meant by the terms *myself*, *will*, *memory*, *love*, *hate*, and so forth; although, to speak exactly, these words do not suggest so many distinct ideas.

ALCIPHRON What would you infer from this?

EUPHRANOR What hath been inferred already – that words may be significant, although they do not stand for ideas. The contrary whereof having been presumed seems to have produced the doctrine of abstract ideas.

ALCIPHRON Will you not allow then that the mind can abstract?

EUPHRANOR I do not deny it may abstract in a certain sense, inasmuch as those things that can really exist, or be really perceived asunder, may be conceived asunder, or abstracted one from the other; for instance, a man's head from his body, colour from motion, figure from weight. But it will not thence follow that the mind can frame abstract general ideas, which appear to be impossible.

ALCIPHRON And yet it is a current opinion that every substantive name marks out and exhibits to the mind one distinct idea separate from all others.

EUPHRANOR Pray, Alciphron, is not the word *number* such a substantive name?

ALCIPHRON It is.

EUPHRANOR Do but try now whether you can frame an idea of number in abstract, exclusive of all signs, words, and things numbered. I profess for my own part I cannot.

ALCIPHRON Can it be so hard a matter to form a simple idea of number, the object of a most evident demonstrable science? Hold, let me see if I can't abstract the idea of number from the numerical names and characters, and all particular numerable things. – Upon which Alciphron paused a while, and then said, To confess the truth I do not find that I can.

EUPHRANOR But, though it seems neither you nor I can form distinct simple ideas of number, we can nevertheless make a very proper and significant use of numeral names. They direct us in the disposition and management of our affairs, and are of such necessary use that we should not know how to do without them. And yet, if other men's faculties may be judged of by mine, to attain a precise simple abstract idea of number is as difficult as to comprehend any mystery in religion.

6

H. L. MANSEL

A Classical Essay on Theological Reserve. *Here is a classical attempt to set out the limits of religious thought, and to argue for the need of caution and reserve in developing theological understanding. The passage contains one of the earliest discussions of the place of metaphor in theological argument, and is one of the earliest occasions on which the logical significance of this grammatical device was acknowledged. Whether in revelation or natural religion, said Mansel, "God is represented under finite conceptions" and theology must use metaphors which "are cumulative terms of the finite, employed at teaching me truths, concerning the infinite, which could neither be taught nor learned in any other manner." These are "lights on the highway of eternal truth, when we take them for what they are – our only guides on that road." Such is the case when we speak of God, even when we speak of him as a Person or a Moral Governor. Mansel, like Kant, considered his concept of God to be "regulative". With echoes of Bishop Butler he rightly complains of "the very irrational error "of those who expect" clearer conceptions and more rigid demonstrations of the invisible things of God, than those which they are content to accept and act upon in the concerns of their daily life."*

What then is the practical lesson which these Lectures are designed to teach concerning the right use of reason in religious questions? and what are the just claims of a reasonable faith, as distinguished from a blind credulity? In the first place, it is obvious that, if there

H. C. Mansel, *The Limits of Religious Thought*, John Murray (Publishers) Ltd. 1859, pp. xi–xiv, xvi–xviii, xix–xx, xxiii–xxvi, xxix–xxx, xxxi–xxxiii, 59.

is any object whatever of which the human mind is unable to form a clear and distinct conception, the inability equally disqualifies us for proving or for disproving a given doctrine, in all cases in which such a conception is an indispensable condition of the argument. If, for example, we can form no positive notion of the Nature of God as an Infinite Being, we are not entitled either to demonstrate the mystery of the Trinity as a necessary property of that Nature, or to reject it as necessarily inconsistent therewith. Such mysteries clearly belong, not to Reason, but to Faith; and the preliminary enquiry which distinguishes a reasonable from an unreasonable belief, must be directed, not to the premises by which the doctrine can be proved or disproved as reasonable or unreasonable, but to the nature of the authority on which it rests, as revealed or unrevealed. The brief summary of Christian Evidences contained in my concluding Lecture, and others which might be added to them, are surely sufficient to form an ample field for the use of Reason, even in regard to those mysteries which it cannot directly examine. If to submit to an authority which can stand the test of such investigations, and to believe it when it tells us of things which we are unable to investigate, – if this be censured as a blind credulity, it is blindness which in these things is a better guide than the opposite quality so justly described by the philosopher as "the sharpsightedness of little souls."

In the second place, a caution is needed concerning the kind of evidence which reason is competent to furnish within the legitimate sphere of its employment. If we have not such a conception of the Divine Nature as is sufficient for the a priori demonstration of religious truths, our rational conviction in any particular case must be regarded not as a certainty, but as a probability. We must remember the Aristotelian rule, to be content with such evidence as the nature of the object-matter allows. A single infallible criterion of all religious truth can be obtained only by the possession of a perfect Philosophy of the Infinite. If such a philosophy is unattainable; if the infinite can only be apprehended under finite symbols, and the authority of those symbols tested by finite evidences, there is always room for error, in consequence of the inadequacy of the conception to express completely the nature of the object. In other words, we must admit that human reason, though not worthless, is at least fallible, in dealing with religious questions; and that the probability of error is always increased in proportion to the partial nature of the evidence with which it deals. Those who set up some supreme criterion of religious truth, their "Christian consciousness", their "religious intuitions", their "moral reason", or any other of the favourite idols of the subjective school of theologians, and who treat with contempt every kind of evidence which does not harmonize with this, are especially liable to be led into error. They use the weight without the counterpoise, to the imminent peril of their mental equilibrium. This is the caution which it was the object of my concluding Lecture to enforce, principally by means of two practical rules; namely, first, that the true evidence for or against a religion, is not to be found in any single criterion, but in the result of many presumptions examined and compared together; and, secondly, that in proportion to the weight of the counter-evidence in favour of a religion, is the probability that we may be mistaken in supposing a particular class of objections to have any real weight at all.

These considerations are no less applicable to moral than to speculative reasonings. The moral faculty, though furnishing undoubtedly some of the most important elements for the solution of the religious problem, is no more entitled than any other single principle of the human mind to be accepted as a sole and sufficient criterion. It is true that to our sense of moral obligation we owe our primary conception of God as a moral Governor: and it is also true that, were man left solely to a priori presumptions in forming his estimate of the nature and attributes of God, the moral sense, as being that one of all human faculties whose judgments are least dependent on experience, would furnish the principal, if not the only characteristics of his highest conception of God. But here, as elsewhere, the original presumption is modified and corrected by subsequent experience. It is a fact which experience forces upon us, and which it is useless, were it possible, to disguise, that the representation of God after the model of the highest human morality which we are capable of conceiving is not sufficient to account for all the phenomena exhibited by the course of His natural Providence. The infliction of physical suffering, the permission of moral evil, the adversity of the good, the prosperity of the wicked, the crimes of the guilty involving the misery of the innocent, the tardy appearance and partial distribution of moral and religious knowledge in the world, – these are facts which no doubt are reconcilable, we know not how, with the infinite Goodness of God; but which certainly are not to be explained on the supposition that its sole and sufficient type is to be found in the finite goodness of man. What right then has the philosopher to assume that a criterion which admits of so many exceptions in the facts of nature may be applied without qualification or exception to the statements of revelation?

It remains to make some remarks on another of the opinions maintained in the following Lectures, on which, to judge by the criticisms to which it has been subjected, a few words of explanation may be desirable. It has been objected by reviewers of very opposite schools, that to deny to man a knowledge of the Infinite is to make Revelation itself impossible, and to leave no room for evidences on which reason can be legitimately employed. The objection would be pertinent, if I had ever maintained that Revelation is or can be a direct manifestation of the Infinite Nature of God. But I have constantly asserted the very reverse. In Revelation, as in Natural Religion, God is represented under finite conceptions, adapted to finite minds; and the evidences on which the authority of Revelation rests are finite and comprehensible also.[1] It is true that in Revelation, no less than in the exercise of our natural faculties, there is indirectly indicated the existence of a higher and more absolute truth, which, as it cannot be grasped by any effort of human thought, cannot be made the vehicle of any valid philosophical criticism. But the comprehension of this higher truth is no more necessary either to a belief in the contents of Revelation or to a reasonable examination of its evidences, than a conception of the infinite divisibility of matter is necessary to the child before it can learn to walk.

But it is a great mistake to suppose, as some of my critics have supposed, that if the Infinite, as an object, is inconceivable, therefore the language which denotes it is wholly without meaning, and the corresponding state of mind one of complete quiescence.

To conceive an object is a very different thing from merely understanding the meaning of a word.[2] The conception of any object as such implies both an identification and a distinction, – a recognition of it as that which it is, and a separation of it from that which it is not. The process therefore necessarily involves a combination of at least two elements – a common feature by which it is known as an object of thought at all, and a distinguishing feature, by which it is known as this object rather than that.

It is thus manifest that, even granting that the Infinite as such is inconceivable, our belief in an Infinite God is not a belief in nothing at all. It is a belief that a certain attribute, whose meaning we know so far at least as it is suggested by its contrary, can and must be combined in some manner with other attributes whose meanings we also know; – though how this combination is effected, and in what manner these attributes can form a consistent whole, we are unable, under the existing laws of human thought, to apprehend. Without such an apprehension of the whole, there can be no conception; though each part, viewed separately, may have an intelligible meaning, as denoting the presence or the absence of some known quality.

What then is meant by the assertion, which has been a stumbling-block to so many critics, that our conception of God, under these conditions of thought, is regulative but not speculative, and does not represent Him as He is in His Absolute Nature. The assertion, far from being a paradox, becomes almost a truism, as soon as we ask ourselves what are the conditions under which speculative truth is possible. My conception of any object is speculatively true, when it corresponds, either completely or as far as it goes, with the characteristics of the object as presented to sense or to some other intuitive faculty. My conception, for example, of any given colour, such as white or black, is speculatively true when it corresponds to the actual appearance of the colour as seen: it is speculatively false when it differs from that appearance. But where an immediate intuition of an object is unattainable, though we may form an indirect conception of it from its supposed resemblance to or difference from something else, such a conception, while it may be sufficient in many ways for our practical guidance, cannot be pronounced speculatively true or speculatively false, from the want of the proper intuition with which it must be compared.

Such is obviously the case with the fundamental conceptions of Theology. To the existence of any religious feeling or duty in man, it is indispensable that he should contemplate the Deity as a Person, and as a Moral Governor. But the attributes which constitute this personality and moral character cannot be apprehended in themselves by a direct intuition of the Divine Mind. We are unable to perceive directly even the intellectual and moral attributes of our fellow men: we can only infer them indirectly, by assuming their resemblance to those of which we are conscious in ourselves. But the close resemblance which may be supposed to exist between the mental attributes of one man and those of another, fails us when we attempt to extend the analogy to the corresponding attributes as they exist in the Divine Mind. In our own consciousness all such attributes are necessarily apprehended as limited; and the condition of limitation adheres to every attempt which we can make to conceive them in other beings. As Infinite Person, or a combination of the several attributes of personality and moral character, each expanded to infinity, appears to human thought to involve similar contradictions to those which may be elicited from the assumption of infinite time or infinite space. We are thus thrown back from the infinite to the indefinite: we are compelled to believe that, to whatever degree we may extend our conceptions of intellectual or moral excellence, they are still bounded by an inconceivable excellence beyond, and, as bounded, do not represent the absolute excellence of the divine perfections. We cannot attempt to conceive a combination of infinite moral attributes without involving ourselves in contradictions; but we believe, nevertheless, that those attributes exist in God without any discord or contradiction at all. Hence the conclusion is inevitable. Neither our positive conception of such attributes as limited, nor our abortive attempt to conceive them as unlimited, is an exact representation of the Divine Nature as it is; though it may be sufficient as a guide to our religious thoughts and feelings and duties. In other words, it is regulative, but not speculative; for a speculative representation of God can only be gained by a direct intuition of the infinite; and a direct intuition of the infinite is unattainable by human consciousness.

But it by no means follows, as some of my critics seem to suppose, that a regulative truth is equivalent to a speculative falsehood. To pronounce a portrait to be unlike the original, as well as to pronounce it to be like, it is necessary that we should have seen the original itself. An intuition of the infinite is thus necessary to the detection of speculative falsehood, no less than to the assertion of speculative truth, in our conceptions of the Divine Nature. We know not how a positive apprehension of infinity would modify our conceptions of certain attributes; for, never having had a positive apprehension of infinity, we have no means of making the trial. We are indeed justified in believing that our faculties are not given us as the instruments of deception: we are justified in believing that the enlargement of our knowledge beyond its present scope would not involve the contradiction of anything that we know now. But we are not warranted in arguing from that belief as if it were identical with the higher knowledge itself: we are not warranted in assuming that every doubt and difficulty with which we are now surrounded would remain hereafter along with the essentials of what we know. We strain our eyes to the utmost limit of their vision, and we behold things dimly and confusedly in the extreme distance. We believe that a keener vision would give us a clearer view of the objects; not that it would increase or retain the dimness and confusion likewise. And so it is with the limitation of our intellectual faculties also. We cannot avoid, in our present condition, the contradictions and confusions which accompany every attempt to conceive the Infinite. Yet we know enough to warrant the belief that these apparent anomalies are but the result of our own limits of thought, and may not be assumed as inherent in the objects which we attempt to conceive.

It is shewn that in all departments of human knowledge alike, – in the laws of thought, in the movement of our limbs, in the perception of our senses, – the truths which guide our practice cannot be reduced to principles which thus satisfy our reason; and that, if religious thought is placed under the same restrictions, this is but in strict analogy to the general conditions to which God has subjected man in his search after truth. One half of the rationalist's objections against revealed religion would fall to the ground, if men would not commit the very irrational error of expecting clearer conceptions and more rigid demonstrations of the invisible things of God, than those which they are content to accept and act upon in the concerns of their earthly life.

I am happy to be able to adduce, in support of the above remarks, the following observations of one of the most learned and intelligent of my critics. "The distinction", says this able writer, "between a knowledge which is speculatively adequate and one which, without being this, is yet practically regulative, has been received by some as if it were a theological heresy of the basest sort. Without entering into the question at present as one of philosophical import, we would only recall to the attention of such, two considerations which may serve to allay their apprehensions of danger from this distinction. The one of these is, that this distinction obtains in matters of ordinary life, and is acted on daily by thousands who follow safely and with advantage practical rules, the theory of which they cannot comprehend; so that, in applying this to our religious interests and relations, we postulate no new principle, but only carry out one to which universal consent has already been obtained. The other consideration is, that it is only on the ground of this distinction that the mode, so plentifully exemplified in Scripture, of representing God as if He were a being of like form, affections, and passions with ourselves, can be explained or justified. We there read that He has eyes, hands, feet – that He is angry, is grieved, repents – that He dwells in a house, sits on a throne, walks in a path, and many other such like representations. Now, viewed speculatively, such modes of representation are beyond all question incorrect; they do not answer to the real nature of God; and, if held as directly true concerning Him, would land us in serious error. What, then, are we to do with them? or how are we to make use of them so as to reap the benefit they are designed to convey to us? To these questions we can see no satisfactory answer without a resort to the distinction between speculative and regulative knowledge."

So, Mansel can say –

It is our duty, then, to think of God as personal; and it is our duty to believe that He is infinite. It is true that we cannot reconcile these two representations with each other; as our conception of personality involves attributes apparently contradictory to the notion of infinity. But it does not follow that this contradiction exists anywhere but in our own minds: it does not follow that it implies any impossibility in the absolute nature of God. The apparent contradiction, in this case, as in those previously noticed, is the necessary consequence of an attempt on the part of the human thinker to transcend the boundaries of his own consciousness. It proves that there are limits to man's power of thought; and it proves no more.

NOTES

1. In confirmation of this view I am happy to be able to quote the following remarks which have appeared since the first publication of these Lectures, from the pen of one of the clearest and profoundest thinkers of the present day.

"What is the treatment which I should give to these symbols? Am I at liberty to say – These are figures, they are metaphors, in the oriental style, and as such, if I am in search of their exact import, they must be shorn of much of their apparent value? The very contrary of this should, as I think, be the rule of interpretation in the case. Oriental writers do indeed indulge themselves in the use of extravagant similes when they are framing adulations for the ear of potentates; but this is not the style of the Biblical writers; and when they are teaching theology in terms and phrases proper to the finite mind, which are the only terms available, or, indeed, possible, they accumulate such figurative terms as substitutes for terms of the Infinite. Thus, in teaching what they teach concerning the Divine Power – they say of the Most High such things as these: That He taketh up the isles as a very little thing; that with Him the mountains are only as the small dust of the balance; that He stays the raging of the sea, and says to its proud waves – Thus far shall ye go, and no further. They say of God – That He spreadeth forth the heavens as a tent to dwell in; and that as a garment, some time hence, He shall roll them together.

. . . These metaphors are cumulative terms of the finite, employed for teaching me truths, concerning the Infinite, which could neither be taught nor learned in any other manner, whether by me or by the loftiest and largest of human minds. . . . The abstractions of the finite reason become delusive fictions when they are put forward as applicable to the Infinite: whereas the figures and (as they might be called) the fictions of a symbolic style are lights on the highway of eternal truth, when we take them for what they are – our only guides on that road." Taylor's *Logic in Theology*, &c., pp. 321–323.

2. A critic in the National Review is of opinion that "relative apprehension is always and necessarily of two terms together"; and "if of the finite, then also of the infinite". This is true as regards the meaning of the words; but by no means as regards the conception of the corresponding objects. If extended to the latter, it should in consistency be asserted that the conception of that which is conceivable involves also the conception of that which is inconceivable; that the consciousness of anything is also a consciousness of nothing; that the intuition of space and time is likewise an intuition of the absence of both.

7

H. LOTZE and F. H. BRADLEY

The Personality of God. *Can we legitimately speak of God as a person? In the passage which follows Lotze considers the argument that we cannot speak of the personality of God because every Ego implies a matching non-Ego, so that to speak of the personality of God demands a limitation of God. He argues on the contrary that personal existence for God, or for man, is given immediately and that such immediate knowledge is presupposed by, and not subsequent to, the distinction of Ego and non-Ego. Selfhood is given to God as to ourselves in a certainty "which is immediately experienced". We are aware of our self-existence earlier than we are aware of the "Ego as opposed to the non-Ego". So Lotze seeks to establish the purpose and existence of God and the infinite, arguing in particular "that the conditions of personality which we meet within finite things, are not lacking to the infinite". Indeed, "perfect personality is in God only, to all finite minds there is allotted but a pale copy thereof". "Personality is an ideal" which "like all that is good appertains to us only conditionally and hence imperfectly".*

It might seem at first sight that Lotze and Bradley are in complete opposition to each other on this theme. It might seem that Lotze is attributing while Bradley is denying personality to God. But in fact they are closer than at first sight appears. Both Lotze and Bradley deny that the personality of God is a finite personality. Lotze talks of God as "a perfect personality". Bradley, who says expressly that "for me a person is infinite or meaningless" appropriately concludes that we must talk of God or the Absolute as supra-personal. But it is plain that both qualify the human model of personality when they use it to speak of God.

It may be that only the being who in thought contrasts with himself a Non-Ego from which he also distinguishes himself, can say I (Ich) to himself, but yet in order that in thus distinguishing he should not mistake and confound himself with the Non-Ego, this discriminating thought of his must be guided by a certainty of self which is immediately experienced, by a self-existence which is earlier than the discriminative relation by which it becomes Ego as opposed to the Non-Ego . . . all self-consciousness rests upon the foundation of direct sense of self which can by no means arise from becoming aware of a contrast with the external world, but is itself the reason that the contrast can be felt as unique, as not comparable to any other distinction between two objects.

It is involved in the notion of a finite being that it has its definite place in the whole, and thus that it is not what any other is, and yet that at the same time it must as a member of the whole in its whole development be related to and must harmonize with that other. Even for the finite being the forms of its activity flow from its inner nature, and neither the content of its sensations nor its feelings, nor the peculiarity of any other of its manifestations, is given to it from without; but the incitements of its action certainly all come to it from that external world, to which, in consequence of the finiteness of its nature, it is related as a part, having the place, time, and character of its development marked out by the determining whole. The same consideration does not hold of the Infinite Being that comprehends in itself all that is finite and is the cause of its nature and reality; this Infinite Being does not need – as we sometimes, with a strange perversion of the right point of view, think – that its life should be called forth by external stimuli, but from the beginning its concept is without that deficiency which seems to us to make such stimuli necessary for the finite being, and its active efficacy thinkable. The Infinite Being, not bound by any obligation to agree in any way with something not itself, will, with perfect self-sufficingness, possess in its own nature the causes of every step forward in the development of its life. An analogy which though weak yet holds in some important points and is to some extent an example of the thing itself, is furnished to us by the course of memory in the finite mind.

H. Lotze, *Microcosmus*, trs. E. Hamilton and E. E. C. Jones, T. and T. Clark 1885, Vol. II, pp. 679–80, 683–88.

The world of our ideas, though certainly called into existence at first by external impressions, spreads out into a stream which, without any fresh stimulation from the external world, produces plenty that is new by the continuous action and reaction of its own movements, and carries out in works of imagination, in the results reached by reflection, and in the conflicts of passion, a great amount of living development – as much, that is, as can be reached by the nature of a finite being without incessantly renewed orientation, by action and reaction with the whole in which it is comprehended; hence the removal of these limits of finiteness does not involve the removal of any producing condition of personality which is not compensated for by the self-sufficingness of the Infinite, but that which is only approximately possible for the finite mind, the conditioning of its life by itself, takes place without limit in God, and no contrast of an external world is necessary for Him.

Of course there remains the question what it is that in God corresponds to the primary impulse which the train of ideas in a finite mind receives from the external world? But the very question involves the answer. For when through the impulse received from without there is imparted to the inner life of the mind an initiatory movement which it subsequently carries on by its own strength, whence comes the movement in the external world which makes it capable of giving that impulse? A brief consideration will suffice to convince us that our theory of the cosmos, whatever it may be, must somehow and somewhere recognize the actual movement itself as an originally given reality, and can never succeed in extracting it from rest. And this indication may suffice for the present, since we wish here to avoid increasing our present difficulties by entering upon the question as to the nature of time. When we characterize the inner life of the Personal God, the current of His thoughts, His feelings, and His will, as everlasting and without beginning, as having never known rest, and having never been roused to movement from some state of quiescence, we call upon imagination to perform a task no other and no greater than that which is required from it by every materialistic or pantheistic view. Without an eternal uncaused movement of the World-Substance, or the assumption of definite initial movements of the countless world-atoms, movements which have to be simply recognized and accepted, neither materialistic nor pantheistic views could attain to any explanation of the existing cosmic course, and all parties will be at last driven to the conviction that the splitting up of reality into a quiescent being and a movement which subsequently takes hold of it, is one of those fictions which, while they are of some use in the ordinary business of reflection, betray their total inadmissibility as soon as we attempt to rise above the reciprocal connection of cosmic particulars to our first notions of the cosmos as a whole.

The ordinary doubts as to the possibility of the personal existence of the Infinite have not made us waver in our conviction. But in seeking to refute them, we have had the feeling that we were occupying a standpoint which could only be regarded as resulting from the strangest perversion of all natural relations. The course of development of philosophic thought has put us who live in this age in the position of being obliged to show that the conditions of personality which we meet with infinite things, are not lacking to the Infinite; whereas the natural concatenation of the matter under discussion would lead us to show that of the full personality which is possible only for the Infinite a feeble reflection is given also to the finite; for the characteristics peculiar to the finite are not producing conditions of self-existence, but obstacles to its unconditioned development, although we are accustomed, unjustifiably, to deduce from these characteristics its capacity of personal existence. The finite being always works with powers with which it did not endow itself, and according to laws which it did not establish – that is, it works by means of a mental organization which is realized not only in it but also in innumerable similar beings. Hence in reflecting on self, it may easily seem to it as though there were in itself some obscure and unknown substance – something which is in the Ego though it is not the Ego itself, and to which, as to its subject, the whole personal development is attached. And hence there arise the questions – never to be quite silenced – What are we ourselves? What is our soul? What is our self – that obscure being, incomprehensible to ourselves, that stirs in our feelings and our passions, and never rises into complete self-consciousness? The fact that these questions can arise shows how far personality is from being developed in us to the extent which its notion admits and requires. It can be perfect only in the Infinite Being which, in surveying all its conditions or actions, never finds any content of that which it suffers or any law of its working, the meaning and origin of which are not transparently plain to it, and capable of being explained by reference to its own nature. Further, the position of the finite mind, which attaches it as a constituent of the whole to some definite place in the cosmic order, requires that its inner life should be awakened by successive stimuli from without, and that its course should proceed according to the laws of a psychical mechanism, in obedience to which individual ideas, feelings, and efforts press upon and supplant one another. Hence the whole self can never be brought together at one moment, our self-conscious-ness never presents to us a complete and perfect picture of our Ego – not even of its whole nature at any moment, and much less of the unity of its development in time. We always appear to ourselves from a one-sided point of view, due to those mental events which happen to be taking place within us at the time – a point of view which only admits of our surveying a small part of our being; we always react upon the stimuli which reach us, in accordance with the one-sided impulses of this accidental and partial self-consciousness; it is only to a limited extent that we can say with truth that *we* act; for the most part action is carried on in us by the individual feelings or groups of ideas to which at any moment the psychical mechanism gives the upper hand. Still less do we exist wholly *for ourselves* in a temporal point of view. There is much that disappears from memory, but most of all individual moods, that escape it by degrees. There are many regions of thought in which while young we were quite at home, which in age we can only bring before our mind as alien phaenomena; feelings in which we once revelled with enthusiasm we can now hardly recover at all, we can now hardly realize even a pale reflection of the power which they once exercised over us; endeavours which once seemed to constitute the most inalienable essence of our Ego seem, when we reach the path along which later life conducts us, to be unintelligible aberrations, the incentives to which we can no longer understand. In point of fact we have little ground for speaking of the personality of finite beings; it is an ideal, which, like all that is ideal, belongs unconditionally only to the Infinite, but like all that is good appertains to us only conditionally and hence imperfectly.

The more simple content of this section hardly needs the brief synoptical repetition in which we now proceed to gather up its results and to add them to those already reached.

Selfhood, the essence of all personality, does not depend upon any opposition that either has happened or is happening of the Ego to a Non-Ego, but it consists in an immediate self-existence which constitutes the basis of the possibility of that contrast wherever it appears. Self-consciousness is the elucidation of this self-existence which is brought about by means of knowledge, and even this is by no means necessarily bound up with the distinction of the Ego from a Non-Ego which is substantially opposed to it.

In the nature of the finite mind as such is to be found the reason why the development of its personal consciousness can take place only through the influences of that cosmic whole which the finite being itself is not, that is through stimulation coming from the Non-Ego, not because it needs the contrast with something *alien* in order to have self-existence, but because in this respect, as in every other, it does not contain in itself the conditions of its existence. We do not find this limitation in the being of the Infinite; hence for it alone is there possible a self-existence, which needs neither to be initiated nor to be continuously developed by something not itself, but which maintains itself within itself with spontaneous action that is eternal and had no beginning.

Perfect Personality is in God only, to all finite minds there is allotted but a pale copy thereof; the finiteness of the finite is not a producing condition of this Personality but a limit and a hindrance of its development.

The Absolute, though known, is higher, in a sense, than our experience and knowledge; and in this connexion I will ask it if has personality. At the point we have reached such a question can be dealt with rapidly. We can answer it at once in the affirmative or negative according to its meaning. Since the Absolute has everything, it of course must possess personality. And if by personality we are to understand the highest form of finite spiritual development, then certainly in an eminent degree the Absolute is personal. For the higher (we may repeat) is always the more real. And, since in the Absolute the very lowest modes of experience are not lost, it seems even absurd to raise such a question about personality.

And this is not the sense in which the question is usually put. "Personal" is employed, in effect with a restrictive meaning; for it is used to exclude what is above, as well as below, personality. The super-personal, in other words, is either openly or tacitly regarded

F. H. Bradley, *Appearance and Reality*, 1930, pp. 470–73 and *Essays on Truth and Reality*, 1914, p. 451. Reprinted by permission of the Clarendon Press, Oxford.

as impossible. Personality is taken as the highest possible way of experience, and naturally, if so, the Absolute cannot be super-personal. This conclusion, with the assumption on which it rests, may be summarily rejected. It has been, indeed, refuted beforehand by previous discussions. If the term "personal" is to bear anything like its ordinary sense, assuredly the Absolute is not merely personal. It is not personal, because it is personal and more. It is, in a word, super-personal.

I intend here not to enquire into the possible meanings of personality. On the nature of the self and of self-consciousness I have spoken already, and I will merely add here that for me a person is finite or is meaningless. But the question raised as to the Absolute may, I think, be more briefly disposed of. If by calling it personal you mean only that it is nothing but experience, that it contains all the highest that we possible can know and feel, and is a unity in which the details are utterly pervaded and embraced – then in this conclusion I am with you. But your employment of the term personal I very much regret. I regret this use mainly, not because I consider it incorrect – that between us would matter little – but because it is misleading and directly serves the cause of dishonesty.

For most of those who insist on what they call "the personality of God", are intellectually dishonest. They desire one conclusion, and, to reach it, they argue for another. But the second, if proved, is quite different, and serves their purpose only because they obscure it and confound it with the first. And it is by their practical purpose that the result may here be judged. The Deity, which they want, is of course finite, a person much like themselves, with thoughts and feelings limited and mutable in the process of time. They desire a person in the sense of a self, amongst and over against other selves, moved by personal relations and feelings towards these others – feelings and relations which are altered by the conduct of the others. And, for their purpose, what is not this, is really nothing. Now with this desire in itself I am not here concerned. Of course for us to ask seriously if the Absolute can be personal in such a way, would be quite absurd. And my business for the moment is not with the truth but with intellectual honesty.

It would be honest first of all to state openly the conclusion aimed at, and then to inquire if this conclusion can be maintained. But what is not honest is to suppress the point really at issue, to desire the personality of the Deity in one sense, and then to contend for it in another, and to do one's best to ignore the chasm which separates the two. Once give up your finite and mutable person, and you have parted with everything which, for you, makes personality important. Nor will you bridge the chasm by the sliding extension of a word. You will only make a fog, where you can cry out that you are on both sides at once. And towards increasing this fog I decline to contribute. It would be useless, in such company and in such an atmosphere, to discuss the meaning of personality – if indeed the word actually has any meaning. For me it is sufficient to know, on one side, that the Absolute is not a finite person. Whether, on the other side, personality in some eviscerated remnant of sense can be applied to it, is a question intellectually unimportant and practically trifling.

With regard to the personality of the Absolute we must guard against two one-sided errors. The Absolute is not personal, nor is it moral, nor is it beautiful or true. And yet in these denials we may be falling into worse mistakes. For it would be far more incorrect to assert that the Absolute is either false, or ugly, or bad, or is something even beneath the application of predicates such as these. And it is better to affim personality than to call the Absolute impersonal. But neither mistake should be necessary. The absolute stands above, and not below, its internal distinctions. It does not eject them, but it includes them as elements in its fullness. To speak in other language, it is not the indifference but the concrete identity of all extremes. But it is better in this connexion to call it super-personal.

A doctrine such as the personality of God may be true, as giving in an imperfect and incorrect manner a most essential feature of reality which cannot as well be given otherwise. And the doctrine may be necessary, perhaps, as being for a certain vital purpose the best idea that we can conceive, and the supreme belief on which we have to act. But, however this may be, if we go further and take personality as being the last word about the Universe, we fall, in my opinion, into serious error.

Theological Reticence. *Here is Bradley's essay into the tentative character of theology. Talk of God and man in relationship, like talk of all terms in relation to each other, presupposes, for Bradley, some unity (the "Absolute") embracing both related terms. Such a view clearly matches the religious man's claim for unity with God. But the implication of all this is that talk of God as an object in relation to men as other subjects, which is the broad structure of most talk about God, will always display inadequacies on philosophical, quite apart from theological grounds. To suppose that we shall ever attain "ultimate theoretical consistency" in theology is (says Bradley) ridiculous. The contrary indeed follows from the very character of the exercise itself.*

Religion naturally implies a relation between Man and God. Now a relation always (as we have seen throughout) is self-contradictory. It implies always two terms which are finite and which claim independence. On the other hand a relation is un-meaning, unless both itself and the relateds are the adjectives of a whole. And to find a solution of this discrepancy would be to pass entirely beyond the relational point of view. This general conclusion may at once be verified in the sphere of religion.

Man is on the one hand a finite subject, who is over against God, and merely "standing in relation". And yet, upon the other hand, apart from God man is merely an abstraction. And religion perceives this truth, and it affirms that man is good and real only through grace, or that again, attempting to be independent, he perishes through wrath. He does not merely "stand in relation", but is moved inly by his opposite, and indeed, apart from that inward working, could not stand at all. God again is a finite object, standing above and apart from man, and is something independent of all relation to his will and intelligence. Hence God, if taken as a thinking and feeling being, has a private personality. But, sundered from those relations which qualify him, God is inconsistent emptiness; and, qualified by his relation to an Other, he is distracted finitude. God is therefore taken, again, as transcending this internal relation. He wills and knows himself, and he finds his reality and self-consciousness, in union with man. Religion is therefore a process with inseparable factors, each appearing on either side. It is the unity of man and God, which, in various stages and forms, wills and knows itself throughout. It parts itself into opposite terms with a relation between them; but in the same breath it denies this provisional sundering, and it asserts and feels in either therm the inward pre-

F. H. Bradley, *Appearance and Reality*, pp. 394–96.

sence of the other. And so religion consists in a practical oscillation, and expresses itself only by the means of theoretical compromise. It would shrink perhaps from the statement that God loves and enjoys himself in human emotion, and it would recoil once more from the assertion that love can be where God is not, and, striving to hug both shores at once, it wavers bewildered. And sin is the hostility of a rebel against a wrathful Ruler. And yet this whole relation too must feel and hate itself in the sinner's heart, while the Ruler also is torn and troubled by conflicting emotions. But to say that sin is a necessary element in the Divine self-consciousness – an element, however, emerging but to be forthwith absorbed, and never liberated as such – this would probably appear to be either nonsense or blasphemy. Religion prefers to put forth statements which it feels are untenable, and to correct them at once by counter-statements which it finds are no better. It is then driven forwards and back between both, like a dog which seeks to follow two masters. A discrepancy worth our notice is the position of God in the universe. We may say that in religion God tends always to pass beyond himself. He is necessarily led to end in the Absolute, which for religion is not God. God, whether a "person" or not, is, on the one hand, a finite being and an object to man. On the other hand, the consummation, sought by the religious consciousness, is the perfect unity of these terms. And, if so, nothing would in the end fall outside God. But to take God as the ceaseless oscillation and changing movement of the process, is out of the question. On the other side the harmony of all these discords demands, as we have shown, the alteration of their finite character. The unity implies a complete suppression of the relation, as such; but, with that suppression, religion and the good have altogether, as such, disappeared. If you identify the Absolute with God, that is not the God of religion. If again you separate them, God becomes a finite factor in the whole. And the effort of religion is to put an end to, and break down, this relation – a relation which, none the less, it essentially presupposes. Hence, short of the Absolute, God cannot rest, and, having reached that goal, he is lost and religion with him.

We may say that God is not God, till he has become all in all, and that a God which is all in all is not the God of religion. God is but an aspect, and that must mean but an appearance, of the Absolute.

Has religion really got to be consistent theoretically? Is ultimate theoretical consistency a thing which is attainable anywhere? And, at all events, is it a thing attainable in life and in practice? This is the fundamental question upon which the whole issue depends. And I need not pause here to ask whether it is quite certain that, when God is limited, the Universe becomes theoretically consistent?

I have elsewhere discussed the question of theoretical consistency. With a certain exception (and how far this is an exception I have explained) I have argued that all truth must be imperfect. Truth cannot in the end become consistent and ultimately true, but, for all that, it is satisfactory in varying degrees. The idea that in the special sciences, and again in practical life, we have absolute truths, must be rejected as illusory. We are everywhere dependent on what may be called useful mythology, and nothing other than these inconsistent ideas could serve our various purposes. These ideas are false in the sense that they are not ultimately true. But they are true in the sense that all that is lacking to them is a greater or lesser extent of completion, which, the more true they are, would the less transform their present character. And, in proportion as the need to which they answer is wider and deeper, these ideas already have attained actual truth.

Viewed thus the question as to what may be called religious ideas is seriously changed. To insist on ultimate theoretical consistency, which in no case can we reach, becomes once for all ridiculous. The main question is as to the real nature and end of religion, and as to the respective importance of those aspects which belong to it. The ideas which best express our highest religious needs and their satisfaction, must certainly be true. Ultimate truth they do not possess, and exactly what in the end it would take to make them perfect we cannot know. But in this respect they are like the whole body of special truths attainable by us, or indeed by any other possible finite beings, whether in this life and world or in any other. What we have to consider is the relative importance of that purpose which the ideas serve, and how well, viewed from all sides, they aid and express its satisfaction. . . .

The demand for a theoretical consistency which mutilates the substance of religion, starts from error in principle and leads in the result to practical discord or sterility.

F. H. Bradley, *Essays on Truth and Reality*, pp. 430–31, 432.

8

RUDOLF OTTO

The first extract contains Otto's classical account of the idea of the holy – as one where to the idea of moral goodness is added the category of the "numinous". The "numinous" is sui generis: *cannot be strictly defined; and can only be evoked – "as everything that comes 'of the spirit' must be awakened". The second extract elucidates further the numinous situation. It is one in which we find ourselves in the presence of a Mystery – a* mysterium tremendum. *Later he adds* fascinans. *Not only is there in the numinous experience "the element of daunting 'awfulness' and 'majesty'". There is also another aspect "in which the (numinous) shows itself as something uniquely attractive and fascinating."*

The third extract is important for the notion of "ideogram" which it contains. "Natural" attributes can be rightly used as "ideograms" for what is properly beyond utterance; but they cannot straightforwardly qualify the numinous since it is non-rational.

. . . We generally take "holy" as meaning "completely good"; it is the absolute moral attribute, denoting the consummation of moral goodness. In this sense Kant calls the will which remains unwaveringly obedient to the moral law from the motive of duty a "holy" will; here clearly we have simply the *perfectly moral* will. In the same way we may speak of the holiness or sanctity of Duty or Law, meaning merely that they are imperative upon conduct and universally obligatory.

But this common usage of the term is inaccurate. It is true that all

Rudolf Otto, *The Idea of the Holy*, trs. J. W. Harvey, Oxford University Press 1924, pp. 5–7, 12–13, 23–24.

this moral significance is contained in the world "holy", but it includes in addition – as even we cannot but feel – a clear overplus of meaning, and this it is now our task to isolate. Nor is this merely a later or acquired meaning; rather, "holy", or at least the equivalent words in Latin and Greek, in Semitic and other ancient languages, denoted first and foremost *only* the overplus: if the ethical element was present at all, at any rate it was not original and never constituted the whole meaning of the word. Any one who uses it today does undoubtedly always feel "the morally good" to be implied in "holy"; and accordingly in our inquiry into that element which is separate and peculiar to the idea of the holy it will be useful, at least for the temporary purpose of the investigation, to invent a special term to stand for "the holy" *minus* its moral factor or "moment", and, as we can now add, minus its "rational" aspect altogether.

It will be our endeavour to suggest this unnamed Something to the reader as far as we may, so that he may himself feel it. There is no religion in which it does not live as the real innermost core, and without it no religion would be worthy of the name. It is pre-eminently a living force in the Semitic religions, and of these again in none has it such vigour as in that of the Bible. Here, too, it has a name of its own, viz. the Hebrew *qādôsh*, to which the Greek ἅγιος and the Latin *sanctus*, and, more accurately still, *sacer*, are the corresponding terms. It is not, of course, disputed, that these terms in all three languages connote, as part of their meaning, *good*, *absolute goodness*, when, that is, the notion has ripened and reached the highest stage in its development. And we then use the word "holy" to translate them. But this "holy" then represents the gradual shaping and filling in with ethical meaning, or what we shall call the "schematization", of what was a unique original feeling-response, which can be in itself ethically neutral and claims consideration in its own right. And when this moment or element first emerges and begins its long development, all those expressions (*qādôsh*, ἅγιος, *sacer*, &c.) mean beyond all question something quite other than "the good". This is universally agreed by contemporary criticism, which rightly explains the rendering of *qādôsh* by "good" as a mistranslation and unwarranted "rationalization" or "moralization" of the term.

Accordingly, it is worth while, as we have said, to find a word to stand for this element in isolation, this "extra" in the meaning of "holy" above and beyond the meaning of goodness. By means of a special term we shall the better be able, first, to keep the meaning clearly apart and distinct, and second, to apprehend and classify connectedly whatever subordinate forms or stages of development it may show. For this purpose I adopt a word coined from the Latin *numen*. *Omen* has given us *ominous*, and there is no reason why from *numen* we should not similarly form a word "*numinous*". I shall speak then of a unique "numinous" category of value and of a definitely "numinous" state of mind, which is always found wherever the category is applied. This mental state is perfectly *sui generis* and irreducible to any other; and therefore, like every absolutely primary and elementary datum, while it admits of being discussed, it cannot be strictly defined. There is only one way to help another to an understanding of it. He must be guided and led on by consideration and discussion of the matter through the ways of his own mind, until he reach the point at which "the numinous" in him perforce begins to stir, to start into life and into consciousness. We can co-operate in this process by bringing before his notice all that can be found in other regions of the mind, already known and familiar, to resemble, or again to afford some special contrast to, the particular experience we wish to elucidate. Then we must add: "This *X* of ours is not precisely *this* experience, but akin to this one and the opposite of that other. Cannot you now realize for yourself what it is?" In other words our *X* cannot, strictly speaking, be taught, it can only be evoked, awakened in the mind; as everything that comes "of the spirit" must be awakened.

We said above that the nature of the numinous can only be suggested by means of the special way in which it is reflected in the mind in terms of feeling. "Its nature is such that it grips or stirs the human mind with this and that determinate affective state." We have now to attempt to give a further indication of these determinate states. We must once again endeavour, by adducing feelings akin to them for the purpose of analogy or contrast, and by the use of metaphor and symbolic expressions, to make the states of mind we are investigating ring out, as it were, of themselves.

Let us consider the deepest and most fundamental element in all strong and sincerely felt religious emotion. Faith unto Salvation, Trust, Love – all these are there. But over and above these is an element which may also on occasion, quite apart from them, profoundly affect us and occupy the mind with a wellnigh bewildering strength. Let us follow it up with every effort of sympathy and imaginative intuition wherever it is to be found, in the lives of those around us, in sudden, strong ebullitions of personal piety and the frames of mind such ebullitions evince, in the fixed and ordered solemnities of rites and liturgies, and again in the atmosphere that clings to old religious monuments and buildings, to temples and to churches. If we do so we shall find we are dealing with something for which there is only one appropriate expression, *mysterium tremendum*. The feeling of it may at times come sweeping like a gentle tide, pervading the mind with a tranquil mood of deepest worship. It may pass over into a more set and lasting attitude of the soul, continuing, as it were, thrillingly vibrant and resonant, until at last it dies away and the soul resumes its "profane", non-religious mood of everyday experience. It may burst in sudden eruption up from the depths of the soul with spasms and convulsions, or lead to the strangest excitements, to intoxicated frenzy, to transport, and to ecstasy. It has its wild and demonic forms and can sink to an almost grisly horror and shuddering. It has its crude, barbaric antecedents and early manifestations, and again it may be developed into something beautiful and pure and glorious. It may become the hushed, trembling, and speechless humility of the creature in the presence of – whom or what? In the presence of that which is a *Mystery* inexpressible and above all creatures.

The *mysterium tremendum* can be characterized not only in terms of "awefulness" and "majesty" but in terms of "energy". Such energy is particularly vividly perceptible in the "ὀργή" or "Wrath"; and it everywhere clothes itself in symbolic expressions – vitality, passion, emotional temper, will, force, movement, excitement, activity, violence. These features are typical and recur again and again from the daemonic level up to the idea of the "living" God. We have here the factor that has everywhere more than any other prompted the fiercest opposition to the "philosophic" God of mere rational speculation, who can be put into a definition. And for their part the philosophers have condemned these expressions of the energy of the numen, whenever they are brought on to the scene, as sheer anthropomorphism. In so far as their opponents have for the most part themselves failed to recognize that the terms they have borrowed from the sphere of human conative and affective life have merely value as analogies, the philosophers are right to condemn them. But they are wrong, in so far as, this error notwithstanding, these terms stood for a genuine aspect of the divine nature – its non-rational aspect – a due consciousness of which served to protect religion itself from being "rationalized" away.

For wherever men have been contending for the "living" God and for voluntarism there, we may be sure, have been non-rationalists fighting rationalists and rationalism. It was so with Luther in his controversy with Erasmus; and Luther's "omnipotentia Dei" in his *De Servo Arbitrio* is nothing but the union of "majesty" – in the sense of absolute supremacy – with this "energy", in the sense of a force that knows not stint nor stay, which is urgent, active, compelling, and alive. In Mysticism, too, this element of "energy" is a very living and vigorous factor, at any rate in the "voluntaristic" Mysticism, the Mysticism of love, where it is very forcibly seen in that "consuming fire" of love whose burning strength the mystic can hardly bear, but begs that the heat that has scorched him may be mitigated, lest he be himself destroyed by it. And in this urgency and pressure the mystic's "love" claims a perceptible kinship with the ὀργή itself, the scorching and consuming wrath of God; it is the same "energy", only differently directed. "Love", says one of the mystics, "is nothing else than quenched Wrath".

The element of "energy" reappears in Fichte's speculations on the Absolute as the gigantic, never-resting, active world-stress, and in Schopenhauer's daemonic "Will". At the same time both these writers are guilty of the same error that is already found in Myth; they transfer "natural" attributes, which ought only to be used as "ideograms" for what is itself properly beyond utterance, to the non-rational as real qualifications of it, and they mistake symbolic expressions of feelings for adequate concepts upon which a "scientific" structure of knowledge may be based.

PART THREE: RECENT EMPIRICISM IN ITS EARLIEST STAGE

9

BERTRAND RUSSELL

Knowledge by acquaintance and knowledge by description. *Bertrand Russell used these phrases to distinguish between an alleged "direct" knowledge of what came to be called coloured patches ("sense data") – a knowledge by acquaintance, and an alleged "indirect" knowledge of physical objects such as tables. This was, in contrast to knowledge by acquaintance, knowledge by description.*

In this way Russell introduced a logical distinction between words ("proper names" in an extended sense of that phrase) whose use in naming was infallible and self-guaranteeing, and phrases which were definite descriptions of the type "the *so-and-so*", *e.g. "the physical object causing the sense data". Definite descriptions only had an indirect contact with the world. What they talked about was only known when they were analyzed into words standing for sense data, words whose reference was incontrovertible. We begin to see here what Russell eventually adumbrated, viz. the notion of a hierarchy of languages built on words for sense-data as their ultimate grounding in the world.*

Thus for Russell, all knowledge rests on acquaintance as its foundation. As the concluding sentences of the extract remarks, on Russell's view: "every proposition which we can understand must be composed wholly of constituents with which we are acquainted". In other words for Russell, every proposition which we can understand must be composed wholly of sense data. To put the point otherwise, on the supposition that the constituents of the world are sense data, then we cannot understand or meaningfully talk about whatever can not be reduced to them. This was the position which led naturally and directly to the verification principle on the basis of which a proposition was meaningful, and only meaningful, if it could be verified by sense experience. On this view many areas of discourse were nonsense, not least theology in its claim to talk about a universe not restricted to the world of sense, as well as some areas of moral discourse.

Acquaintance and Description

We shall say that we have *acquaintance* with anything of which we are directly aware, without the intermediary of any process of inference or any knowledge of truths. Thus in the presence of my table I am acquainted with the sense data that make up the appearance of my table – its colour, shape, hardness, smoothness, etc.; all these are things of which I am immediately conscious when I am seeing and touching my table. The particular shade of colour that I am seeing may have many things said about it – I may say that it is brown, that it is rather dark, and so on. But such statements, though they make me know truths about the colour, do not make me know the colour itself any better than I did before: so far as concerns knowledge of the colour itself, as opposed to knowledge of truths about it, I know the colour perfectly and completely when I see it, and no further knowledge of it itself is even theoretically possible. Thus the sense-data which make up the appearance of my table are things with which I have acquaintance, things immediately known to me just as they are.

My knowledge of the table as a physical object, on the contrary, is not direct knowledge. Such as it is, it is obtained through acquaintance with the sense-data that make up the appearance of the table. We have seen that it is possible, without absurdity, to doubt whether there is a table at all, whereas it is not possible to doubt the sense-data. My knowledge of the table is of the kind which we shall call "knowledge by description". The table is "the physical object which causes such-and-such sense-data". This *describes* the table by means of the sense-data. In order to know anything about the table, we must know truths connecting it with things with which we have acquaintance: we must know that "such-and-such sense-data

Bertrand Russell, *The Problems of Philosophy*, 1946, pp. 46–48, 51, 52, 53, 57.

are caused by a physical object". There is no state of mind in which we are directly aware of the table; all our knowledge of the table is really knowledge of *truths*, and the actual thing which is the table is not, strictly speaking, known to us at all. We know a description, and we know that there is just one object to which this description applies, though the object itself is not directly known to us. In such a case, we say that our knowledge of the object is knowledge by description.

All our knowledge, both knowledge of things and knowledge of truths, rests upon acquaintance as its foundation. . . .

Knowledge by acquaintance

We have acquaintance in sensation with the data of the outer senses, and in introspection with the data of what may be called the inner sense-thoughts, feelings, desires, etc.; we have acquaintance in memory with things which have been data either of the outer senses or of the inner sense. Further, it is probable, though not certain, that we have acquaintance with Self, as that which is aware of things or has desires towards things.

In addition to our acquaintance with particular existing things, we also have acquaintance with what we shall call *universals*, that is to say, general ideas, such as *whiteness*, *diversity*, *brotherhood*, and so on.

It will be seen that among the objects with which we are acquainted are not included physical objects (as opposed to sense-data), nor other people's minds. These things are known to us by what I call "knowledge by description", which we must now consider.

Knowledge by description

We shall say that an object is "known by description" when we know that it is "the 'so-and-so' ", i.e. when we know that there is one object, and no more, having a certain property, and it will generally be implied that we do not have knowledge of the same object by acquaintance. We know that the man with the iron mask existed, and many propositions are known about him; but we do not know who he was.

The primacy of "acquaintance"

It will be seen that there are various stages in the removal from acquaintance with particulars: there is Bismarck to people who knew him; Bismarck to those who only know of him through history; the man with iron mask; the longest-lived of men. These are progressively further removed from acquaintance with particulars; the first comes as near to acquaintance as is possible in regard to another person; in the second, we shall still be said to know "who Bismarck was"; in the third, we do not know who was the man with the iron mask, though we can know many propositions about him which are not logically deducible from the fact that he wore an iron mask; in the fourth, finally, we know nothing beyond what is logically deducible from the definition of the man. There is a similar hierarchy in the region of universals. Many universals, like many particulars, are only known to us by description. But here, as in the case of particulars, knowledge concerning what is known by description is ultimately reducible to knowledge concerning what is known by acquaintance.

The fundamental principle in the analysis of propositions containing descriptions is this: *Every proposition which we can understand must be composed wholly of constituents with which we were acquainted.*

The Notion of "Incomplete Symbols". *For Russell, as we have seen earlier, a "proper name" understood in a logical sense directly describes quite unambiguously some object. All other language is "incomplete". Thus the notion of completeness becomes attached to symbols (or assertions) which specify what "really exists", or what for Russell was supposed to be "the meaning". So he could argue that "incomplete assertions" meant nothing. It is plain, however, that such an assertion is only an approximation to the truth, though it might well lead us (whether in Russell's own form or not) to the notion of a language hierarchy, which was not all that far from F. H. Bradley's idea of "degrees of meaning and truth". Further, if we took our involvement in a situation as the unit of "reality", or as yielding our basic existential posit, then even a third person assertion would be "incomplete", having to be set within a first person frame for the full "meaning" of a situation to be given.*

By an "incomplete" symbol we mean a symbol which is not supposed to have any meaning in isolation, but is only defined in certain

Bertrand Russell and A. N. Whitehead, *Principia Mathematica*, Cambridge University Press, 1910, Vol. I, pp. 69, 70.

contexts. In ordinary mathematics, for example, $\frac{d}{dx}$ and $\int_a^b$ are incomplete symbols: something has to be supplied before we have anything significant. Such symbols have what may be called a "definition in use". This distinguishes such symbols from what (in a generalized sense) we may call proper names: "Socrates", for example, stands for a certain man, and therefore has a meaning by itself, without the need of any context. If we supply a context, as in "Socrates is mortal", these words express a fact of which Socrates himself is a constituent: there is a certain object, namely Socrates, which does have the property of mortality, and this object is a constituent of the complex fact which we assert when we say "Socrates is mortal". But in other cases, this simple analysis fails us. Suppose we say: "The round square does not exist". It seems plain that this is a true proposition, yet we cannot regard it as denying the existence of a certain object called "the round square". For if there were such an object, it would exist: We cannot first assume that there is a certain object, and then proceed to deny that there is such an object. Whenever the grammatical subject of a proposition can be supposed not to exist without rendering the proposition meaningless, it is plain that the grammatical subject is not a proper name, i.e. not a name directly representing some object. Thus in all such cases, the proposition must be capable of being so analysed that what was the grammatical subject shall have disappeared. Thus when we say "the round square does not exist", we may, as a first attempt at such analysis, substitute "it is false that there is an object x which is both round and square".

It might be suggested that "Scott is the author of Waverley" asserts that "Scott" and "the author of Waverley" are two names for the same object. But a little reflection will show that this would be a mistake. For if that were the meaning of "Scott is the author of Waverley", what would be required for its truth would be that Scott should have been called the author of Waverley: if he had been so called, the proposition would be true, even if someone else had written Waverley; while if no one called him so, the proposition would be false, even if he had written Waverley. But in fact he was the author of Waverley at a time when no one called him so, and he would not have been the author if every one had called him so but some one else had written Waverley. Thus the proposition "Scott is the author of Waverley" is not a proposition about names, like "Napoleon is Bonaparte"; and this illustrates the sense in which "the author of Waverley" differs from a true proper name.

Thus all phrases (other than propositions) containing the word the (in the singular) are incomplete symbols: they have a meaning in use, but not in isolation. For "the author of Waverley" cannot mean the same as "Scott", or "Scott is the author of Waverley" would mean the same as "Scott is Scott", which it plainly does not; nor can "the author of Waverley" mean anything other than "Scott", or "Scott is the author of Waverley" would be false. Hence "the author of Waverley" means nothing.

IO

G. E. MOORE

Earlier Empiricism : Philosophy as Clarificatory. *This extract provides a good illustration of the persistent questioning, the penetrating analysis and the constant search for clarity which characterized G. E. Moore's approach to philosophical problems. The definitive question in all his philosophizing was "What do we mean by so-and-so ?"*

When I ask the question "How do we know that other people exist?" I do not mean: "How does our belief in their existence arise?"

But if I do not mean this what do I mean? I have said that I mean to ask a question with regard to the truth of that belief; and the particular question which I mean to ask might be expressed in the words: What reason have we for our belief in the existence of other persons? But these are words which themselves need some explanation, and I will try to give it.

In the first place, then, when I talk of "a reason", I mean only a good reason and not a bad one. A bad reason is, no doubt, a reason, in one sense of the word; but I mean to use the word "reason" exclusively in the sense in which it is equivalent to "good reason". But what, then, is meant by a good reason for a belief? I think I can express sufficiently accurately what I mean by it in this connection, as follows: A good reason for a belief is a proposition which is true, and which would not be true unless the belief were also true. We should, I think, commonly say that when a man knows such a proposition, he has a good reason for his belief; and, when he

G. E. Moore, *Philosophical Studies*, 1922, pp. 34–40. Reprinted by permission of Routledge & Kegan Paul, London and Humanities Press Inc., New York.

knows no such proposition, we should say that he has no reason for it. When he knows such a proposition, we should say he knows something which is a reason for thinking his belief to be true – something from which it could be validly inferred. And if, in answer to the question "How do you know so and so?" he were to state such a proposition, we should, I think, feel that he had answered the question which we meant to ask. Suppose, for instance, in answer to the question "How do you know that?" he were to say "I saw it in the Times". Then, if we believed that he had seen it in the Times, and also believed that it would not have been in the Times, unless it had been true, we should admit that he had answered our question. We should no longer doubt that he did know what he asserted, we should no longer doubt that his belief was true. But if, on the other hand, we believed that he had not seen it in the Times – if, for instance, we had reason to believe that what he saw was not the statement which he made, but some other statement which he mistook for it; or if we believed that the kind of statement in question was one with regard to which there was no presumption that, being in the Times, it would be true; in either of these cases we should, I think, feel that he had not answered our question. We should still doubt whether what he had said was true. We should still doubt whether he knew what he asserted; and since a man cannot tell you how he knows a thing unless he does know that thing, we should think that, though he might have told us truly how he came to believe it, he had certainly not told us how he knew it. But though we should thus hold that he had not told us how he knew what he had asserted, and that he had given us no reason for believing it to be true; we must yet admit that he had given us a reason in a sense – a bad reason, a reason which was no reason because it had no tendency to show that what he believed was true; and we might also be perfectly convinced that he had given us the reason why he believed it – the proposition by believing which he was induced also to believe his original assertion.

I mean, then, by my question, "How do we know that other people exist?" what, I believe, is ordinarily meant, namely, "What reason have we for believing that they exist?" and by this again I mean, what I also believe is ordinarily meant, namely, "What proposition do we believe, which is both true itself and is also such that it would not be true, unless other people existed?" And I hope it is plain that this question, thus explained, is quite a different question from the psychological question, which I said I did not mean to ask – from the question, "How does our belief in the existence of other people arise?" My illustration, I hope, has made this plain. For I have pointed out that we may quite well hold that a man has told us how a belief of his arises, and even what was the reason which made him adopt that belief, and yet may have failed to give us any good reason for his belief – any proposition which is both true itself, and also such that the truth of his belief follows from it. And, indeed, it is plain that if any one ever believes what is false, he is believing something for which there is no good reason, in the sense which I have explained, and for which, therefore, he cannot possibly have a good reason; and yet it plainly does not follow that his belief did not arise in anyway whatever, nor even that he had no reason for it – no bad reason. It is plain that false beliefs do arise in some way or other – they have origins and causes: and many people who hold them have bad reasons for holding them – their belief does arise (by inference or otherwise) from their belief in some other proposition, which is not itself true, or else is not a good reason for holding that, which they infer from it, or which, in some other way, it induces them to believe. I submit, therefore, that the question, "What good reason have we for believing in the existence of other people?" is different from the question "How does that belief arise?" But when I say this, I must not be misunderstood; I must not be understood to affirm that the answer to both questions may not, in a sense, be the same. I fully admit that the very same fact, which suggests to us the belief in the existence of other people, may also be a good reason for believing that they do exist. All that I maintain is that the question whether it is a good reason for that belief is a different question from the question whether it suggests that belief: if we assert that a certain fact both suggests our belief in the existence of other persons and is also a good reason for holding that belief, we are asserting two different things and not only one. And hence, when I assert, as I shall assert, that we have a good reason for our belief in the existence of other persons, I must not be understood also to assert either that we infer the existence of other persons from this good reason, or that our belief in that good reason suggests our belief in the existence of other persons in any other way. It is plain, I think, that a man may believe two true propositions, of which the one would not be true, unless the other were true too, without, in any sense whatever, having arrived at his belief in the one from his belief in the other; and it is plain, at all events, that the question whether his belief in the one did arise from his belief in the other, is a different question from the question whether the truth of the one belief follows from the truth of the other.

I hope, then, that I have made it a little clearer what I mean by the question: "What reason have we for believing in the existence of other people?" and that what I mean by it is at all events different from what is meant by the question: "How does our belief in the existence of other people arise?"

But I am sorry to say that I have not yet reached the end of my explanations as to what my meaning is. I am afraid that the subject may seem very tedious. I can assure you that I have found it excessively tedious to try to make my meaning clear to myself. I have constantly found that I was confusing one question with another, and that, where I had thought I had a good reason for some assertion, I had in reality no good reason. But I may perhaps remind you that this question, "How do we know so and so?" "What reason have we for believing it?" is one of which philosophy is full; and one to which the most various answers have been given. Philosophy largely consists in giving reasons; and the question what are good reasons for a particular conclusion and what are bad, is one upon which philosophers have disagreed as much as on any other question. For one and the same conclusion different philosophers have given not only different, but incompatible, reasons; and conversely different philosophers have maintained that one and the same fact is a reason for incompatible conclusions. We are apt, I think, sometimes to pay too little attention to this fact. When we have taken, perhaps, no little pains to assure ourselves that our own reasoning is correct, and especially when we know that a great many other philosophers agree with us, we are apt to assume that the arguments of those philosophers, who have come to a contradictory conclusion, are scarcely worthy of serious consideration. And yet, I think, there is scarcely a single reasoned conclusion in philosophy, as to which we shall not find that some other philosopher, who has, so far as we know, bestowed equal pains on his reasoning, and with equal ability, has reached a conclusion incompatible with ours. We may be satisfied that we are right, and we may, in fact, be so; but it is certain that both cannot be right: either our opponent or we must have mistaken bad reasons for good. And this being, so, however satisfied we may be that it is not we who have done so, I think we should at least draw the conclusion that it is by no means easy to avoid mistaking bad reasons for good; and that no process, however laborious, which is in the least likely to help us in avoiding this should be evaded. But it is at least possible that one source of error lies in mistaking one kind of reason for another – in supposing that, because there is, in one sense, a reason for a given conclusion, there is also a reason in another, or that because there is, in one sense, no reason for a given conclusion, there is, therefore, no reason at all. I believe myself that this is a very frequent source of error: but it is at least a possible one. And where, as disagreements show, there certainly is error on one side or the other, and reason, too, to suppose that the error is not easy to detect, I think we should spare no pains in investigating any source, from which it is even possible that the error may arise.

II

LUDWIG WITTGENSTEIN

This extract from Wittgenstein's Tractatus *illustrates a philosophical attitude and method that was to be very influential in the development of empirical philosophy over some four decades. The earlier Wittgenstein had a view of facts and language very like Russell who did in fact contribute an introduction to the first edition of the* Tractatus. *But already here there are hints at developments which are to come, and the sections of the following extract, which are especially significant are:*

4.112	*Philosophy as an Activity.*
4.116	*The ideal of clarity.*
4.1212	*The notion of "showing" as being something wider than saying.*
6.521	*The possibility of pseudo-problems and pseudo-questions.*
6.4311	*A section pointing to the odd logic of talk of death, and end of life or eternity.*
6.432	*Expressing the kind of judgment on the world that lies behind much secularity, as well as the "Death of God" movement.*
6.522	*Besides "the totality of facts" which make up the world there are, said Wittgenstein, things which "make themselves manifest", things which show themselves. Perhaps here there are links with my own concept of disclosure.*
7.	*The notion that some parts of philosophy are best done in silence – a reflection that made some to think of theology as the inexpressible.*

Philosophy and the World: Clarity or Mysticism

1 The world is all that is the case.

1.1 The world is the totality of facts, not of things.

1.11 The world is determined by the facts, and by their being *all* the facts.

1.12 For the totality of facts determines what is the case, and also whatever is not the case.

1.13 The facts in logical space are the world.

1.2 The world divides into facts.

1.21 Each item can be the case or not the case while everything else remains the same.

2 What is the case – a fact – is the existence of states of affairs.

4.1 Propositions represent the existence and non-existence of states of affairs.

4.11 The totality of true propositions is the whole of natural science (or the whole corpus of the natural sciences).

4.111 Philosophy is not one of the natural sciences.

(The word "philosophy" must mean something whose place is above or below the natural sciences, not beside them.)

4.112 Philosophy aims at the logical clarification of thoughts.

Philosophy is not a body of doctrine but an activity.

A philosophical work consists essentially of elucidations.

Philosophy does not result in "philosophical propositions", but rather in the clarification of propositions.

Without philosophy, thoughts are, as it were, cloudy and indistinct: its task is to make them clear and to give them sharp boundaries.

4.1121 Psychology is no more closely related to philosophy than any other natural science.

Theory of knowledge is the philosophy of psychology.

Does not my study of sign-language correspond to the study of thought-processes, which philosophers used to consider so essential to the philosophy of logic? Only in

Ludwig Wittgenstein, *Tractatus Logico-Philosophicus*, new trs. by D. F. Pears and B. F. McGuinness, 1961, pp. 7, 47–51, 147–51. Reprinted by permission of Routledge & Kegan Paul, London and Humanities Press Inc., New York.

most cases they got entangled in unessential psychological investigations, and with my method too there is an analogous risk.

4.1122 Darwin's theory has no more to do with philosophy than any other hypothesis in natural science.

4.113 Philosophy settles controversies about the limits of natural science.

4.114 It must set limits to what can be thought; and, in doing so, to what cannot be thought.

It must set limits to what cannot be thought by working outwards through what can be thought.

4.115 It will signify what cannot be said, by presenting clearly what can be said.

4.116 Everything that can be thought at all can be thought clearly. Everything that can be put into words can be put clearly.

4.12 Propositions can represent the whole of reality, but they cannot represent what they must have in common with reality in order to be able to represent it – logical form.

In order to be able to represent logical form, we should have to be able to station ourselves with propositions somewhere outside logic, that is to say outside the world.

4.121 Propositions cannot represent logical form: it is mirrored in them.

What finds its reflection in language, language cannot represent.

What expresses *itself* in language, *we* cannot express by means of language.

Propositions *show* the logical form of reality.

They display it.

4.1211 Thus one proposition "*fa*" shows that the object *a* occurs in its sense, two propositions "*fa*" and "*ga*" show that the same object is mentioned in both of them.

If two propositions contradict one another, then their structure shows it; the same is true if one of them follows from the other. And so on.

4.1212 What *can* be shown, *cannot* be said.

6.4311 Death is not an event in life: we do not live to experience death.

If we take eternity to mean not infinite temporal duration

but timelessness, then eternal life belongs to those who live in the present.

Our life has no end in just the way in which our visual field has no limits.

6.4312 Not only is there no guarantee of the temporal immortality of the human soul, that is to say of its eternal survival after death; but, in any case, this assumption completely fails to accomplish the purposes for which it has always been intended. Or is some riddle solved by my surviving for ever? Is not this eternal life itself as much of a riddle as our present life? The solution of the riddle of life in space and time lies *outside* space and time.

(It is certainly not the solution of any problems of natural science that is required.)

6.432 *How* things are in the world is a matter of complete indifference for what is higher. God does not reveal himself *in* the world.

6.4321 The facts all contribute only to setting the problem, not to its solution.

6.44 It is not *how* things are in the world that is mystical, but *that* it exists.

6.45 To view the world *sub specie aeterni* is to view it as a whole – a limited whole.

Feeling the world as a limited whole – it is this that is mystical.

6.5 When the answer cannot be put into words, neither can the question be put into words.

The riddle does not exist.

If a question can be framed at all, it is also possible to answer it.

6.51 Scepticism is *not* irrefutable, but obviously nonsensical, when it tries to raise doubts where no questions can be asked.

For doubt can exist only where a question exists, a question only where an answer exists, and an answer only where something *can be said.*

6.52 We feel that even when *all possible* scientific questions have been answered, the problems of life remain untouched. Of course there are then no questions left, and this itself is the answer.

6.521 The solution of the problem of life is seen in the vanishing of the problem.

(Is not this the reason why those who have found after a long period of doubt that the sense of life became clear to them have then been unable to say what constituted that sense?)

6.522 There are, indeed, things that cannot be put into words. They *make themselves manifest*. They are what is mystical.

6.53 The correct method in philosophy would really be the following: to say nothing except what can be said, i.e. propositions of natural science – i.e. something that has nothing to do with philosophy – and then, whenever someone else wanted to say something metaphysical, to demonstrate to him that he had failed to give a meaning to certain signs in his propositions. Although it would not be satisfying to the other person – he would not have the feeling that we were teaching him philosophy – *this* method would be the only strictly correct one.

6.54 My propositions serve as elucidations in the following way: anyone who understands me eventually recognizes them as nonsensical, when he has used them – as steps – to climb up beyond them. (He must, so to speak, throw away the ladder after he has climbed up it.)

He must transcend these propositions, and then he will see the world aright.

7. What we cannot speak about we must consign to silence.

12

A. J. AYER

The Verification Principle and Belief in God. *Here is Ayer's developed expression of the verification principle which as originally expressed claimed that propositions have meaning if, and only if they are verifiable in principle by experience. On this view virtually all theology, and much of ethics, was nonsense. But here Ayer argues that putative statements of fact are only nonsense if no observations are relevant to their truth or falsity. The problem for theological and metaphysical assertions is then to establish some empirical relevance. Yet, as one may remark this will, a fortiori, not be according to the scientific pattern. For if it were theological assertions would be about nothing but the visible world.*

The criterion which we use to test the genuineness of apparent statements of fact is the criterion of verifiability. We say that a sentence is factually significant to any given person, if, and only if, he knows how to verify the proposition which it purports to express – that is, if he knows what observations would lead him, under certain conditions, to accept the proposition as being true, or reject it as being false. If, on the other hand, the putative proposition is of such a character that the assumption of its truth, or falsehood, is consistent with any assumption whatsoever concerning the nature of his future experience, then, as far as he is concerned, it is, if not a tautology, a mere pseudo-proposition. The sentence expressing it may be emotionally significant to him; but it is not literally significant. And with regard to questions the procedure is the same.

A. J. Ayer, *Language, Truth and Logic*, Victor Gollanz, London and Dover Publications Inc., New York, 1950, pp. 35–38. Reprinted by permission of the publishers.

We enquire in every case what observations would lead us to answer the question, one way or the other; and, if none can be discovered, we must conclude that the sentence under consideration does not, as far as we are concerned, express a genuine question, however strongly its grammatical appearance may suggest that it does. As the adoption of this procedure is an essential factor in the argument of this book, it needs to be examined in detail.

In the first place, it is necessary to draw a distinction between practical verifiability, and verifiability in principle. Plainly we all understand, in many cases believe, propositions which we have not in fact taken steps to verify. Many of these are propositions which we could verify if we took enough trouble. But there remain a number of significant propositions, concerning matters of fact, which we could not verify even if we chose; simply because we lack the practical means of placing ourselves in the situation where the relevant observations could be made. A simple and familiar example of such a proposition is the proposition that there are mountains on the farther side of the moon. No rocket has yet been invented which would enable me to go and look at the farther side of the moon, so that I am unable to decide the matter by actual observation. But I do know what observations would decide it for me, if, as is theoretically conceivable, I were once in a position to make them. And therefore I say that the proposition is verifiable in principle, if not in practice, and is accordingly significant. On the other hand, such a metaphysical pseudo-proposition as "the Absolute enters into, but is itself incapable of, evolution and progress,"[1] is not even in principle verifiable. For one cannot conceive of an observation which would enable one to determine whether the Absolute did, or did not, enter into evolution and progress. Of course it is possible that the author of such a remark is using English words in a way in which they are not commonly used by English-speaking people, and that he does, in fact, intend to assert something which could be empirically verified. But until he makes us understand how the proposition that he wishes to express would be verified, he fails to communicate anything to us. And if he admits, as I think the author of the remark in question would have admitted, that his words were not intended to express either a tautology or a proposition which was capable, at least in principle, of being verified, then it follows that he has made an utterance which has no literal significance even for himself.

A further distinction which we must make is the distinction between the "strong" and the "weak" sense of the term "verifiable". A proposition is said to be verifiable, in the strong sense of the term, if, and only if, its truth could be conclusively established in experience. But it is verifiable, in the weak sense, if it is possible for experience to render it probable. In which sense are we using the term when we say that a putative proposition is genuine only if it is verifiable?

It seems to me that if we adopt conclusive verifiability as our criterion of significance, as some positivists have proposed,[2] our argument will prove too much. Consider, for example, the case of general propositions of law – such propositions, namely, as "arsenic is poisonous"; "all men are mortal"; "a body tends to expand when it is heated". It is of the very nature of these propositions that their truth cannot be established with certainty by any finite series of observations. But if it is recognized that such general propositions of law are designed to cover an infinite number of cases, then it must be admitted that they cannot, even in principle, be verified conclusively. And then, if we adopt conclusive verifiability as our criterion of significance, we are logically obliged to treat these general propositions of law in the same fashion as we treat the statements of the metaphysician.

In face of this difficulty, some positivists[3] have adopted the heroic course of saying that these general propositions are indeed pieces of nonsense, albeit an essentially important type of nonsense. But here the introduction of the term "important" is simply an attempt to hedge. It serves only to mark the authors' recognition that their view is somewhat too paradoxical, without in any way removing the paradox. Besides, the difficulty is not confined to the case of general propositions of law, though it is there revealed most plainly. It is hardly less obvious in the case of propositions about the remote past. For it must surely be admitted that, however strong the evidence in favour of historical statements may be, their truth can never become more than highly probable. And to maintain that they also constituted an important, or unimportant, type of nonsense would be unplausible, to say the very least. Indeed, it will be our contention that no proposition, other than a tautology, can possibly be anything more than a probable hypothesis. And if this is correct, the principle that a sentence can be factually significant only if it expresses what is conclusively verifiable is self-stultifying as a criterion of significance. For it leads to the conclusion that it is impossible to make a significant statement of fact at all.

Nor can we accept the suggestion that a sentence should be allowed to be factually significant if, and only if, it expresses something which is definitely confutable by experience.[4] Those who adopt this course assume that, although no finite series of observations is ever sufficient to establish the truth of a hypothesis beyond all possibility of doubt, there are crucial cases in which a single observation, or series of observations, can definitely confute it. But, as we shall show later on, this assumption is false. A hypothesis cannot be conclusively confuted any more than it can be conclusively verified. For when we take the occurrence of certain observations as proof that a given hypothesis is false, we presuppose the existence of certain conditions. And though, in any given case, it may be extremely improbable that this assumption is false, it is not logically impossible. We shall see that there need be no self-contradiction in holding that some of the relevant circumstances are other than we have taken them to be, and consequently that the hypothesis has not really broken down. And if it is not the case that any hypothesis can be definitely confuted, we cannot hold that the genuineness of a proposition depends on the possibility of its definite confutation.

Accordingly, we fall back on the weaker sense of verification. We say that the question that must be asked about any putative statement of fact is not, Would any observations make its truth or falsehood logically certain? but simply, Would any observations be relevant to the determination of its truth or falsehood? And it is only if a negative answer is given to this second question that we conclude that the statement under consideration is nonsensical.

Refutation of belief in God. *The following passage which gives the positivist refutation of belief in God arises from supposing –*

(*a*) *that there can be no deductive argument leading to a conclusion that God exists, for this assertion is, if it is about anything at all, an empirical assertion;*
(*b*) *that "God exists" cannot be an empirical assertion because since God is transcendent it has to be metaphysical;*
(*c*) *that metaphysical transcendence must be about another world altogether. God is, on Ayer's view, "held to be superior to the empirical world, and so outside it". Therefore, statements about*

God are devoid of empirical relevance and therefore non-sensical.

But at the end it is abundantly clear that Ayer so uses "truth" and "matter-of-fact" as to allow no "truth about any matter-of-fact" which does not issue in scientific assertions. In other words, his rejection of theology is not a conclusion so much as an unexamined presupposition of the argument.

The only answer to this position is to show, if possible, that there are situations which are already empirical and more, but not "more" in the sense of having more empirical features, nor "more" in having a segregated metaphysical adjunct. The problem of theology is basically to show the possibility of this kind of situation, and this is what I myself have sought to provide, successfully or not, in the concept of a disclosure situation.

It is now generally admitted, at any rate by philosophers, that the existence of a being having the attributes which define the god of any non-animistic religion cannot be demonstratively proved. To see that this is so, we have only to ask ourselves what are the premises from which the existence of such a god could be deduced. If the conclusion that a god exists is to be demonstratively certain, then these premises must be certain; for, as the conclusion of a deductive argument is already contained in the premises, any uncertainty there may be about the truth of the premises is necessarily shared by it. But we know that no empirical proposition can ever be anything more than probable. It is only *a priori* propositions that are logically certain. But we cannot deduce the existence of a god from an *a priori* proposition. For we know that the reason why *a priori* propositions are certain in that they are tautologies. And from a set of tautologies nothing but a further tautology can be validly deduced. It follows that there is no possibility of demonstrating the existence of a god.

What is not so generally recognized is that there can be no way of proving that the existence of a god, such as the God of Christianity, is even probable. Yet this also is easily shown. For if the existence of such a god were probable, then the proposition that he existed would be an empirical hypothesis. And in that case it would be possible to deduce from it, and other empirical hypotheses, certain experiential

Language, Truth and Logic, pp. 114–20.

propositions which were not deducible from those other hypotheses alone. But in fact this is not possible. It is sometimes claimed, indeed, that the existence of a certain sort of regularity in nature constitutes sufficient evidence for the existence of a god. But if the sentence "God exists" entails no more than that certain types of phenomena occur in certain sequences, then to assert the existence of a god will be simply equivalent to asserting that there is the requisite regularity in nature; and no religious man would admit that this was all he intended to assert in asserting the existence of a god. He would say that in talking about God, he was talking about a transcendent being who might be known through certain empirical manifestations, but certainly could not be defined in terms of those manifestations. But in that case the term "god" is a metaphysical term. And if "god" is a metaphysical term, then it cannot be even probable that a god exists. For to say that "God exists" is to make a metaphysical utterance which cannot be either true or false. And by the same criterion, no sentence which purports to describe the nature of a transcendent god can possess any literal significance.

It is important not to confuse this view of religious assertions with the view that is adopted by atheists, or agnostics. For it is characteristic of an agnostic to hold that the existence of a god is a possibility in which there is no good reason either to believe or disbelieve; and it is characteristic of an atheist to hold that it is at least probable that no god exists. And our view that all utterances about the nature of God are nonsensical, so far from being identical with, or even lending any support to, either of these familiar contentions, is actually incompatible with them. For if the assertion that there is a god is nonsensical, then the atheist's assertion that there is no god is equally nonsensical, since it is only a significant proposition that can be significantly contradicted. As for the agnostic, although he refrains from saying either that there is or that there is not a god, he does not deny that the question whether a transcendent god exists is a genuine question. He does not deny that the two sentences "There is a transcendent god" and "There is no transcendent god" express propositions one of which is actually true and the other false. All he says is that we have no means of telling which of them is true, and therefore ought not to commit ourselves to either. But we have seen that the sentences in question do not express propositions at all. And this means that agnosticism also is ruled out.

Thus we offer the theist the same comfort as we gave to the

moralist. His assertions cannot possibly be valid, but they cannot be invalid either. As he says nothing at all about the world, he cannot justly be accused of saying anything false, or anything for which he has insufficient grounds. It is only when the theist claims that in asserting the existence of a transcendent god he is expressing a genuine proposition that we are entitled to disagree with him.

It is to be remarked that in cases where deities are identified with natural objects, assertions concerning them may be allowed to be significant. If, for example, a man tells me that the occurrence of thunder is alone both necessary and sufficient to establish the truth of the proposition that Jehovah is angry, I may conclude that, in his usage of words, the sentence "Jehovah is angry" is equivalent to "It is thundering". But in sophisticated religions, though they may be to some extent based on men's awe of natural process which they cannot sufficiently understand, the "person" who is supposed to control the empirical world is not himself located in it; he is held to be superior to the empirical world, and so outside it; and he is endowed with super-empirical attributes. But the notion of a person whose essential attributes are non-empirical is not an intelligible notion at all. We may have a word which is used as if it named this "person", but, unless the sentences in which it occurs express propositions which are empirically verifiable, it cannot be said to symbolize anything. And this is the case with regard to the word "god", in the usage in which it is intended to refer to a transcendent object. The mere existence of the noun is enough to foster the illusion that there is a real, or at any rate a possible entity corresponding to it. It is only when we enquire what God's attributes are that we discover that "God", in this usage, is not a genuine name.

It is common to find belief in a transcendent god conjoined with belief in an after-life. But, in the form which it usually takes, the content of this belief is not a genuine hypothesis. To say that men do not ever die, or that the state of death is merely a state of prolonged insensibility, is indeed to express a significant proposition, though all the available evidence goes to show that it is false. But to say that there is something imperceptible inside a man, which is his soul or his real self, and that it goes on living after he is dead, is to make a metaphysical assertion which has no more factual content than the assertion that there is a transcendent god.

It is worth mentioning that, according to the account which we have given of religious assertions, there is no logical ground for antagonism between religion and natural science. As far as the question of truth or falsehood is concerned, there is no opposition between the natural scientist and the theist who believes in a transcendent god. For since the religious utterances of the theist are not genuine propositions at all, they cannot stand in any logical relation to the propositions of science. Such antagonism as there is between religion and science appears to consist in the fact that science takes away one of the motives which make men religious. For it is acknowledged that one of the ultimate sources of religious feeling lies in the inability of men to determine their own destiny; and science tends to destroy the feeling of awe with which men regard an alien world, by making them believe that they can understand and anticipate the course of natural phenomena, and even to some extent control it. The fact that it has recently become fashionable for physicists themselves to be sympathetic towards religion is a point in favour of this hypothesis. For this sympathy towards religion marks the physicists' own lack of confidence in the validity of their hypotheses, which is a reaction on their part from the anti-religious dogmatism of nineteenth-century scientists, and a natural outcome of the crisis through which physics has just passed.

It is not within the scope of this enquiry to enter more deeply into the causes of religious feeling, or to discuss the probability of the continuance of religious belief. We are concerned only to answer those questions which arise out of our discussion of the possibility of religious knowledge. The point which we wish to establish is that there cannot be any transcendent truths of religion. For the sentences which the theist uses to express such "truths" are not literally significant.

An interesting feature of this conclusion is that it accords with what many theists are accustomed to say themselves. For we are often told that the nature of God is a mystery which transcends the human understanding. But to say that something transcends the human understanding is to say that it is unintelligible. And what is unintelligible cannot significantly be described. Again, we are told that God is not an object of reason but an object of faith. This may be nothing more than an admission that the existence of God must be taken on trust, since it cannot be proved. But it may also be an assertion that God is the object of a purely mystical intuition, and cannot therefore be defined in terms which are intelligible to the reason. And I think there are many theists who would assert this.

But if one allows that it is impossible to define God in intelligible terms, then one is allowing that it is impossible for a sentence both to be significant and to be about God. If a mystic admits that the object of his vision is something which cannot be described, then he must also admit that he is bound to talk nonsense when he describes it.

For his part, the mystic may protest that his intuition does reveal truths to him, even though he cannot explain to others what these truths are; and that we do not possess this faculty of intuition can have no ground for denying that it is a cognitive faculty. For we can hardly maintain *a priori* that there are no ways of discovering true propositions except those which we ourselves employ. The answer is that we set no limit to the number of ways in which one may come to formulate a true proposition. We do not in any way deny that a synthetic truth may be discovered by purely intuitive methods as well as by the rational method of induction. But we do say that every synthetic proposition, however it may have been arrived at, must be subject to the test of actual experience. We do not deny *a priori* that the mystic is able to discover truths by his own special methods. We wait to hear what are the propositions which embody his discoveries, in order to see whether they are verified or confuted by our empirical observations. But the mystic, so far from producing propositions which are empirically verified, is unable to produce any intelligible propositions at all. And therefore we say that his intuition has not revealed to him any facts. It is no use his saying that he has apprehended facts but is unable to express them. For we know that if he really had acquired any information, he would be able to express it. He would be able to indicate in some way or other how the genuineness of his discovery might be empirically determined. The fact that he cannot reveal what he "knows", or even himself devise an empirical test to validate his "knowledge", shows that his state of mystical intuition is not a genuinely cognitive state. So that in describing his vision the mystic does not give us any information about the external world; he merely gives us indirect information about the condition of his own mind.

These considerations dispose of the argument from religious experience, which many philosophers still regard as a valid argument in favour of the existence of a god. They say that it is logically possible for men to be immediately acquainted with God, as they are immediately acquainted with a sense-content, and that there is no reason why one should be prepared to believe a man when he says that he is seeing a yellow patch, and refuse to believe him when he says that he is seeing God. The answer to this is that if the man who asserts that he is seeing God is merely asserting that he is experiencing a peculiar kind of sense-content, then we do not for a moment deny that his assertion may be true. But, ordinarily, the man who says that he is seeing God is saying not merely that he is experiencing a religious emotion, but also that there exists a transcendent being who is the object of this emotion; just as the man who says that he sees a yellow patch is ordinarily saying not merely that his visual sense-field contains a yellow sense-content, but also that there exists a yellow object to which the sense-content belongs. And it is not irrational to be prepared to believe a man when he asserts the existence of a yellow object, and to refuse to believe him when he asserts the existence of a transcendent god. For whereas the sentence "There exists here a yellow-coloured material thing" expresses a genuine synthetic proposition which could be empirically verified, the sentence "There exists a transcendent god" has, as we have seen, no literal significance.

We conclude, therefore, that the argument from religious experience is altogether fallacious. The fact that people have religious experiences is interesting from the psychological point of view, but it does not in any way imply that there is such a thing as religious knowledge, any more than our having moral experiences implies that there is such a thing as moral knowledge. The theist, like the moralist, may believe that his experiences are cognitive experiences, but, unless he can formulate his "knowledge" in propositions that are empirically verifiable, we may be sure that he is deceiving himself. It follows that those philosophers who fill their books with assertions that they intuitively "know" this or that moral or religious "truth" are merely providing material for the psychoanalyst. For no act of intuition can be said to reveal a truth about any matter of fact unless it issues in verifiable propositions. And all such propositions are to be incorporated in the system of empirical propositions which constitutes science.

NOTES

1. A remark taken at random from *Appearance and Reality*, by F. H. Bradley.
2. e.g. M. Schlick, "Positivismus und Realismus," *Erkenntnis*, Vol. I, 1930. F. Weissmann, "Logische Analyse des Wahrscheinlichkeitsbegriffs," *Erkenntnis*, Vol. I, 1930.
3. e.g. M. Schlick, "Die Kausalität in der gegenwärtigen Physik," *Naturwissenschaft*, Vol. 19, 1931.
4. This has been proposed by Karl Popper in his *Logik der Forschung*.

PART FOUR: RECENT EMPIRICISM: ITS LATER BROADENING

13

BERTRAND RUSSELL

Quite apart from its particular argument, this passage will be helpful as giving a background to Dr Waismann's paper. But in giving some account of Russell's concept of a hierarchy of languages, it also affords a link with some of Russell's earlier views on object language, the primary language which on his view is associated with "knowledge by acquaintance". Whether however, there is any such "primary language", and whether any words ever occur "in isolation" as Russell supposes, are questions for discussion. For my own part, I would see Russell's logical insights which he develops here as completely destructive of his own, earlier crude ontology which we may characterize as "physical realism", and which took sense-data as the building bricks of the universe.

Tarski, in his important book *Der Wahrheitsbegriff in den formalisierten Sprachen*, has shown that the words "true" and "false", as applied to the sentences of a given language, always require another language, of higher order, for their adequate definition. The conception of a hierarchy of languages is involved in the theory of types, which, in some form, is necessary for the solution of the paradoxes; it plays an important part in Carnap's work as well as in Tarski's. I suggested it in my introduction to Wittgenstein's Tractatus, as

Bertrand Russell, *An Inquiry into Meaning and Truth*, Allen Unwin 1948 pp. 62–65.

an escape from his theory that syntax can only be "shown", not expressed in words. The arguments for the necessity of a hierarchy of languages are overwhelming, and I shall henceforth assume their validity.

The hierarchy must extend upwards indefinitely, but not downwards, since, if it did, language could never get started. There must, therefore, be a language of lowest type. I shall define one such language, not the only possible one. I shall call this sometimes the "object-language", sometimes the "primary language". My purpose, in the present chapter, is to define and describe this basic language. The languages which follow in the hierarchy I shall call secondary, tertiary, and so on; it is to be understood that each language contains all its predecessors.

The primary language, we shall find, can be defined both logically and psychologically; but before attempting formal definitions it will be well to make a preliminary informal exploration.

It is clear, from Tarski's argument, that the words "true" and "false" cannot occur in the primary language; for these words, as applied to sentences in the nth language, belong to the $(n-1)^{th}$ language. This does not mean that sentences in the primary language are neither true nor false, but that, if "p" is a sentence in this language, the two sentences "p is true" and "p is false" belong to the secondary language. This is, indeed, obvious apart from Tarski's argument. For, if there is a primary language, its words must not be such as presuppose the existence of a language. Now "true" and "false" are words applicable to sentences, and thus presuppose the existence of language. (I do not mean to deny that a memory consisting of images, not words, may be "true" or "false"; but this is in a somewhat different sense, which need not concern us at present.) In the primary language, therefore, though we can make assertions, we cannot say that our own assertions or those of others are either true or false.

When I say that we make assertions in the primary language, I must guard against a misunderstanding, for the word "assertion" is ambiguous. It is used, sometimes, as the antithesis of denial, and in this sense it cannot occur in the primary language. Denial presupposes a form of words, and proceeds to state that this form of words is false. The word "not" is only significant when attached to a sentence, and therefore presupposes language. Consequently, if "p" is a sentence of the primary language, "not-p" is a sentence of the secondary language. It is easy to fall into confusion, since "p", without verbal alteration, may express a sentence only possible in the secondary language. Suppose, for example, you have taken salt by mistake instead of sugar, and you exclaim "this is *not* sugar". This is a denial, and belongs to the secondary language. You now use a different sprinkler, and say with relief "this *is* sugar". Psychologically, you are answering affirmatively the question "is this sugar?" You are in fact saying, as unpedantically as you can: "the sentence 'this is sugar' is true". Therefore what you mean is something which cannot be said in the primary language, although the same form of words can express a sentence in the primary language. The assertion which is the antithesis of denial belongs to the secondary language; the assertion which belongs to the primary language has no antithesis.

Just the same kind of considerations as apply to "not" apply to "or" and "but" and conjunctions generally. Conjunctions, as their their name implies, join other words, and have no meaning in isolation; they therefore presuppose the existence of a language. The same applies to "all" and "some"; you can only have all of something, or some of something, and in the absence of other words "all" and "some" are meaningless. This argument also applies to "the".

Thus logical words, without exception, are absent from the primary language. All of them, in fact, presuppose propositional forms: "not" and conjunctions presuppose propositions, while "all" and "some" and "the" presuppose propositional functions.

Ordinary language contains a number of purely syntactical words, such as "is" and "than", which must obviously be excluded from the primary language. Such words, unlike those that we have hitherto considered, are in fact wholly unnecessary, and do not appear in symbolic logical languages. Instead of "A is earlier than B" we say "A precedes B"; instead of "A is yellow" a logical language will say "yellow (A)"; instead of "there are smiling villains" we say: it is false that all values of "either x does not smile or x is not a villain" are false. "Existence" and "Being", as they occur in traditional metaphysics, are hypostatized forms of certain meanings of "is". Since "is" does not belong to the primary language, "existence" and "being", if they are to mean anything, must be linguistic concepts not directly applicable to objects.

There is another very important class of words that must be at least provisionally excluded, namely such words as "believe", "desire", "doubt", all of which, when they occur in a sentence, must be followed by a subordinate sentence telling what it is that is believed or desired or doubted. Such words, so far as I have been able to discover, are always psychological, and involve what I call "propositional attitudes". For the present, I will merely point out that they differ from such words as "or" in an important respect, namely that they are necessary for the description of observable phenomena. If I want to see the paper, that is a fact which I can easily observe, and yet "want" is a word which has to be followed by a subordinate sentence if anything significant is to result. Such words raise problems, and are perhaps capable of being analysed in such a way as to make them able to take their place in the primary language. But as this is not *prima facie* possible, I shall for the present assume that they are to be excluded. I shall devote a later chapter to the discussion of this subject.

We can now partially define the primary or object-language as a language consisting wholly of "object-words", where "object-words" are defined, logically, as words having meaning in isolation, and, psychologically, as words which have been learnt without its being necessary to have previously learnt any other words.

14

F. WAISMANN

The Broadening of Empiricism. *This essay by Dr Waismann, a one-time member of the Vienna Circle, who was brought up in a positivist tradition, is important as representing the broadening of the empirical approach beyond the narrow confines of the verification principle. Dr Waismann argues that language is no homogeneous area with words as fixed points, but ought rather to be pictured as an interweaving of various strands, with words working in and between different contexts. Against this background we come to see that terms like "meaning", "truth", "verification", are often being used in different senses, and we see the futility in particular of supposing there to be sharp lines between meaning and meaninglessness.*

The essay is also important for its introduction to logical paradoxes and not least to Russell's theory of types, which itself leads us to think of language as being logically variegated rather than as being altogether homogeneous in character.

1. *Types of Ambiguity*

Both vagueness and "open texture" must be distinguished from, and likened to, another sort of lack of definition; ambiguity. Of the many types of ambiguity a few examples may be mentioned.

(i) A word may have two altogether different meanings, or better, there may be two words which have the sound in common; thus someone might say, "How long it is since I have seen the Alps!

F. Waismann, "Language Strata", *Logic and Language* (Second Series), ed. A. G. N. Flew, Blackwells 1953, pp. 11–26. Reprinted by permission of the publisher and the Waismann Trust Fund.

How I long to see them." This fact makes possible certain puns – as when a crying child is called the "Prince of Wails".

(ii) An extreme case of ambiguity is what is called the *antithetical sense* of primal words. There is evidence that in the oldest languages opposites such as: strong—weak, light—dark, large—small were expressed by the same root word. Thus, in ancient Egyptian *keu* stood for both strong and weak. In Latin *altus* means high and deep, *sacer* both sacred and accursed. Compare further *clamare*, to shout, and *clam*, quietly, secretly, or *siccus*, dry and *succus*, juice. Nor is it only the ancient languages which have retained as relics words capable of meaning either of two opposites. The same applies to present-day languages. "To cleave" means to split, but in the phrase "cleave to" it means to adhere. The word "without", originally carrying with it both a positive and a negative connotation, is used today in the negative sense only. That "with" has not only the sense of "adding to" but also that of "depriving of" is clear from the compounds "withdraw" and "withhold".

(iii) It is commonly impossible to distinguish between different senses of a word without considering how it is used in context. When used in different contexts, the same word may assume different senses. Take as an example the transitive and intransitive use of a verb: "I smell the lilac", "The lilac smells lovely". But even when a verb is used transitively, it may take on different meanings when connected with words of different types: "I caught him", "I caught measles". We use the word "like" often in the sense of "similar"; we say, for instance, "That man is like his brother", and in this context we may also say "very like", "amazingly like", "so like that one cannot tell them apart". On the other hand, it would be amazing to learn of two triangles "so alike that one cannot tell them apart". In the one case the word admits of degrees of comparison, in the other it does not. Compare the phrase "Find the key which –" with "Find the number which – ". In spite of the sameness of the construction the difference in meaning is clearly felt. Thus I might have said "Compute the number which – ", but not "Compute the key which – ", a sign that the word is used according to different substitution rules. Again, compare "I am trying to solve this equation", "I am trying to remember a forgotten name", "I am trying to fall asleep".

(iv) A word which is used in a quite definite way and in quite definite contexts may be used in a new sort of context: with this change of use often goes a change in meaning. For instance: "the fruit of a tree", "the fruit of his labour", "the fruit of hism editations"; "to sow seed", "to sow distrust". What we use is a picture. If the image becomes a stereotyped figure of speech, we talk of "figurative meaning". (This is one of the means by which language grows. A speaker may, on the spur of the moment, place a word in a new collocation, thus giving rise to a new meaning – a process over which there is little control.) Now the point of this is that it is not always possible to say exactly where the metaphor ends and where the word starts having an independent meaning. The phrase "to sow distrust" is felt to be a metaphor, perhaps also "the fruit of his meditations", but not "a fruitless attempt". Here the pictorial element has faded. Glance through the following list and consider whether you would venture to draw a sharp line between a figure that is still a live image and one which has become a well-worn metaphor: "The birth of tragedy", "Drowned in sorrow", "An abyss of grief", "A radiant spirit", "A flight of phantasy", "A fiery temper".

(v) A word may be used in a "figurative sense". Remember that almost all terms denoting the mental are derived from words whose primary connotation was sensuous. Thus we speak of an idea "floating in the mind", we "call it to mind", we say it is still "hazy"; an idea is "engraved upon my memory", it "makes an impression upon me"; something "moves us", "touches us", so that we are "carried away"; we feel "stirred", "beside ourselves"; we talk of a "brilliant idea", a "flash of wit"; and so on.

This rising of the meaning of a word from the sphere of the sensuous to that of the mental continues to the present day. Think of expressions such as "split personality", "the layers of the subconscious", twilight of consciousness", etc. A sensuous element gleams through most of the phrases which denote emotions. We talk of "shady", "volcanic", "unbridled", "ebullient" characters; "wooden", "unpolished", "crabbed" individuals; of an "oily", "smooth" manner, a "stiff" attitude, a "lukewarm", "cool", "icy" reception; of an "arid", "sparkling", "will-o'-the-wisp" spirit.

The fact that language develops out of the sensuous into the mental produces a peculiar phenomenon: we seem at times to glimpse behind a word another sense, deeper and half hidden, and to hear faintly the entry of another meaning, in and with which others begin to sound, and all accompany the original meaning of the word like the sympathetic chimes of a bell. Hence that deep and sonorous ring in words which is lacking in artificial and invented languages; and hence also the multiplicity of meaning, the indefiniteness, the strange suggestiveness and evasiveness of so much poetry. Hugo von Hofmannsthal once described this phenomenon.

> It leads us into the innermost nature of Oriental poetry, into the very mystery and being of language. For this mysteriousness is the deepest element in Eastern language and poetry alike, in so far as everything in it is metaphorical, everything remotely descended from ancient roots. The original root is sensuous, primitive, concise and strong, but the word moves away from it by subtle transitions to new, related meanings, and then to meanings only remotely related: yet in the remotest meaning there is still some echo of the original sound of the word, still some darkly mirrored image of the first sensuous impression . . . In the limitless detail and particularity of description the subject matter itself seems to oppress and overwhelm us: but what would come so close to us as to hurt us, were we limited to immediate meanings, resolves itself by virtue of the multiplicity of meaning in the words into a magic cloud, and so behind the immediate meaning we divine another which is derived from it. Thus it is that we do not lose sight of the proper and original sense: where, however, this sense was commonplace and mean, it loses its implicit commonplaceness, and often, as we contemplate the word, we hesitate in our perceptive awareness between the particular reality which it symbolizes and a higher reality, and this in a flash leads up to the great and the sublime.

(vi) There are other cases in which the meanings cannot be as clearly separated out as, for instance, in the case of the word "cold" (where I may say of a day or of a reception that it is cold). Consider a word like "haughty". That there is a difference in its use is shown in the fact that the word can be combined with words of very different logical types; thus we may speak of a haughty smile, a haughty tone of voice, a haughty face, a haughty look, a haughty bearing, a haughty speech, a haughty person. So there *is* a difference in meaning. Yet all these meanings are connected – in saying of somebody that he is haughty, at least part of what we mean is that he has a haughty face, or a haughty bearing, etc. So the meanings interpenetrate, and unite into a larger whole, a sort of cloud in which the several precise conceits are lost. We may say that they *dissolve into vagueness*. Such an example shows how ambiguity may gradually pass into vagueness.

"But shouldn't we still try to distinguish as clearly as possible all the different shades of meaning the word can assume?" Try, and you'll see how puzzling it is. Paul Valéry put this point very well when he said:

> You must . . . at some time or another, have noticed this curious fact – that a given word, which may be perfectly obvious when used in the ordinary course of communication, which presents no difficulties whatever when caught up in the give and take of normal conversation, has a way of becoming almost magically embarrassing, strangely resistant and quite unmanageable in definition, as soon as you withdraw it from circulation with the object of examining it closely and apart from its neighbours, as soon, that is, as you try to establish its meaning in isolation from its momentary function. It is almost comic to note the difficulty with which we are confronted when we try to establish the *precise* meaning of a word which, in the ordinary routine of life, we use daily to our complete satisfaction . . . But isolate it, clip its wings and it turns and rends you. You soon become convinced that the number of its meanings is far in excess of its functions. Formerly it was only a *means*, but now it is an *end*, the object of a terrible philosophical desire. It is something entirely different from what it was, an enigma, an abyss, a source of mental torment.

(vii) Next, consider a number of statements made by psychologists: "We perceive the surface of the metal, it is true, but its colour seems to lie *behind* this surface". "Lustre-light does not lie *in* the plane of the object to which it belongs, but appears rather either *before* the object or *superimposed on* it". "When a shadow moves it moves not *in* the surface of the object but *across* it". "When a person is speaking with someone in complete darkness, the voice of the one who answers usually sounds distinctly *behind* the darkness, not *in* the darkness". "If you look at a colour disk which turns round quickly, it is better to say that there is a flickering *across* the disk or *before* it in space than to say that the disk *itself* is flickering". Notice that in all these cases the prepositions which symbolize spatial relations take on a somewhat new sense. In the last example, for instance, to say that there is a flickering *before* the disk in space is to use "before" in a peculiar way, namely so as to make it *meaningless* to ask exactly what distance, precisely how many millimetres before the surface it lies. Here we have a sense of "before" or "in front of" which differs from the ordinary sense. The same holds of the "behind" in our first example. There are intermediate ones: thus a growing piece of iron is seen as luminous *throughout* its mass; a rainbow, though extended in space before the observer, does not possess a surface. One feels that one can penetrate more or less deeply *into* the spectral colours, whereas when one looks at the colour of a paper the surface presents a sort of barrier beyond which the gaze cannot pass. The words "throughout" and "into" come here closer to, though they have not exactly, the ordinary meaning. Many more examples could be collected, but these will do. "The English prepositions", says Empson, "from being used in so many ways and in combination with so many verbs, have acquired not so much a number of meanings as a body of meaning continuous in several directions". Exactly, there are so many senses and they are so firmly interlocked that they seem to form one continuous body. Thus many words which we wouldn't suspect turn out to be ambiguous. One can hardly make too much of this ambiguity of language through which we often seem to see words like shapes in a mist.

(viii) Then there is such a thing as *systematic ambiguity*. This expression was first coined by Bertrand Russell in connection with his Theory of Types. Without entering into it here we can say that his idea, roughly speaking, is that we must distinguish between different *logical types of symbols*. Beginning with names which stand for "individuals", we come next to predicates which possibly apply to those names, and then to second-order predicates which possibly apply to the first-order predicates, and so on. We are thus led to consider a hierarchy of symbols which, theoretically, goes on without end. This hierarchy corresponds to a similar hierarchy of *statements*. And statements are divided into different types according to whether they are statements about an individual, or statements about a class of individuals, or statements about a class of classes of individuals, and so on. A statement such as "Socrates is mortal" is true when there is a corresponding fact, and false when there is no corresponding fact. But take now such a statement as "All men are mortal". The truth of it can no longer consist in its correspondence to a single fact, for there are indefinitely many facts such as "Socrates is mortal", "Plato is mortal", etc. Now Russell's point is that the meaning of "truth" which is applicable to the latter sort of proposition is *not the same* as the meaning of "truth" which is applicable to the proposition "All men are mortal"; i.e. each type of statement has its own sort of truth.

The main ground for accepting that distinction is that it offers an escape from the paradoxes or antinomies which were a threat to logic.

> The imaginary sceptic, who asserts that he knows nothing, and is refuted by being asked if he knows that he knows nothing, has asserted nonsense, and has been fallaciously refuted by an argument which involves a vicious-circle fallacy. In order that the sceptic's assertion may become significant, it is necessary to place some limitation upon the things of which he is asserting his ignorance, because the things of which it is possible to be ignorant form an illegitimate totality. *Principia Mathematica* (Vol. I, Introduction).

Take the case of the Liar, that is of a man who says "I am lying"; if he is lying he is speaking the truth, and if he is speaking the truth he is lying. We may interpret his statement as saying, "All propositions which I assert are false". Is this proposition itself true or false? To clear up the paradox we must distinguish between elementary propositions which do not refer to a totality of propositions, first-order propositions which do refer to a totality of elementary propositions, second-order propositions which do refer to a totality of first-order propositions, and so on. Now if the liar asserts that all propositions which he asserts are false he is making a first-order statement which does not fall within its own scope, and therefore no contradiction emerges. The decisive point to realize is that the phrase "all propositions" is an illegitimate totality. As soon as a suitable limitation has been put upon the collection of propositions we are considering, as soon as they are broken up into different orders, the contradiction disappears. We may put it like this: if somebody were to tell us that he is a liar, we could ask him, "Well, a liar of what order?" If he says he is a liar of the first order he is making a statement of the second order, and this statement may be perfectly true. When he says "I am a liar of the second order" (including the totality of first-order statements) this would be a statement of the third order; and so on. However far he may extend the scope of propositions to which he is referring, his statement about their falsehood will represent a proposition of higher order. Once we reach this stage, there is no contradiction.

Russell's solution is thus based on the ground that "true" and "false" are ambiguous, and that, in order to make them unambiguous, we must specify the order of truth or falsehood which we ascribe to a proposition. Similar considerations apply to negation and disjunction, and indeed to any logical particle. It might seem that they were symbols which had throughout the same meaning. But this is due to a systematic ambiguity in the meanings of "not", "or", etc., by which they adjust themselves to propositions of any order.

The ambiguity about which I want to speak is not connected with the Theory of Types but with what may be called the "many-level structure" of language. I shall first of all explain what I understand by a *language stratum*.

2. *Language Strata*

Let me begin by introducing a distinction between two paths a logical inquiry may follow. It will perhaps be best to illustrate my point with a picture. In studying the geometry of a curve we may wish to find out its behaviour *at some particular point* – for instance, whether it has a tangent there, whether it is continuous there, what its measure of curvature is there, and the like. Then we are studying *local* properties of the curve. Or we may wish to study the behaviour of the curve *as a whole* – for instance, whether it is closed or not, and, if it is closed, whether it is convex, etc. Then we are studying its properties *at large*. This picture suggests two different types of investigation in logic. The one takes its orientation from the logical relations which hold between a number of given propositions; a question of this sort is to ask whether a given proposition follows from another one, or contradicts it, or is independent of it, etc. We are then concerned with the logical nexus *on a small scale*, so to speak with *local* relations between propositions. Suppose, on the other hand, considering a certain deductive theory based upon a number of suitable axioms, say Euclidean Geometry or the Theory of Deduction, we ask whether the system under consideration is *free from contradiction*, that is, whether it is ever possible to prove a certain theorem and its contradictory. This is a question of quite a different kind. Suppose we say, "The theory in question contains no contradiction", then we are making an assertion, not about the relations between two or three or more single propositions, but about the theory *as a whole*. Again, we may inquire whether the deductive theory we are considering is *complete*, i.e. whether any statements that can be constructed in accordance with the given rules (of the theory) can always be decided (in one way or the other) by the means of the theory and decided in a finite number of steps; we may also be investigating whether two given theories are isomorphic (i.e. of the same logical structure so that to each proposition of the one there corresponds precisely one proposition of the other, and vice versa, and that all the logical relations of the propositions in the one are retained in the other). Now in pursuing such questions we are concerned with what may be called the *macrological* features of such theories, in contrast with questions concerning the *micrological* connections of single statements.

A technique has been worked out to deal with problems of that macrological kind. Naturally, these methods – called "metalogical" and "metamathematical" – only apply to *deductive systems*. However, it does seem to me that there is also good sense in talking of macro- and micrological features of a *language*. Language, it is true, is not organized in the way a deductive system is; compared with such a system it is of a much more loosely knitted texture. And yet one feels a marked difference when one compares such statements as: a material object statement, a sense-datum statement, a law of nature, a geometrical proposition, a statement describing national characteristics, a statement describing a half-faded memory picture, a statement describing a dream, a proverb, and so forth. It is as if each of these statements was constructed in a different *logical style*. (I will explain presently what I mean by this.) We may set ourselves the task of grouping statements of our language according to the similarity of their usage in distinct domains, in *language-strata* as I shall venture to call them. Thus laws will form one language stratum, material object statements another one, sense datum statements yet another one, and so on. Now the question which I want to consider is this: Is it possible to develop out of that vague feeling that "each of them is built in a different logical style" something more precise? Is it possible, say, by characterizing each stratum on the basis of its intrinsic internal fabric or logical texture? To make this clearer let me return to the picture taken from geometry. It was a memorable achievement of mathematical thought when Gauss succeeded in characterizing a curved surface merely "from within" without any reference to space outside, which amounted to this, that he showed that if two-dimensional beings were living on the surface of a sphere, an egg or a wine-glass, etc., they could, merely through carrying out certain measuring operations within their abode, find out in what sort of surface they were living; in other words, they could learn the "intrinsic geometry" of their habitation without any reference to three-dimensional space. Now the analogous problem in our case would be this: Can a given language stratum be characterized; not by reference to something outside the subject-matter by dubbing it "material object", "memory picture" or the like, but by purely formal motifs? Let us see what means we have at our disposal for such a programme.

We may first investigate the nature of the concepts which a given stratum contains: whether they are absolutely precise and definable with mathematical rigour, or vague, or of an open texture. We may next consider the statements themselves and ask what sort of logic is valid for them. By "logic" I mean logic in the strict sense, the laws of inference. Aristotelian logic, including the modernized and refined form of its presentation in *Principia Mathematica*, has gone the same way as Euclidean geometry – a number of different "logics" have grown up alongside it, more or less akin to it, just as Euclidean geometry is now surrounded by a number of similar and cognate systems. One effect of this development is the disappearance of that disturbing air of uniqueness that had puzzled philosophers for so long. Birkhoff and von Neumann, for instance, have indicated a system, different from classical logic, which seems to be in better harmony with the structure of quantum mechanics. On the suggestion of Brouwer a logic has been constructed different from classical logic in which is actually employed mathematical demonstration, a logic in which the law of excluded middle is no longer universally true. And, notice, when we pass from the one logic to the other, we get an altogether different mathematics; which goes to show that the sort of logic we apply is an important characteristic ingrained in a certain field of propositions. Change the logic and then the propositions will take on new meanings. Take another example – the logic of half-faded memory pictures. Here the situation is such that we are often unable to call to mind one or the other point of detail, that is, that we are often unable to decide an alternative. What did that bathroom look like I saw the other day on a visit? Was it ivory, was it cream or pale biscuit or maize? Suppose a pattern-book were shown to me, and I was later asked whether *this* was the colour I had seen, perhaps I would not be able to decide. If I were pressed I might have to say, "I can't remember so distinctly"; if another different shade of yellow were shown to me then I might give the same reply, finally adding, "all I know is that it was some light yellowish colour". Notice that, in this case, it is quite natural to use a *vague* term ("light colour") to express the indeterminacy of the impression. If language was such that each and every word was particular and each colour word had a definite, clearly defined meaning, we should find we could not use it. That is, we should come up against alternatives: "Was it this colour or not?" – which we could not decide. I cannot get back to the impression I had then, it cannot be pinned down and preserved under glass for inspection like a dead beetle. To insist, in these circumstances, on the law of excluded middle, without any means of deciding the issue, is paying lip service to the laws of logic. There are only two alternatives open to us: We must either be prepared to drop the law of excluded middle when we wish to use a language with precisely defined terms; or we shall have to use a language whose words are in one way or another blurred. But we can't have it both ways. Another way of bringing out this point is to say that, if several colours are shown to me which differ only slightly, they do not necessarily exclude one another. This shows particularly clearly that our attitude towards a half-faded memory image is radically different from that towards a material object. No one would dream of ascribing two different lengths to the table in this room (a *real* table), and saying that both were right. One statement, if it proves true, excludes the other. Whereas it is perfectly correct to say of two slightly different colour statements, when applied to an indeterminate memory picture, that both are compatible; which just shows that the logic of colour words, when applied in this language stratum, is different from their usual logic.

Again, the logic of aphorisms seems to be very peculiar. A man who writes aphorisms may say a thing, and, on another occasion, the very opposite of it without being guilty of a contradiction. For each aphorism, as it stands, is quite complete in itself. Two different aphorisms are not parts of one and the same communication. Suppose you go to a museum where several paintings are hung on the wall. Would you complain that they are not correlated and do not fit into one and the same perspective? Well now, each painting has a pictorial space of its own; what is represented in two paintings, though the paintings may be adjacent, is not in the same pictorial space. It is the first aim of Art, it has been said, to set a frame around Nature. Sometimes the frame is large, sometimes small, but always it is there. An aphorism is Literature and done with ink instead of colours. Of two aphorisms each is in a frame of its own; hence no clash. It would be interesting to penetrate the logic of poems, or of mysticism. Here a contradiction may be a perfectly legitimate means to point to what cannot be said in language. No: seeming contradictions are not always absurd.

To return to our subject: I said that the examples given suggest looking upon a logic as a characteristic which sets its stamp upon a particular language stratum. But there are two further characteristics: truth and verifiability.

3. *Systematic Ambiguity of Truth and Verifiability*

Compare a variety of statements such as: a sense-datum statement, a material object statement, a law of nature, description of something half forgotten, a statement of my own motives, a conjecture as to the motives by which someone else was actuated, quotation of the exact words so-and-so was using, brief summary of the tenor of a political speech, characterization of the *Zeitgeist* of a certain historical period, a proverb, a poetic metaphor, a mathematical proposition, and so on. Now what I want to emphasize is that the idea of truth varies with the kind of statement; that it has a systematic ambiguity. Take, for instance, a mathematical proposition, say a theorem of geometry. To say that it is true simply means that it can be deduced from such-and-such axioms. As a consequence of this, it may be true in one system of geometry and false in another. And the axioms themselves? They are no concern of the pure mathematician: all he is concerned with is that *if* these and these axioms apply, *then* the theorems apply too. But whether the axioms actually do apply, is not for him to decide. He leaves that to applied mathematics. Hence Russell's definition of mathematics as "the subject in which we never know what we are talking about, nor whether what we are saying is true". Here, then, is a very good case for the "coherence theory of truth".

Again, a law of nature is never true in the same sense in which, say, "There is a fire burning in this room" is, nor in the sense in which "He is an amusing fellow" may be; and the two latter statements are not true in the same sense in which "I've got a headache" is. Truth, when applied to a physical law, means roughly speaking that it is well established by experimental evidence or other observation, that it brings widely different things into a close connection and makes us "understand" what seemed a mystery before; that it simplifies our theoretical system, and further, that it is fruitful in leading us to predictions and new discoveries. (That is, incidentally, why the pragmatist identifies truth with usefulness: he has really got hold of one facet, but of one facet only.) Truth, in this case, it may be said, is not *one* idea but a whole bundle of ideas. Nothing of this applies to truth in the case of a simple observation. Suppose you have to make sure that the light is on in your room. Now when you go and look and say "All right, it's on", your statement is true, *not* because it brings widely different things into connection, *not* because it simplifies I don't know what, *not* because it is fruitful or suggestive – no, nothing of the sort; it is just true because it says so-and-so is as you say it is.

Again, in what sense is one to say of a proverb that it is true? Have you ever tried to put some rare and subtle experience, or some half-forgotten (but strong) impression into words? If you do, you will find that truth, in this case, is inseparably tied up with the literary quality of your writing: it needs no less than a poet to express fully and faithfully such fragile states of mind, How you say it matters even more than what you say.

Similar remarks apply to verification. A law of nature can be verified by experimental evidence, though not conclusively. Whether a material object statement is capable of conclusive verification is a moot point. Take next a case such as "I've got a terrible toothache". Suppose I go to the dentist, he examines my teeth and says, "All right, there's nothing wrong with them". Would I then reply, "Oh, I beg your pardon, I *thought* that I've got a toothache, but now I see that I was mistaken"? My toothache cannot be argued away or refuted by examining my teeth, my nerves, etc. If I were asked how I know that I've got a toothache, I might be tempted to reply, "Because I *feel* it". What a queer sort of reply! Is there anything else I can do with a toothache but feel it? What my reply aimed at, however, was something different, namely to *shake off* the whole question as improper, beside the point. How do I know? I've simply got toothache, and that's the end of it. I do not grant that I may have fallen victim to a delusion, I do not recognize a medical examination, an observation of my teeth, any psychological tests, a court of experts – no dentist in heaven or earth can refute me. In saying "I just *feel it*" I am expressing the fact that the toothache is something *given in immediate experience*, not a thing *inferred from something else* on the strength of certain evidences. The first person singular has, amongst other uses, the function to indicate the character of *immediacy* of an experience.

Take the statement, "There are sea serpents". How would you verify it? Is it enough that some person has seen them? Perhaps for him; for you the situation is different: you have so far only a man who *says* that he has seen them. So you must check up what he says – you may test his eyesight, go into his past and examine his reliability, and so on. The result of this checking will be a number of statements each of which, in its turn, may again be checked: the expert who examined the man's eyesight may himself be examined, the witnesses who testified may in their turn be scrutinized, etc. In following up the threads of verification we nowhere come to an absolute end, that is, we can never say, "Now it is conclusively proved that the man was right". What this particular example shows applies in general. At some point we do stop, it is true, for practical reasons, when the evidence seems to be sufficient. But theoretically we may go on checking and rechecking our statements as long as we please. So long as we move amongst statements concerning such evidences as illustrated above, verification has no natural end, but refers continually to ever new statements. In pursuing these fibres, however, we see how secondary lines branch off into other regions: the points where they come to a sudden end represent those immediate experiences which an observer has the moment he experiences them, and which, in this moment, cannot be checked against other evidences. These experiences, expressed in "I"-sentences, are, so to speak, end points of verification – but of verification in a quite different sense. For if we try to use this verification later, it turns to dust. It lives in the moment, and is gone. Still these experiences are the moments of ultimate fulfilment. It is they from which all light of knowledge flows forth. Or, to change the metaphor, they are the points in which knowledge makes direct contact with reality. Without them all our sentences would float in the air cut off from actual facts. What establishes a connection between sentences and reality are these last points of verification, transitory though they may be. Thus a statement may be verified in two quite different senses: either by checking it against other statements, or by appealing to immediate experience. In the case of a material object statement, for instance, some lines refer to other material object statements, i.e. they lead from statement to statement within the same language stratum; some others branch off and penetrate into a different stratum, the "I"-statements. Thus verification weaves a complicated net, a ramified pattern of lines.

It is easily seen that the term "meaningful" displays the same ambiguity: its sense varies with the stratum. For instance, a sentence in a novel is meaningful, if (1) it is correct English, i.e. not a broth of words, and (2) it fits in with the other sentences. This meaningfulness has nothing whatever to do with verifiability. (That, by the way, is why Fiction is not false.) This criterion, however, does not apply to experiential statements where verifiability is of some relevance, although it would not be right to equate meaningfulness with verifiability. Again, in which sense is a rule, a definition, a request, a question meaningful? There may even be a sense in which metaphysical statements have a meaning. The trouble with the Logical Positivists was that they attached too rigid an import to "meaningfulness" and lost sight of its ambiguity. By virtue of the multiplicity of meaning in this word they lost themselves in a magic cloud out of which they condemned everything that did not conform to their standards. In actual fact they had no machinery, such as they thought they had, by which the senselessness of metaphysics could be *proved;* though it must be admitted that metaphysicians made the greatest efforts to supply them with plausible arguments for such a view. I am afraid that what has been said on this subject was of a profound shallowness.

To sum up this point: Statements may be *true* in different senses, *verifiable* in different senses, *meaningful* in different senses. Therefore the attempts at defining "truth", or at drawing a sharp line between the meaningful and the meaningless, etc., are doomed to fail.

15

GILBERT RYLE

Some Logical Insights into Language: Systematically Misleading Expressions. *With special reference to existential assertions Professor Ryle shows here how the grammatical or verbal form of sentences can mislead the philosopher. Very often, and not least in the case of assertions about existence, the* grammatical *or* verbal *form is no guide to the* logical *form of an assertion, i.e. as to how they are to be rightly understood.*

I. *Quasi-Ontological Statements*

Since Kant, we have, most of us, paid lip service to the doctrine that "existence is not a quality" and so we have rejected the pseudo-implication of the ontological argument; "God is perfect, being perfect entails being existent, . . . God exists". For if existence is not a quality, it is not the sort of thing that can be entailed by a quality.

But until fairly recently it was not noticed that if in "God exists" "exists" is not a predicate (save in grammar), then in the same statement "God" cannot be (save in grammar) the subject of the predication. The realization of this came from examining negative existential propositions like "Satan does not exist" or "unicorns are non-existent". If there is no Satan, then the statement "Satan does not exist" cannot be about Satan in the way in which "I am sleepy" is about me. Despite appearances the word "Satan" cannot be signifying a subject of attributes.

Gilbert Ryle, "Systematically Misleading Expressions", *Logic and Language* (First Series), ed. A. G. N. Flew, Blackwells 1952, pp. 15-20. Reprinted by permission of the author.

Philosophers have toyed with theories which would enable them to continue to say that "Satan does not exist" is none the less still somehow about Satan, and that "exists" still signifies some sort of attribute or character, although not a quality.

So some argued that the statement was about something described as "the idea of Satan", others that it was about a subsistent but non-actual entity called "Satan". Both theories in effect try to show that something may be (whether as being "merely mental" or as being in "the realm of subsistents"), but not be in existence. But as we can say "round squares do not exist", and "real nonentities do not exist", this sort of interpretation of negative existentials is bound to fill either the realm of subsistents or the realm of ideas with walking self-contradictions. So the theories had to be dropped and a new analysis of existential propositions had to begin.

Suppose I assert of (apparently) the general subject "carnivorous cows" that they "do not exist", and my assertion is true, I cannot really be talking about carnivorous cows, for there are none. So it follows that the expression "carnivorous cows" is not really being used, though the grammatical appearances are to the contrary, to denote the thing or things of which the predicate is being asserted. And in the same way as the verb "exists" is not signifying the character asserted, although grammatically it looks as if it was, the real predicate must be looked for elsewhere.

So the clue of the grammar has to be rejected and the analysis has been suggested that "carnivorous cows do not exist" means what is meant by "no cows are carnivorous" or "no carnivorous beasts are cows". But a further improvement seems to be required.

"Unicorns do not exist" seems to mean what is meant by "nothing is both a quadruped and herbivorous and the wearer of one horn" (or whatever the marks of being a unicorn are). And this does not seem to imply that there are some quadrupeds or herbivorous animals.

So "carnivorous cows do not exist" ought to be rendered "nothing is both a cow and carnivorous", which does not as it stands imply that anything is either.

Take now an apparently singular subject as in "God exists" or "Satan does not exist". If the former analysis was right, then here too: "God" and "Satan" are in fact, despite grammatical appearance, predicative expressions. That is to say, they are that element in the assertion that something has a specified character, which signifies the character by which the subject is being asserted to be characterized. "God exists" must mean what is meant by "Something, and one thing only, is omniscient, omnipotent, and infinitely good" (or whatever else are the characters summed in the compound character of being a god and the only god). And "Satan does not exist" must mean what is meant by "nothing is both devilish and alone in being devilish", or perhaps "nothing is both devilish and called 'Satan' ", or even " 'Satan' is not the proper name of anything". To put it roughly, "*x* exists" and *x* does not exist" do not assert or deny that a given subject of attributes *x* has the attribute of existing, but assert or deny the attribute of being *x*-ish or being an *x* of something not named in the statement.

Now I can show my hand. I say that expressions such as "carnivorous cows do not exist" are systematically misleading and that the expressions by which we paraphrased them are not or are not in the same way or to the same extent systematically misleading. But they are not false, nor are they senseless. They are true, and they really do mean what their less systematically misleading paraphrases mean. Nor (save in a special class of cases) is the non-philosophical author of such expressions ignorant or doubtful of the nature of the state of affairs which his expression records. He is not a whit misled. There is a trap, however, in the form of his expression, but a trap which only threatens the man who has begun to generalize about sorts or types of states of affairs and assumes that every statement gives in its syntax a clue to the logical form of the fact that it records. I refer here not merely nor even primarily to the philosopher, but to any man who embarks on abstraction.

But before developing this theme I want to generalize the results of our examination of what we must now describe as "so-called existential statements". It is the more necessary in that, while most philosophers are now forewarned by Kant against the systematic misleadingness of "God exists", few of them have observed that the same taint infects a whole host of other expressions.

If "God exists" means what we have said it means, then patently "God is an existent", "God is an entity", "God has being", or "existence" require the same analysis. So ". . . is an existent", " . . . is an entity" are only bogus predicates, and that of which (in grammar) they are asserted is only a bogus subject.

And the same will be true of all the items in the following pair of lists.

Mr. Baldwin –	Mr. Pickwick –
is a being.	is a nonentity.
is real, or a reality.	is unreal or an unreality or an appearance.
is a genuine entity.	is a bogus or sham entity.
is a substance.	is not a substance.
is an actual object or entity.	is an unreal object or entity.
is objective.	is not objective or is subjective.
is a concrete reality.	is a fiction or figment.
is an object.	is an imaginary object.
is.	is not.
	is a mere idea.
	is an abstraction.
	is a logical construction.

None of these statements is really about Mr. Pickwick. For if they are true, there is no such person for them to be about. Nor is any of them about Mr. Baldwin. For if they were false, there would be no one for them to be about. Nor in any of them is the grammatical predicate that element in the statement which signifies the character that is being asserted to be characterizing or not to be characterizing something.

I formulate the conclusion in this rather clumsy way. There is a class of statements of which the grammatical predicate appears to signify not the having of a specified character but the having (or not having) of a specified status. But in all such statements the appearance is a purely grammatical one, and what the statements really record can be stated in statements embodying no such quasi-ontological predicates.

And, again, in all such quasi-ontological statements the grammatical subject-word or phrase appears to denote or refer to something as that of which the quasi-ontological predicate is being predicated; but in fact the apparent subject term is a concealed predicative expression, and what is really recorded in such statements can be re-stated in statements no part of which even appears to refer to any such subject.

In a word, all quasi-ontological statements are systematically misleading. (If I am right in this, then the conclusion follows, which I accept, that those metaphysical philosophers are the greatest sinners, who, as if they were saying something of importance, make

"Reality" or "Being" the subject of their propositions, or "real" the predicate. For at best what they say is systematically misleading, which is the one thing which a philosopher's propositions have no right to be; and at worst it is meaningless.)

I must give warning again, that the naïve employer of such quasi-ontological expressions is not necessarily and not even probably misled. He has said what he wanted to say, and anyone who knew English would understand what he was saying. Moreover, I would add, in the cases that I have listed, the statements are not merely significant, but true. Each of them records a real state of affairs. Nor need they mislead the philosopher. We, for instance, I hope are not misled. But the point is that anyone, the philosopher included, who abstracts and generalizes and so tries to consider what different facts of the same type (i.e. facts of the same type about different things) have in common, is compelled to use the common grammatical form of the statements of those facts as handles with which to grasp the common logical form of the facts themselves. For (what we shall see later) as the way in which a fact ought to be recorded in expressions would be a clue to the form of that fact, we jump to the assumption that the way in which a fact is recorded is such a clue. And very often the clue is misleading and suggests that the fact is of a different form from what really is its form. "Satan is not a reality" from its grammatical form looks as if it recorded the same sort of fact as "Capone is not a philosopher", and so was just as much denying a character of a somebody called "Satan" as the latter does deny a character of a somebody called "Capone". But it turns out that the suggestion is a fraud; for the fact recorded would have been properly or less improperly recorded in the statement " 'Satan' is not a proper name" or "No one is called 'Satan' " or "No one is both called 'Satan' and is infinitely malevolent, etc.", or perhaps "Some people believe that someone is both called 'Satan' and infinitely malevolent, but their belief is false". And none of these statements even pretend to be "about Satan". Instead, they are and are patently about the noise "Satan" or else about people who misuse it.

In the same way, while it is significant, true, and directly "intelligible to say 'Mr. Pickwick is a fiction' ", it is a systematically misleading expression (i.e. an expression misleading in virtue of a formal property which it does or might share with other expressions); for it does not really record, as it appears to record, a fact of the same sort as is recorded in "Mr. Baldwin is a statesman". The world does not contain fictions in the way in which it contains statesmen. There is no subject of attributes of which we can say "there is a fiction". What we can do is to say of Dickens "there is a story-teller", or of Pickwick Papers "there is a pack of lies"; or of a sentence in that novel, which contains the pseudo-name "Mr. Pickwick" "there is a fable". And when we say things of this sort we are recording just what we recorded when we said "Mr. Pickwick is a fiction", only our new expressions do not suggest what our old one did that some subject of attributes has the two attributes of being called "Mr. Pickwick" and of being a fiction, but instead that some subject of attributes has the attributes of being called Dickens and being a coiner of false propositions and pseudo-proper names, or, on the other analysis, of being a book or a sentence which could only be true or false if someone was called "Mr. Pickwick". The proposition "Mr. Pickwick is a fiction" is really, despite its *prima facies*, about Dickens or else about Pickwick Papers. But the fact that it is so is concealed and not exhibited by the form of the expression in which it is said.

It must be noted that the sense in which such quasi-ontological statements are misleading is not that they are false and not even that any word in them is equivocal or vague, but only that they are formally improper to facts of the logical form which they are employed to record and proper to facts of quite another logical form. What the implications are of these notions of formal propriety or formal impropriety we shall see later on.

In what is now a classical work, Professor Ryle illustrates how logical insights, enshrined in concepts like that of "logical type" and "category mistake", can be used with profit in the discussion of traditional problems like that of the body mind relationship.

There is a doctrine about the nature and place of minds which is so prevalent among theorists and even among laymen that it deserves to be described as the official theory. Most philosophers, psychologists and religious teachers subscribe, with minor reservations, to its main articles and, although they admit certain theoretical

Gilbert Ryle, *The Concept of Mind*, Hutchinson's University Library 1949, pp. 13, 17–20, 23–24. Reprinted by permission of the Hutchinson Publishing Group Ltd., London and Barnes & Noble Inc., New York.

difficulties in it, they tend to assume that these can be overcome without serious modifications being made to the architecture of the theory. It will be argued here that the central principles of the doctrine are unsound and conflict with the whole body of what we know about minds when we are not speculating about them.

The official doctrine, which hails chiefly from Descartes, is something like this. With the doubtful exceptions of idiots and infants in arms every human being has both a body and a mind. Some would prefer to say that every human being is both a body and a mind. His body and his mind are ordinarily harnessed together, but after the death of the body his mind may continue to exist and function.

Such in outline is the official theory. I shall often speak of it, with deliberate abusiveness, as "the dogma of the Ghost in the Machine". I hope to prove that it is entirely false, and false not in detail but in principle. It is not merely an assemblage of particular mistakes. It is one big mistake and a mistake of a special kind. It is, namely, a category-mistake. It represents the facts of mental life as if they belonged to one logical type or category (or range of types or categories), when they actually belong to another. The dogma is therefore a philosopher's myth. In attempting to explode the myth I shall probably be taken to be denying well-known facts about the mental life of human beings, and my plea that I aim at doing nothing more than rectify the logic of mental-conduct concepts will probably be disallowed as mere subterfuge.

I must first indicate what is meant by the phrase "Category-mistake". This I do in a series of illustrations.

A foreigner visiting Oxford or Cambridge for the first time is shown a number of colleges, libraries, playing fields, museums, scientific departments and administrative offices. He then asks "But where is the University? I have seen where the members of the Colleges live, where the Registrar works, where the scientists experiment and the rest. But I have not yet seen the University in which reside and work the members of your University." It has then to be explained to him that the University is not another collateral institution, some ulterior counterpart to the colleges, laboratories and offices which he has seen. The University is just the way in which all that he has already seen is organized. When they are seen and when their co-ordination is understood, the University has been seen. His mistake lay in his innocent assumption that it was correct to speak of Christ Church, the Bodleian Library, the Ashmolean Museum *and* the University, to speak, that is, as if "the University" stood for an extra member of the class of which these other units are members. He was mistakenly allocating the University to the same category as that to which the other institutions belong.

The same mistake would be made by a child witnessing the march-past of a division, who, having had pointed out to him such and such battalions, batteries, squadrons, etc., asked when the division was going to appear. He would be supposing that a division was a counterpart to the units already seen, partly similar to them and partly unlike them. He would be shown his mistake by being told that in watching the battalions, batteries and squadrons marching past he had been watching the division marching past. The march-past was not a parade of battalions, batteries, squadrons *and* a division; it was a parade of the battalions, batteries and squadrons *of* a division.

One more illustration. A foreigner watching his first game of cricket learns what are the functions of the bowlers, the batsmen, the fielders, the umpires and the scorers. He then says "But there is no one left on the field to contribute the famous element of team-spirit. I see who does the bowling, the batting and the wicket-keeping; but I do not see whose role it is to exercise *esprit de corps*". Once more, it would have to be explained that he was looking for the wrong type of thing. Team-spirit is not another cricketing-operation supplementary to all of the other special tasks. It is, roughly, the keenness with which each of the special tasks is performed, and performing a task keenly is not performing two tasks. Certainly exhibiting team-spirit is not the same thing as bowling or catching, but nor is it a third thing such that we can say that the bowler first bowls *and* then exhibits team-spirit or that a fielder is at a given moment *either* catching *or* displaying *esprit de corps*.

These illustrations of category-mistakes have a common feature which must be noticed. The mistakes were made by people who did not know how to wield the concepts *University*, *division* and *team-spirit*. Their puzzles arose from inability to use certain items in the English vocabulary.

The theoretically interesting category-mistakes are those made by people who are perfectly competent to apply concepts, at least in the situations with which they are familiar, but are still liable in their abstract thinking to allocate those concepts to logical types to which they do not belong. An instance of a mistake of this sort would be the following story. A student of politics has learned the main differences between the British, the French, and the American Constitutions, and has learned also the differences and connexions between the Cabinet, Parliament, the various Ministries, the Judicature and the Church of England. But he still became embarrassed when asked questions about the connexions between the Church of England, the Home Office and the British Constitution. For while the Church and the Home Office are institutions, the British Constitution is not another institution in the same sense of that noun. So inter-institutional relations which can be asserted or denied to hold between the Church and the Home Office cannot be asserted or denied to hold between either of them and the British Constitution. "The British Constitution" is not a term of the same logical type as "the Home Office" and "the Church of England". In a partially similar way, John Doe may be a relative, a friend, an enemy or a stranger to Richard Roe; but he cannot be any of these things to the Average Taxpayer. He knows how to talk sense in certain sorts of discussion about the Average Taxpayer, but he is baffled to say why he could not come across him in the street as he can come across Richard Roe.

It is pertinent to our main subject to notice that, so long as the student of politics continues to think of the British Constitution as a counterpart to the other institutions, he will tend to describe it as a mysteriously occult institution; and so long as John Doe continues to think of the Average Taxpayer as a fellow-citizen, he will tend to think of him as an elusive insubstantial man, a ghost who is everywhere yet nowhere.

My destructive purpose is to show that a family of radical category-mistakes is the source of the double-life theory. The representation of a person as a ghost mysteriously ensconced in a machine derives from this argument. Because, as is true, a person's thinking, feeling and purposive doing cannot be described solely in the idioms of physics, chemistry and physiology, therefore they must be described in counterpart idioms. As the human body is a complex organized unit, so the human mind must be another complex organized unit, though one made of a different sort of stuff and with a different sort of structure. Or, again, as the human body, like any other parcel of matter, is a field of causes and effects, so the mind must be another field of causes and effects, though not (Heaven be praised) mechanical causes and effects.

When two terms belong to the same category, it is proper to construct conjunctive propositions embodying them. Thus a purchaser may say that he bought a left-hand glove and a right-hand glove, but not that he bought a left-hand glove, a right-hand glove and a pair of gloves. "She came home in a flood of tears and a sedan-chair" is a well-known joke based on the absurdity of conjoining terms of different types. It would have been equally ridiculous to construct the disjunction, "She came home either in a flood of tears or else in a sedan-chair". Now the dogma of the Ghost in the Machine does just this. It maintains that there exist both bodies and minds; that there occur physical processes and mental processes; that there are mechanical causes of corporeal movements and mental causes of corporeal movements. I shall argue that these and other analogous conjunctions are absurd; but, it must be noticed, the argument will not show that either of the illegitimately conjoined propositions is absurd in itself. I am not, for example, denying that there occur mental processes. Doing long division is a mental process and so is making a joke. But I am saying that the phrase "there occur mental processes" does not mean the same sort of thing as "there occur physical processes", and, therefore, that it makes no sense to conjoin or disjoin the two.

If my argument is successful, there will follow some interesting consequences. First, the hallowed contrast between Mind and Matter will be dissipated, but dissipated not by either of the equally hallowed absorptions of Mind by Matter or of Matter by Mind, but in quite a different way. For the seeming contrast of the two will be shown to be as illegitimate as would be the contrast of "she came home in a flood of tears" and "she came home in a sedan-chair". The belief that there is a polar opposition between Mind and Matter is the belief that they are terms of the same logical type.

It will also follow that both Idealism and Materialism are answers to an improper question. The "reduction" of the material world to mental states and processes, as well as the "reduction" of mental states and processes to physical states and processes, presupposes the legitimacy of the disjunction, "Either there exist minds or there exist bodies (but not both)". It would be like saying, "Either she bought a left-hand and right-hand glove or she bought a pair of gloves (but not both)".

It is perfectly proper to say, in one logical tone of voice, that there exist minds and to say, in another logical tone of voice, that there exist bodies. but these expressions do not indicate two different species of existence, for "existence" is not a generic word like "coloured" or "sexed". They indicate two different senses of "exist", somewhat as "rising" has different senses in "the tide is rising", "hopes are rising", and "the average age of death is rising". A man would be thought to be making a poor joke who said that three things are now rising, namely the tide, hopes and the average age of death. It would be just as good or bad a joke to say that there exist prime numbers and Wednesdays and public opinions and navies; or that there exist both minds and bodies.

16

P. F. STRAWSON

This extract illustrates the change there has been in our approach to, and understanding of, logic, and includes a very helpful example which illuminates the relationship which contemporary philosophers consider holds between formal logic and ordinary language.

This ideal of system has been present in formal logic from the start. The earliest logicians had seen that with the help of just a few logical principles, they could, taking a small number of patterns of valid inference as basic, *prove* the validity of a larger number of other patterns; that is, they could apply logic within logic, use it to systematize itself. And it is this ideal of systematization which has most profoundly influenced the modern development of logic; so profoundly that the original conception of simply codifying the most general principles we appeal to in making our logical appraisals has pretty well been lost sight of. For the expressions of ordinary speech, such as "if", "and", "not", "all", "some", "or", which figured so prominently as logical constants in the inference-patterns of early logicians, lack, as they are ordinarily used, not only the stability, but also the simplicity, of meaning which would make them the ideal candidates for the roles of constants in logical systems of the now desired kind. So their place tends to be taken by fabricated expressions to which are assigned just the kinds of meaning needed to meet the requirements of system. The logical uses of these fabricated expressions correspond in part with, and diverge in part from, some uses of some expressions in ordinary speech; the correspondence and the divergence being revealed in a partial parallelism and a

P. F. Strawson, *Introduction to Logical Theory*, Methuen 1952, pp. 57–58.

partial discrepancy between the rules to which we appeal in our logical appraisals of ordinary talk, and the rules governing the new expressions. The latter are written as symbols, not as words. And the change is itself symbolic; for there are few, if any, words which have just, and only, the meaning assigned to the symbols.

To put this another way. The formal logician now aims at an exact and highly systematic logic, comparable in these respects with mathematics. But he cannot give the exact and systematic logic of expressions of everyday speech; for these expressions have no exact and systematic logic. What he can, and does, do is to devise a set of rules which satisfies his requirements, and, at the same time, while not doing full justice to the complexities of ordinary usage, and diverging from it in many ways, does touch ordinary usage at some vital points. The formal logician, in relation to ordinary language, might be compared with a man ostensibly mapping a piece of country of which the main contours are highly irregular and shifting. But the man is passionately addicted to geometry, and insists on using in his drawings only geometrical figures for which rules of construction can be given; and on using as few of such rules as he can. Naturally his maps will never quite fit. But a good many landmarks are identifiable on his drawing, and there is a rough correspondence between some of the main features of the country and some of the main lines of the map. The logician, we may say, manufactures the elements of a language of his own, which, unlike ordinary language, is subject to rigid and systematically connected rules, and some of the symbols of which exhibit logical analogies to familiar expressions of ordinary speech, as these expressions are commonly, though not always, used. And in the process of system-construction he may, and does – if only by contrast – teach us a good deal about the logic of ordinary discourse.

This discussion of the logic of persons – an example of what Strawson calls "descriptive" as opposed to "revisionary" metaphysics, metaphysics no longer being a forbidden pursuit, provides a context for seeing afresh the point of the doctrine of the resurrection of the body. P-predicates are those predicates which belong distinctly to persons, as distinct from those predicates which "are also properly applied to material bodies". As example of P-predicates, Strawson gives "is smiling", "is going for a walk", "is in pain", "is thinking hard", "believes in God" by contrast with "weighs ten stone", "is in the drawing room" and so on. (*p. 104 loc. cit.*)

Now our perplexities may take a different form, the form of the question: "But how can one ascribe to oneself, not on the basis of observation, the very same thing that others may have, on the basis of observation, reasons of a logically adequate kind for ascribing to one?" This question may be absorbed in a wider one, which might be phrased: "How are P-predicates possible?" or: "How is the concept of a person possible?" This is the question by which we replace those two earlier questions, viz.: "Why are states of consciousness ascribed at all, ascribed to anything?" and "Why are they ascribed to the very same thing as certain corporeal characteristics &c.?" For the answer to these two initial questions is to be found nowhere else but in the admission of the primitiveness of the concept of a person, and hence of the unique character of P-predicates. So residual perplexities have to frame themselves in this new way. For when we have acknowledged the primitiveness of the concept of a person, and, with it, the unique character of P-predicates, we may still want to ask what it is in the natural facts that makes it intelligible that we should have this concept, and to ask this in the hope of a non-trivial answer, i.e. in the hope of an answer which does not *merely* say: "Well, there are people in the world". I do not pretend to be able to satisfy this demand at all fully. But I may mention two very different things which might count as beginnings or fragments of an answer.

First, I think a beginning can be made by moving a certain class of P-predicates to a central position in the picture. They are predicates, roughly, which involve doing something, which clearly imply intention or a state of mind or at least consciousness in general, and which indicate a characteristic pattern, or range of patterns, of bodily movement, while not indicating at all precisely any very definite sensation or experience. I mean such things as "going for a walk", "coiling a rope", "playing ball", "writing a letter". Such predicates have the interesting characteristic of many P-predicates, that one does not, in general, ascribe them to oneself on the strength of observation, whereas one does ascribe them to others on the strength of observation. But, in the case of these predicates, one feels minimal reluctance to concede that what is ascribed in these two different ways is the same. This is because of the marked domi-

P. F. Strawson, *Individuals*, Methuen 1959, pp. 110–16.

nance of a fairly definite pattern of bodily movement in what they ascribe, and the marked absence of any distinctive experience. They release us from the idea that the only things we can know about without observation or inference, or both, are private experiences; we can know, without telling by either of these means, about the present and future movements of a body. Yet bodily movements are certainly also things we can know about by observation and inference. Among the things that we observe, as opposed to the things we know about without observation, are the movements of bodies similar to that about which we have knowledge not based on observation. It is important that we should understand such movements, for they bear on the condition our own; and in fact we understand them, we interpret them, only by seeing them as elements in just such plans or schemes of action as those of which we know the present course and future development without observation of the relevant present movements. But this is to say that we see such movements as *actions*, that we interpret them in terms of intention, that we see them as movements of individuals of a type to which also belongs that individual whose present and future movements we know about without observation; it is to say that we see others as self-ascribers, not on the basis of observation, of what we ascribe to them on this basis.

These remarks are not intended to suggest how the "problem of other minds" could be solved, or our beliefs about others given a general philosophical "justification". I have already argued that such a "solution" or "justification" is impossible, that the demand for it cannot be coherently stated. Nor are these remarks intended as *a priori* genetic psychology. They are simply intended to help to make it seem intelligible to us, at this stage in the history of the philosophy of this subject, that we have the conceptual scheme we have. What I am suggesting is that it is easier to understand how we can see each other, and ourselves, as persons, if we think first of the fact that we act, and act on each other, and act in accordance with a common human nature. Now "to see each other as persons" is a lot of things, but not a lot of separate and unconnected things. The class of P-predicates that I have moved into the centre of the picture are not unconnectedly there, detached from others irrelevant to them. On the contrary, they are inextricably bound up with the others, interwoven with them. The topic of the mind does not divide into unconnected subjects.

I spoke just now of a common human nature. But there is also a sense in which a condition of the existence of the conceptual scheme we have is that human nature should not be common – should not be, that is, a community nature. Philosophers used to discuss the question of whether there was, or could be, such a thing as a "group mind". For some the idea had a peculiar fascination, while to others it seemed utterly absurd and nonsensical and at the same time, curiously enough, pernicious. It is easy to see why these last found it pernicious: they found something horrible in the thought that people should cease to have to individual persons the kind of attitudes that they did have, and instead have attitudes in some way analogous towards groups; and that they might cease to decide individual courses of action for themselves and instead merely participate in corporate activities. But their finding it pernicious showed that they understood the idea they claimed to be absurd only too well. The fact that we find it natural to individuate as persons the members of a certain class of moving natural objects does not mean that such a conceptual scheme is inevitable for any class of beings not utterly unlike ourselves. A technique similar to that which I used in the last chapter to decide whether there was a place in the restricted auditory world for the concept of the self, is available to determine whether we might not construct the idea of a special kind of social world in which the concept of an individual person is replaced by that of a group. Think, to begin with, of certain aspects of actual human existence. Think, for example, of two groups of human beings engaged in some competitive, but corporate activity, such as battle, for which they have been exceedingly well trained. We may even suppose that orders are superfluous, though information is passed. It is easy to suppose that, while absorbed in such activity, the members of the groups make no references to individual persons at all, have no use for personal names or pronouns. They do, however, refer to the groups and apply to them predicates analogous to those predicates ascribing purposive activity which we normally apply to individual persons. They may *in fact* use in such circumstances the plural forms "we" and "they"; but these are not genuine plurals, they are plurals without a singular, such as occur in sentences like: "We have taken the citadel", "We have lost the game". They may also refer to elements in the group, to members of the group, but exclusively in terms which get their sense from the parts played by these elements in the corporate activity. Thus we sometimes refer to what are in fact persons as "stroke" or "square-leg".

When we think of such cases, we see that we ourselves, over a part of our social lives – not, happily, a very large part – do work with a set of ideas from which that of the individual person is excluded, in which its place is taken by that of the group. But might we not think of communities or groups such that this part of the lives of their members was the dominant part – or was not merely a part, but the whole? It sometimes happens, with groups of human beings, that, as *we* say, their members think, feel and act "as one". I suggest it is a condition for the existence of the concept of an individual person, that this should happen only sometimes.

It is quite useless to say, at this point: "But all the same, even if it happened all the time, every member of the group would *have* an individual consciousness, would embody an individual subject of experience." For, once more, there is no sense in speaking of the individual consciousness just as such, of the individual subject of experience just as such; there is no way of identifying such pure entities. It is true, of course, that, in suggesting the fantasy of total absorption in the group, I took our concept of an individual person as a starting point. It is this fact which makes the useless reaction a natural one. But suppose someone seriously advanced the following "hypothesis": that each part of the human body, each organ and each member, had an individual consciousness, was a separate centre of experiences. The "hypothesis" would be useless in the same way as the above remark, only more obviously so. Let us now suppose that there is a class of moving natural objects, divided into groups, each group exhibiting the same characteristic pattern of activity. Within each group there are certain differentiations of appearance accompanying differentiations of function, and in particular there is one member of each group with a distinctive appearance. Cannot one imagine different sets of observations which might lead us in the one case to think of the particular member as the spokesman of the group, as its mouthpiece; and in the other case to think of him as its mouth, to think of the group as a single *scattered* body? The important point is that as soon as we adopt the latter way of thinking, then we abandon the former; we are no longer influenced by the human analogy in its first form, but only in its second; we are no longer tempted to say: Perhaps the members have consciousness. It is helpful here to remember the startling ambiguity of the phrase, "a body and its members".

Earlier, when I was discussing the concept of a pure individual consciousness, I said that though it could not exist as a primary concept to be used in the explanation of the concept of a person (so that there is no mind–body problem, as traditionally conceived), yet it might have a logically secondary existence. Thus, from within our actual conceptual scheme, each of us can quite intelligibly conceive of his or her individual survival of bodily death. The effort of imagination is not even great. One has simply to think of oneself as having thoughts and memories as at present, visual and auditory experiences largely as at present, even, perhaps – though this involves certain complications – some quasi-tactual and organic sensations as at present, whilst (*a*) having no perceptions of a body related to one's experience as one's own body is, and (*b*) having no powers of initiating changes in the physical condition of the world, such as one at present does with one's hands, shoulders, feet and vocal chords. Condition (*a*) must be expanded by adding that no one else exhibits reactions indicating that he perceives a body at the point which one's body would be occupying if one were seeing and hearing in an embodied state from the point from which one is seeing and hearing in a disembodied state. One could, of course, imagine condition (*a*) being fulfilled, in both its parts, without condition (*b*) being fulfilled. This would be a rather vulgar fancy, in the class of the table-tapping spirits with familiar voices. But suppose we take disembodiment strictly in the sense that we imagine both (*a*) and (*b*) fulfilled. Then two consequences follow, one of which is commonly noted, the other of which is perhaps insufficiently attended to. The first is that the strictly disembodied individual is strictly solitary, and it must remain for him indeed an utterly empty, though not meaningless, speculation, as to whether there are any other members of his class. The other, and less commonly noticed point, is that in order to retain his idea of himself as an individual, he must always think of himself as *dis*embodied, as a *former* person. That is to say, he must contrive still to have the idea of himself as a member of a class or type of entities with whom, however, he is now debarred from entering into any of those transactions the past fact of which was the condition of his having any idea of himself at all. Since then he has, as it were, no personal life of his own to lead, he must live much in the memories of the personal life he did lead; or he might, when this living in the past loses its appeal, achieve some kind of attenuated vicarious personal existence by taking a certain kind of interest in the human affairs of which he is a mute and invisible witness – much like that kind of spectator at a play who says to himself: "That's what I should have done (or said)" or "If I were he, I should . . .". In proportion as the memories fade, and this vicarious living palls, to that degree his concept of himself as an individual becomes attenuated. At the limit of attenuation there is, *from the point of view of his survival as an individual*, no difference between the continuance of experience and its cessation. Disembodied survival, on such terms as these, may well seem unattractive. No doubt it is for this reason that the orthodox have wisely insisted on the resurrection of the body.

17

J. L. AUSTIN

Performative Utterances. *In introducing his concept of performatives Professor J. L. Austin singled out a most important and significant feature of the logical landscape, and one which helps us to understand much better what we are doing when we use words. At the same time, I think he was too nervous of the element of first person involvement, for the apparent exceptions he gives are scarcely concealed first person utterances. The third extract shows how in the end Professor Austin introduces the concept of illocutionary (or performative) force. In other words, instead of regarding an utterance as in itself a performative he regards it as having illocutionary force along, for example, with descriptive (or "constative") force. With performatives the degree of illocutionary force is a maximum and the degree of descriptive force a minimum. In a subsequent extract Professor Donald Evans shows how this concept of performatives in its full analysis can be of great use in helping to elucidate the character of theological assertions.*

I want to discuss a kind of utterance which looks like a statement and grammatically, I suppose, would be classed as a statement, which is not nonsensical, and yet is not true or false. These are not going to be utterances which contain curious verbs like "could" or "might", or curious words like "good", which many philosophers regard nowadays simply as danger signals. They will be perfectly straightforward utterances, with ordinary verbs in the first person singular

J. L. Austin, *Philosophical Papers*, ed. J. O. Urmson and G. J. Warnock, 1961, pp. 222–23, 228–30, 237–39. Reprinted by permission of the Clarendon Press, Oxford.

present indicative active, and yet we shall see at once that they could not possibly be true or false. Furthermore, if a person makes an utterance of this sort we should say that he is *doing* something rather than merely *saying* something. This may sound a little odd, but the examples I shall give will in fact not be odd at all, and may even seem decidedly dull. Here are three or four. Suppose, for example, that in the course of a marriage ceremony I say, as people will, "I do" – (take this woman to be my lawful wedded wife). Or again, suppose that I tread on your toe and say "I apologize". Or again, suppose that I have the bottle of champagne in my hand and say "I name this ship the *Queen Elizabeth*". Or suppose I say "I bet you sixpence it will rain tomorrow". In all these cases it would be absurd to regard the thing that I say as a report of the performance of the action which is undoubtedly done – the action of betting, or christening or apologizing. We should say rather that, in saying what I do, I actually perform that action. When I say "I name this ship the *Queen Elizabeth*" I do not describe the christening ceremony, I actually perform the christening; and when I say "I do" (take this woman to be my lawful wedded wife), I am not reporting on a marriage, I am indulging in it.

Now these kinds of utterance are the ones that we call *performative* utterances. This is rather an ugly word, and a new word, but there seems to be no word already in existence to do the job. The nearest approach that I can think of is the word "operative" as used by lawyers. Lawyers when talking about legal instruments will distinguish between the preamble, which recites the circumstances in which a transaction is effected, and on the other hand the operative part – the part of it which actually performs the legal act which it is the purpose of the instrument to perform. So the word "operative" is very near to what we want. "I give and bequeath my watch to my brother" would be an operative clause and is a performative utterance. However, the word "operative" has other uses, and it seems preferable to have a word specially designed for the use we want.

Now at this point one might protest, perhaps even with some alarm, that I seem to be suggesting that marrying is simply saying a few words, that just saying a few words *is* marrying. Well, that certainly is not the case. The words have to be said in the appropriate circumstances, and this is a matter that will come up again later. But the one thing we must not suppose is that what is needed in addition to the saying of the words in such cases is the performance of some internal spiritual act, of which the words then are to be the report. It's very easy to slip into this view at least in difficult, portentous cases, though perhaps not so easy in simple cases like apologizing. In the case of promising – for example, "I promise to be there tomorrow" – it's very easy to think that the utterance is simply the outward and visible (that is, verbal) sign of the performance of some inward spiritual act of promising, and this view has certainly been expressed in many classic places. There is the case of Euripides' Hippolytus, who said "My tongue swore to, but my heart did not" – perhaps it should be "mind" or "spirit" rather than "heart", but at any rate some kind of backstage artiste. Now it is clear from this sort of example that, if we slip into thinking that such utterances are reports, true or false, of the performance of inward and spiritual acts, we open a loophole to perjurers and welshers and bigamists and so on, so that there are disadvantages in being excessively solemn in this way. It is better, perhaps, to stick to the old saying that our word is our bond.

How can we be sure, how can we tell, whether any utterance is to be classed as a performative or not? Surely, we feel, we ought to be able to do that. And we should obviously very much like to be able to say that there is a grammatical criterion for this, some grammatical means of deciding whether an utterance is performative. All the examples I have given hitherto do in fact have the same grammatical form; they all of them begin with the verb in the first person singular present indicative active – not just any kind of verb of course, but still they all are in fact of that form. Furthermore, with these verbs that I have used there is a typical asymmetry between the use of this person and tense of the verb and the use of the same verb in other persons and other tenses, and this asymmetry is rather an important clue.

For example, when we say "I promise that . . .", the case is very different from when we say "He promises that . . .", or in the past tense "I promised that . . .". For when we say "I promise that . . ." we do perform an act of promising – we give a promise. What we do *not* do is to report on somebody's performing an act of promising – in particular, we do not report on somebody's use of the expression "I promise". We actually do use it and do the promising. But if I say "He promises", or in the past tense "I promised", I precisely do report on an act of promising, that is to say an act of using this formula "I promise" – I report on a present act of promising by him, or on a past act of my own. There is thus a clear difference between our first person singular present indicative active, and other persons and tenses. This is brought out by the typical incident of little Willie whose uncle says he'll give him half-a-crown if he promises never to smoke till he's 55. Little Willie's anxious parent will say "Of course he promises, don't you, Willie?" giving him a nudge, and little Willie just doesn't vouchsafe. The point here is that he must do the promising himself by saying "I promise", and his parent is going too fast in saying he promises.

That, then, is a bit of a test for whether an utterance is performative or not, but it would not do to suppose that every performative utterance has to take this standard form. There is at least one other standard form, every bit as common as this one, where the verb is in the passive voice and in the second or third person, not in the first. The sort of case I mean is that of a notice inscribed "Passengers are warned to cross the line by the bridge only", or of a document reading "You are hereby authorized" to do so-and-so. These are undoubtedly performative, and in fact a signature is often required in order to show who it is that is doing the act of warning, or authorizing, or whatever it may be. Very typical of this kind of performative – especially liable to occur in written documents of course – is that the little word "hereby" either actually occurs or might naturally be inserted.

Unfortunately, however, we still can't possibly suggest that every utterance which is to be classed as a performative has to take one or another of these two, as we might call them, standard forms. After all it would be a very typical performative utterance to say "I order you to shut the door". This satisfies all the criteria. It is performing the act of ordering you to shut the door, and it is not true or false. But in the appropriate circumstances surely we could perform exactly the same act by simply saying "Shut the door", in the imperative. Or again, suppose that somebody sticks up a notice "This bull is dangerous", or simply "Dangerous bull", or simply "Bull". Does this necessarily differ from sticking up a notice, appropriately signed, saying "You are hereby warned that this bull is dangerous"? It seems that the simple notice "Bull" can do just the same job as the more elaborate formula. Of course the difference is that if we just stick up "Bull" it would not be quite clear that it is a warning; it might be there just for interest or information, like

"Wallaby" on the cage at the zoo, or "Ancient Monument". No doubt we should know from the nature of the case that it was a warning, but it would not be explicit.

Well, in view of this break-down of grammatical criteria, what we should like to suppose – and there is a good deal in this – is that any utterance which is performative could be reduced or expanded or analysed into one of these two standard forms beginning "I . . ." so and so or beginning "You (or he) hereby . . ." so and so. If there was any justification for this hope, as to some extent there is, then we might hope to make a list of all the verbs which can appear in these standard forms, and then we might classify the kinds of acts that can be performed by performative utterances.

Then let us look for a moment at our original contrast between the performative and the statement from the other side. In handling performatives we have been putting it all the time as though the only thing that a performative utterance had to do was to be felicitous, to come off, not to be a misfire, not to be an abuse. Yes, but that's not the end of the matter. At least in the case of many utterances which, on what we have said, we should have to class as performatives – cases where we say "I warn you to . . .", "I advise you to . . ." and so on – there will be other questions besides simply: was it in order, was it all right, as a piece of advice or a warning, did it come off? After that surely there will be the question: was it good or sound advice? Was it a justified warning? Or in the case, let us say, of a verdict or an estimate: was it a good estimate, or a sound verdict? And these are questions that can only be decided by considering how the content of the verdict or estimate is related in some way to fact, or to evidence available about the facts. This is to say that we do require to assess at least a great many performative utterances in a general dimension of correspondence with fact. It may still be said, of course, that this does not make them *very* like statements because still they are not true or false, and that's a little black and white speciality that distinguishes statements as a class apart. But actually – though it would take too long to go on about this – the more you think about truth and falsity the more you find that very few statements that we ever utter are just true or just false. Usually there is the question are they fair or are they not fair, are they adequate or not adequate, are they exaggerated or not exaggerated? Are they too rough, or are they perfectly precise, accurate, and so on? "True" and "false" are just general labels for a whole dimension of different appraisals which have something or other to do with the relation between what we say and the facts. If, then, we loosen up our ideas of truth and falsity we shall see that statements, when assessed in relation to the facts, are not so very different after all from pieces of advice, warnings, verdicts, and so on.

We see then that stating something is performing an act just as much as is giving an order or giving a warning; and we see, on the other hand, that, when we give an order or a warning or a piece of advice, there is a question about how this is related to fact which is not perhaps so very different from the kind of question that arises when we discuss how a statement is related to fact. Well, this seems to mean that in its original form our distinction between the performative and the statement is considerably weakened, and indeed breaks down. I will just make a suggestion as to how to handle this matter. We need to go very much farther back, to consider all the ways and senses in which saying anything at all is doing this or that – because of course it is always doing a good many different things. And one thing that emerges when we do this is that, besides the question that has been very much studied in the past as to what a certain utterance *means*, there is a further question distinct from this as to what was the *force*, as we may call it, of the utterance. We may be quite clear what "Shut the door" means, but not yet at all clear on the further point as to whether as uttered at a certain time it was an order, an entreaty or whatnot. What we need besides the old doctrine about meanings is a new doctrine about all the possible forces of utterances, towards the discovery of which our proposed list of explicit performative verbs would be a very great help; and then, going on from there, an investigation of the various terms of appraisal that we use in discussing speech-acts of this, that, or the other precise kind – orders, warnings, and the like.

The notions that we have considered then, are the performative, the infelicity, the explicit performative, and lastly, rather hurriedly, the notion of the forces of utterances. I dare say that all this seems a little unremunerative, a little complicated. Well, I suppose in some ways it is unremunerative, and I suppose it ought to be remunerative. At least, though, I think that if we pay attention to these matters we can clear up some mistakes in philosophy; and after all philosophy is used as a scapegoat, it parades mistakes which are really the mistakes of everybody. We might even clear up some mistakes in grammar, which perhaps is a little more respectable.

And is it complicated? Well, it is complicated a bit; but life and truth and things do tend to be complicated. It's not things, it's philosophers that are simple. You will have heard it said, I expect, that over-simplification is the occupational disease of philosophers, and in a way one might agree with that. But for a sneaking suspicion that it's their occupation.

There is a certain amount of overlap between these extracts and the others from Professor Austin's work, but it is an overlap which I think will illuminate his position further. It is plain that Austin as a contemporary empiricist was very nervous about what he calls "fictitious inward states". But he does not see that the first person involvement of a performative utterance may in its uttering realize, and witness to, a further dimension beyond "observed behaviour". It is true that with performatives we may be more or less involved. But in so far as there is a true performative which involves myself in its utterance, then equally in its utterance there is an expression of my subjectivity, and to know its meaning fully the listener must make it his own, which means that for him it will only be fully understood when it has served to evoke that subjectivity in which his own uniqueness is grounded. In other words, it would seem that the whole doctrine of performative utterances has metaphysical implications, and this point could well be granted while agreeing with Austin that traditional stylings of these implications have been both misleading and erroneous.

When Professor Austin developed his concept of performatives in this way, it was to introduce the notion of an utterance as a speech-act so that the "constative" (or "plain descriptive") utterances is to be regarded as an abstraction from such a speech-act when all illocutionary and perlocutionary aspects have been thought away; whereas when we speak of the performative utterance we are rather concentrating attention on its illocutionary force. Further, truth and falsity "depend not merely on the meanings of words but on what act you were performing in what circumstances".

When we originally contrasted the performative with the constative utterance we said that

J. L. Austin, *How to do Things with Words*, ed. J. O. Urmson, 1962, pp. 132–46. Reprinted by permission of the Clarendon Press, Oxford.

1. the performative should be doing something as opposed to just saying something; and
2. the performative is happy or unhappy as opposed to true or false.

Were these distinctions really sound? Our subsequent discussion of doing and saying certainly seems to point to the conclusion that whenever I "say" anything (except perhaps a mere exclamation like "damn" or "ouch") I shall be performing both locutionary and illocutionary acts, and these two kinds of acts seem to be the very things which we tried to use as a means of distinguishing, under the names of "doing" and "saying", performatives from constatives. If we are in general always doing both things, how can our distinction survive?

Let us first reconsider the contrast from the side of constative utterances: Of these, we were content to refer to "statements" as the typical or paradigm case. Would it be correct to say that when we state something

1. we are doing something as well as and distinct from just saying something, and
2. our utterance is liable to be happy or unhappy (as well as, if you will, true or false)?

1. Surely to state is every bit as much to perform an illocutionary act as, say, to warn or to pronounce. Of course it is not to perform an act in some specially physical way, other than in so far as it involves, when verbal, the making of movements of vocal organs; but then nor, as we have seen, is to warn, to protest, to promise or to name. "Stating" seems to meet all the criteria we had for distinguishing the illocutionary act. Consider such an unexceptionable remark as the following:

> In saying that it was raining, I was not betting or arguing or warning: I was simply stating it as a fact.

Here "stating" is put absolutely on a level with arguing, betting, and warning. Or again:

> In saying that it was leading to unemployment, I was not warning or protesting: I was simply stating the facts.

Or to take a different type of test also used earlier, surely

> I state that he did not do it

is exactly on a level with

I argue that he did not do it,
I suggest that he did not do it,
I bet that he did not do it, &c.

If I simply use the primary or non-explicit form of utterance:

He did not do it.

we may make explicit what we were doing in saying this, or specify the illocutionary force of the utterance, equally by saying any of the above three (or more) things.

Moreover, although the utterance "He did not do it" is often issued as a statement, and is then undoubtedly true or false (*this* is if anything is), it does not seem possible to say that it differs from "I state that he did not do it" in this respect. If someone says "I state that he did not do it", we investigate the truth of his statement in just the same way as if he had said "He did not do it" *simpliciter*, when we took that to be, as we naturally often should, a statement. That is, to say "I state that he did not" is to make the very same statement as to say "He did not": it is not to make a different statement about what "I" state (except in exceptional cases: the historic and habitual present, &c.). As notoriously, when I say even "I think he did it" someone is being rude if he says "That's a statement about you": and this might conceivably be about myself, whereas the statement could not. So that there is no necessary conflict between

(*a*) our issuing the utterance being the doing of something
(*b*) our utterance being true or false.

For that matter compare, for example, "I warn you that it is going to charge", where likewise it is both a warning and true or false that it is going to charge; and that comes in in appraising the warning just as much as, though not quite in the same way as, in appraising the statement.

On mere inspection, "I state that" does not appear to differ in any essential way from "I maintain that" (to say which is to maintain that), "I inform you that", "I testify that", &c. Possibly some "essential" differences may yet be established between such verbs: but nothing has been done towards this yet.

2. Moreover, if we think of the second alleged contrast, according to which performatives are happy or unhappy and statements true or false, again from the side of supposed constative utterances,

notably statements, we find that statements *are* liable to every kind of infelicity to which performatives are liable. Let us look back again and consider whether statements are not liable to precisely the same disabilities as, say, warnings by way of what we called "infelicities" – that is various disabilities which make an utterance unhappy without, however, making it true or false.

We have already noted that sense in which saying or stating "The cat is on the mat" implies that I believe that the cat is on the mat. This is parallel to the sense – is the same sense – as that in which "I promise to be there" implies that I intend to be there and that I believe I shall be able to be there. So the statement is liable to the *insincerity* form of infelicity; and even to the *breach* form of infelicity in this sense, that saying or stating that the cat is on the mat commits me to saying or stating "The mat is underneath the cat" just as much as the performative 'I define X as Y" (in that *fiat* sense say) commits me to using those terms in special ways in future discourse, and we can see how this is connected with such acts as promising. This means that statements can give rise to infelicities of our two *I* kinds.

Now what about infelicities of the A and B kinds, which rendered the act – warning, undertaking, &c. – null and void?: can a thing that looks like a statement be null and void as much as a putative contract? The answer seems to be Yes, importantly. The first cases are A. 1 and A. 2, where there is no convention (or not an accepted convention) or where the circumstances are not appropriate for its invocation by the speaker. Many infelicities of just this type do infect statements.

We have already noticed the case of a putative statement *presupposing* (as it is called) the existence of that which it refers to; if no such thing exists, "the statement" is not about anything. Now some say that in these circumstances, if, for example, someone asserts that the present King of France is bald, "the question whether he is bald does not arise"; but it is better to say that the putative statement is null and void, exactly as when I say that I sell you something but it is not mine or (having been burnt) is not any longer in existence. Contracts often are void because the objects they are about do not exist, which involves a breakdown of reference (total ambiguity).

But it is important to notice also that "statements" too are liable to infelicity of this kind in other ways also parallel to contracts, promises, warnings, &c. Just as we often say, for example, "You cannot order me", in the sense "You have not the right to order me", which is equivalent to saying that you are not in the appropriate position to do so: so often there are things you cannot state – have no right to state – are not in a position to state. You *cannot* now state how many people there are in the next room; if you say "There are fifty people in the next room", I can only regard you as guessing or conjecturing (just as sometimes you are not ordering me, which would be inconceivable, but possibly asking me to rather impolitely, so here you are "hazarding a guess" rather oddly). Here there is something you might, in other circumstances, be in a position to state; but what about statements about other persons' feelings or about the future? Is a forecast or even a prediction about, say, persons' behaviour really a statement? It is important to take the speech-situation as a whole.

Just as sometimes we cannot appoint but only confirm an appointment already made, so sometimes we cannot state but only confirm a statement already made. Putative statements are also liable to infelicities of type B, flaws, and hitches. Somebody "says something he did not really mean" – uses the wrong word – says "the cat is on the mat" when he meant to say "bat". Other similar trivialities arise – or rather not entirely trivialities; because it is possible to discuss such utterances entirely in terms of meaning or sense and reference and so get confused about them, though they are really easy to understand.

Once we realize that what we have to study is *not* the sentence but the issuing of an utterance in a speech situation, there can hardly be any longer a possibility of not seeing that stating is performing an act. Moreover, comparing stating to what we have said about the illocutionary act, it is an act to which, just as much as to other illocutionary acts, it is essential to "secure uptake": the doubt about whether I stated something if it was not heard or understood is just the same as the doubt about whether I warned *sotto voce* or protested if someone did not take it as a protest, &c. And statements do "take effect" just as much as "namings", say: if I have stated something, then that commits me to other statements: other statements made by me will be in order or out of order. Also some statements or remarks made by you will be henceforward contradicting me or not contradicting me, rebutting me or not rebutting me, and so forth. If perhaps a statement does not invite a response, that is not essential to all illocutionary acts anyway. And certainly in stating we are or may be performing perlocutionary acts of all kinds.

The most that might be argued, and with some plausibility, is that there is no perlocutionary *object* specifically associated with stating, as there is with informing, arguing, &c.; and this comparative purity may be one reason why we give "statements" a certain special position. But this certainly would not justify giving, say, "descriptions", if properly used, a similar priority, and it is in any case true of many illocutionary acts.

However, looking at the matter from the side of performatives, we may still feel that they lack something which statements have, even if, as we have shown, the converse is not so. Performatives are, of course, incidentally saying something as well as doing something, but we may feel that they are not essentially true or false as statements are. We may feel that there is here a dimension in which we judge, assess, or appraise the constative utterance (granting as a preliminary that it is felicitous) which does not arise with non-constative or performative utterances. Let us agree that all these circumstances of situation have to be in order for me to have succeeded in stating something, yet when I have, *the* question arises, was what I stated true or false? And this we feel, speaking in popular terms, is now the question of whether the statement "corresponds with the facts". With this I agree: attempts to say that the use of the expression "is true" is equivalent to endorsing or the like are no good. So we have here a new dimension of criticism of the accomplished statement.

But now

1. Doesn't just such a similar objective assessment of the accomplished utterance arise, at least in many cases, with other utterances which seem typically performative; and

2. Is not this account of statements a little over-simplified?

First, there is an obvious slide towards truth or falsity in the case of, for example, verdictives, such as estimating, finding, and pronouncing. Thus we may:

estimate	rightly or wrongly	for example, that it is half past two,
find	correctly or incorrectly	for example, that he is guilty,
pronounce	correctly or incorrectly	for example, that the batsman is out.

We shall not say "truly" in the case of verdictives, but we shall certainly address ourselves to the same question; and such adverbs as "rightly", "wrongly", "correctly", and "incorrectly" are used with statements too.

Or again there is a parallel between inferring and arguing soundly or validly and stating truly. It is not just a question of whether he did argue or infer but also of whether he had a right to, and did he succeed. Warning and advising may be done correctly or incorrectly, well or badly. Similar considerations arise about praise, blame, and congratulation. Blame is not in order, if, say, you have done the same thing yourself; and the question always arises whether the praise, blame, or congratulation was merited or unmerited: it is not enough to say that you have blamed him and there's an end on't – still one act is, with reason, preferred to another. The question whether praise and blame are merited is quite different from the question whether they are opportune, and the same distinction can be made in the case of advice. It is a different thing to say that advice is good or bad from saying that it is opportune or inopportune, though the timing of advice is more important to its goodness than the timing of blame is to its being merited.

Can we be sure that stating truly is a different *class* of assessment from arguing soundly, advising well, judging fairly, and blaming justifiably? Do these not have something to do in complicated ways with facts? The same is true also of exercitives such as naming, appointing, bequeathing, and betting. Facts come in as well as our knowledge or opinion about facts.

Well, of course, attempts are constantly made to effect this distinction. The soundness of arguments (if they are not deductive arguments which are "valid") and the meritedness of blame are not objective matters, it is alleged; or in warning, we are told, we should distinguish the "statement" that the bull is about to charge from the warning itself. But consider also for a moment whether the question of truth or falsity is so very objective. We ask: "Is it a *fair* statement?", and are the good reasons and good evidence for stating and saying so very different from the good reasons and evidence for performative acts like arguing, warning, and judging? Is the constative, then, always true or false? When a constative is confronted with the facts, we in fact appraise it in ways involving the employment of a vast array of terms which overlap with those that we use in the appraisal of performatives. In real life, as opposed to the simple situations envisaged in logical theory, one cannot always answer in a simple manner whether it is true or false.

Suppose that we confront "France is hexagonal" with the facts, in this case, I suppose, with France, is it true or false? Well, if you like, up to a point; of course I can see what you mean by saying that it is true for certain intents and purposes. It is good enough for a top-ranking general, perhaps, but not for a geographer. "Naturally it is pretty rough", we should say, "and pretty good as a pretty rough statement". But then someone says: "But is it true or is it false? I don't mind whether it is rough or not; of course it's rough, but it has to be true or false – it's a statement, isn't it?" How can one answer this question, whether it is true or false that France is hexagonal? It is just rough, and that is the right and final answer to the question of the relation of "France is hexagonal" to France. It is a rough description; it is not a true or a false one.

Again, in the case of stating truly or falsely, just as much as in the case of advising well or badly, the intents and purposes of the utterance and its context are important; what is judged true in a school book may not be so judged in a work of historical research. Consider the constative, "Lord Raglan won the battle of Alma", remembering that Alma was a soldier's battle if ever there was one and that Lord Raglan's orders were never transmitted to some of his subordinates. Did Lord Raglan then win the battle of Alma or did he not? Of course in some contexts, perhaps in a school book, it is perfectly justifiable to say so – it is something of an exaggeration, maybe, and there would be no question of giving Raglan a medal for it. As "France is hexagonal" is rough, so "Lord Raglan won the battle of Alma" is exaggerated and suitable to some contexts and not to others; it would be pointless to insist on its truth or falsity.

Thirdly, let us consider the question whether it is true that all snow geese migrate to Labrador, given that perhaps one maimed sometimes fails when migrating to get quite the whole way. Faced with such problems, many have claimed, with much justice, that utterances such as those beginning "All . . ." are prescriptive definitions or advice to adopt a rule. But what rule? This idea arises partly through not understanding the reference of such statements, which is limited to the known; we cannot quite make the simple statement that the truth of statements depends on facts as distinct from knowledge of facts. Suppose that before Australia is discovered

X says "All swans are white". If you later find a black swan in Australia, is *X* refuted? Is his statement false now? Not necessarily: he will take it back but he could say "I wasn't talking about swans absolutely everywhere; for example, I was not making a statement about possible swans on Mars". Reference depends on knowledge at the time of utterance.

The truth or falsity of statements is affected by what they leave out or put in and by their being misleading, and so on. Thus, for example, descriptions, which are said to be true or false or, if you like, are "statements", are surely liable to these criticisms, since they are selective and uttered for a purpose. It is essential to realize that "true" and "false", like "free" and "unfree", do not stand for anything simple at all; but only for a general dimension of being a right or proper thing to say as opposed to a wrong thing, in these circumstances, to this audience, for these purposes and with these intentions.

In general we may say this: with both statements (and, for example, descriptions) *and* warnings, &c., the question of whether, granting that you did warn and had the right to warn, did state, or did advise, you were *right* to state or warn or advise, can arise – not in the sense of whether it was opportune or expedient, but whether, on the facts and your knowledge of the facts and the purposes for which you were speaking, and so on, this was the proper thing to say.

This doctrine is quite different from much that the pragmatists have said, to the effect that the true is what works, &c.

The truth or falsity of a statement depends not merely on the meanings of words but on what act you were performing in what circumstances.

What then finally is left of the distinction of the performative and constative utterance? Really we may say that what we had in mind here was this:

(*a*) With the constative utterance, we abstract from the illocutionary (let alone the perlocutionary) aspects of the speech act, and we concentrate on the locutionary: moreover, we use an over-simplified notion of correspondence with the facts – over-simplified because essentially it brings in the illocutionary aspect. We aim at the ideal of what would be right to say in all circumstances, for any purpose, to any audience, &c. Perhaps this is sometimes realized.

(*b*) With the performative utterance, we attend as much as possible to the illocutionary force of the utterance, and abstract from the dimension of correspondence with facts.

Perhaps neither of these abstractions is so very expedient: perhaps we have here not really two poles, but rather an historical development. Now in certain cases, perhaps with mathematical formulas in physics books as examples of constatives, or with the issuing of simple executive orders or the giving of simple names, say, as examples of performatives, we approximate in real life to finding such things. It was examples of this kind, like "I apologize", and "The cat is on the mat", said for no conceivable reason, extreme marginal cases, that gave rise to the idea of two distinct utterances. But the real conclusion must surely be that we need (*a*) to distinguish between locutionary and illocutionary acts, and (*b*) specially and critically to establish with respect to each kind of illocutionary act-warnings, estimates, verdicts, statements, and descriptions – what if any is the specific way in which they are intended, first to be in order or not in order, and second, to be "right" or "wrong"; what terms of appraisal and disappraisal are used for each and what they mean. This is a wide field and certainly will not lead to a simple distinction of "true" and "false"; nor will it lead to a distinction of statements from the rest, for stating is only one among very numerous speech acts of the illocutionary class.

Furthermore, in general the locutionary act as much as the illocutionary is an abstraction only: every genuine speech act is both.

18

R. M. HARE

The Language of Morals: A Possible Clue to the Logic of Theology. *This extract illustrates how sentences in the language of morals are both descriptive and evaluative and can have both these features in varying proportions. Besides having its own independent significance, it is also important in showing how superficial and restricted a view of meaningful language was embodied in the verification principle.*

. . . I have been in the past, and still am, a stout defender of Hume's doctrine that one cannot deduce moral judgements from non-moral statements of fact; and also of that particular application of the doctrine which says that one cannot deduce moral judgements of substance from statements about the uses of words or about the logical relations between concepts. Yet I have not drawn the conclusion from this thesis which so many have drawn, namely that the only kind of cogent moral argument is one which has as a premise a moral principle already accepted by both parties to the argument. On the contrary, I have maintained that, once the logical character of the moral concepts is understood, there can be useful and compelling moral argument even between people who have, before it begins, no substantive moral principles in common.

Let us consider various forms of this objection. It may be said, first of all, that I am open to the same sort of attack as I, and those of like opinion, bring against the naturalists. The essence of naturalism is to say "If you understand the meaning of such and such a moral word, you cannot deny such and such a moral assertion".

R. M. Hare, *Freedom and Reason*, 1963, pp. 25, 186–91. Reprinted by permission of the Clarendon Press, Oxford.

It will certainly be objected that I have been saying this very thing. The most fundamental objection against naturalism is that it makes moral questions depend upon conceptual ones – whereas we feel that to adopt a certain conceptual apparatus is one thing, and to adopt a certain system of moral principles another, though there are some concepts which we shall not employ unless our moral principles are of a certain stamp. Consider again, for example, the thesis, typical of recent naturalists, that at any rate the more specialized moral words like "courageous" (on which they are inclined to fix their attention) are tied by their meaning to certain evaluations and to certain descriptions – thus firmly tying the evaluations to the descriptions. If, they say, one does not evaluate highly a certain kind of acts, then one will just have to give up using the word "courageous". Conversely, if one continues to use the word, that commits one to certain evaluations. If a man, in a battle, deliberately disregards his own safety in order to preserve that of his fellow soldiers, one cannot, if one has the word in one's vocabulary, deny that he has been courageous. But "courageous" is, by its very meaning, a term of commendation; therefore, by using it, one expresses a favourable evaluation of the act. So, once we have this word or concept in use, we are led ineluctably, despite Hume, from a description to an evaluation.

We shall not, however, be so attracted by this naturalist argument if we take as an example, not a concept which incapsulates evaluations that we are all disposed to make, but one incapsulating attitudes which most of us abhor. Consider an example used earlier – the word "nigger". A naturalist might put forward an argument, identical in form with the one just summarized, to show that we have to despise negroes. If, he might argue, a man has curly hair and a black skin and thick lips, and is descended from people with similar features, then we cannot deny that he is a nigger. But "nigger" is a term of contempt. Therefore, if we have the word "nigger" in use, we are led ineluctably from factual propositions about his skin-colour, &c., to the indubitably evaluative proposition that he is a nigger. If one knows that he has a black skin, &c., one cannot but (logically cannot but) despise him.

To this argument, a person who is not inclined to despise people just because they are negroes will reply that, simply because the user of the word "nigger" is led along this path, he prefers not to use the word "nigger". By abandoning the concept, he becomes no longer committeed to the attitude. He substitutes, let us suppose, the neutral word "negro". Then, though he cannot deny that the man with black skin, &c., is a negro, this does not commit him to thinking of him as inferior.

The only reason why such a course with the word "courageous" would seem to us strange is that we are, most of us, very firmly wedded to the attitude which the word incapsulates. If there were a person who was not in the least disposed to commend those who preserved the safety of others by disregarding their own, then he could say, as before, "I prefer not to use the word 'courageous', just because it incapsulates this attitude to which I do not subscribe. I prefer the longer, morally neutral expression, 'disregarding one's own safety in order to preserve that of others'. This, though it is not equivalent to 'courageous', even descriptively, is in fact all that we can be logically compelled to admit of a person, once he has done the 'courageous' act referred to. To go on to call the act courageous is, strictly speaking, an additional step which I am not disposed to take, because I do not share the evaluations of those who take it. It is true that there is no single evaluatively neutral word, like 'negro', which in the present case can be used to describe such actions without committing the describer to any evaluation; but we could have such a word. What I shall actually do, in default of an invented word, is to use the same word 'courageous', but to make it clear by my tone of voice or by putting quotation marks round it, that I am using it in a purely descriptive sense, implying thereby no commendation whatever."

We must note that it is secondarily evaluative words which occur most naturally in arguments of the type which we have been considering – that is to say, words which have their descriptive meaning more firmly tied to them than their evaluation. Naturalists have sometimes sought to maintain that the same sort of argument could by analogy be extended to the more general moral words like "good"; but we must be careful to notice just what is happening in such extensions. We have these more general, primarily evaluative words just because we do not want to be the prisoners of our own conceptual apparatus. If a man wishes to reject the evaluations which are incapsulated in the word "nigger", he can do so explicitly by using another value-word – often a more general one; he may say "A man can be a negro, and be none the worse for that". Here the value-word "worse", just because it is not tied to any particular evaluative attitude, can be used to reject the one to which the word "nigger" is tired. Similarly a man might say, "Blasphemy is sometimes a duty", indicating by his tone or by the context that he was using the word "blasphemy" in a purely descriptive way. And in the same fashion a man who did not believe in sacrificing his own safety to that of others might say "It's wrong to indulge in these heroics; a man's first duty is to himself."

The naturalist is, nevertheless, quite right if he claims that what can easily happen to the word "nigger" can be made to happen, though with more reluctance, even to the most general value-words. If the evaluations which are expressed by a certain word are so unanimous in a given society that its descriptive meaning gets firmly tied to it (the evaluation comes to be incapsulated in the word), then, even if it is a general word like "good", it can either "get into inverted commas" or become "conventional". Since, however, it is always, even with the most general value-words, open to anyone who rejects the evaluation that is incapsulated in a word to go on using the word, but in inverted commas, it is never the case, as naturalists seem to claim that it is, that our mere possession of a certain word commits us to certain evaluations. It is true that, given that a word has, through the unanimity of people's evaluations, got a certain descriptive meaning very securely tied to it, it is possible to derive judgements containing the word from non-evaluative statements; but, if this is done, nobody can be compelled logically to accept the evaluation which is normally incapsulated in the word; he can only be compelled to accept what is implied in the descriptive meaning of the word. Thus, though what is normally a value-word occurs in the conclusion of the naturalist's argument, the victory is barren, since the evaluation can always be down-graded so that it becomes no evaluation at all, but a mere repetition of the premiss; and this, indeed, is all that was really entailed by the original description.

The upshot is that the mere existence of a certain conceptual apparatus cannot compel anybody to accept any particular evaluation, although it is more difficult to break away from evaluations which are incapsulated in the very language which we use – hence the potency of Newspeak.[1] For we can, at any rate in this respect, alter our conceptual apparatus – by treating as descriptive a word which used to be evaluative. It follows that the insights of the naturalists are not sufficiently fundamental to give us help when we are in doubt about accepting the evaluations which are incapsulated in our language. To a southerner who was in process of breaking away from the attitude towards negroes current in his society, it would be unhelpful to appeal to the word "nigger" to ease his doubts. If his doubts still persist and grow, and he comes to think that negroes are the equals of whites, the word "nigger" will be the first casualty. Word-usage can delay changes in attitudes; it cannot postpone them indefinitely. And the same would be true if we came to alter our attitude to actions that are now called "courageous", or even to those now called "duties". If the attitudes go, the vocabulary will go, or lose its evaluative meaning, or acquire a new descriptive meaning.

NOTE

1. Orwell's Newspeak in 1984 was a language so designed that in it dangerous thoughts could not be expressed. Much of Oldspeak is like this too – if we want, in the Southern States, to speak to a negro as an equal, we cannot do so by addressing him as a nigger; the word "nigger" incapsulates the standards of the society, and, if we were confined to it, we could not break free of those standards. But fortunately we are not so confined; our language, as we have it, can be a vehicle for new ideas (*Freedom and Reason*, p. 25).

19

C. K. OGDEN and I. A. RICHARDS

This passage is not only of interest in relation to the logic of metaphors. It also emphasizes the importance of context, and in distinguishing between the reference of a word and its contextual setting we are reminded of Frege's distinction between "reference" (Bedeutung) and "sense" (Sinn). This distinction may be alternatively expressed as one between naming and meaning, between knowing what a concept denotes or stands for, and understanding the concept. Thus "Morning Star" or "Evening Star" name the same thing; but "the two phrases", as W. V. O. Quine reminds us (From a Logical Point of View; *Harvard 1953*), *"cannot be regarded as having the same meaning. . . . The meanings, then, being different from one another, must be other than the named object, which is one and the same in both cases" (loc. cit. p. 9). For a translation of Frege's essay, I refer the reader to* Uber Sinn und Bedeutung [*on sense and* Nominatum] *in H. Freigl and W. S. Sellars,* Readings in Philosophical Analysis, *Appleton-Century Crofts Inc., N.Y.* 1949, *pp. 89–102.*

In highly developed languages the means by which complex symbols are formed, by which they receive their structure as symbols, are very many and various. Complex symbols with the same referent may be given alternative forms even when the simple symbols, the names, contained remain unaltered. The study of these forms is a part of grammar, but a more genuine interest in, and awareness of, psychological problems than it is usual for grammarians to possess is required if they are to be fruitfully discussed.

We may now consider a few of the easier cases of these complex symbols. Let us begin with the contrast between proper names and descriptive phrases. We saw above that particular references require contexts of a much simpler form than general references, and any descriptive phrase involves for its understanding a context of the more complicated form. To use such a symbol as the name of an individual – let us call him *Thomas* – we need merely that the name shall be in a context with Thomas-experiences. A few such experiences are usually sufficient to establish this conjunction; for every such experience, since we rarely encounter an acquaintance without realizing that he has a name and what that name is, will help to form the context. Contrast with this the understanding of such a descriptive name as "my relatives". Here the experiences required will not be in all cases the same. At one time a grandfather, at another a niece will present themselves; but not upon all occasions will their relationship to us be in any degree a dominant feature, nor is the relationship which they agree in bearing to their grandson and uncle respectively an obvious one. Thus a range of experiences differing very widely one from another is necessary if the required context is to be built up.

"Relatives" is in fact an abstraction, in the sense that the reference which it symbolizes cannot be formed simply and directly by one grouping of experience, but is the result of varied groupings of experiences whose very difference enables their common elements to survive in isolation. This process of selection and elimination is always at work in the acquisition of a vocabulary and the development of thought. It is rare for words to be formed into contexts with non-symbolic experience directly, for as a rule they are learnt only through other words. We early begin to use language in order to learn language, but since it is no mere matter of the acquisition of synonyms or alternative locutions, the same stressing of similarities between references and elimination of their differences through conflict is required. By these means we develop references of greater and greater abstractness, and metaphor, the primitive symbolization of abstraction, becomes possible Metaphor, in the most general sense, is the use of one reference to a group of things between which a given relation holds, for the purpose of facilitating the discrimination of an analogous relation in another group. In the understanding of metaphorical language one reference borrows part of the context of another in an abstract form.

There are two ways in which one reference may appropriate part of the context of another. Thus a reference to man may be joined with a reference to sea, the result being a reference to seamen. No metaphor is involved in this. When, on the other hand, we take arms against a sea of troubles, that part of the context of the reference to sea which is combined with the other references appears in an abstract form, i.e., the relevant characters of the sea will not include attraction by the moon or being the resort of fishes. The poetic value of the metaphor depends in this case chiefly on the way in which the ceaseless recurrence of the waves accentuates the sense of hopelessness already present – as the Cuchulain legend well shows.

In fact the use of metaphor involves the same kind of contexts as abstract thought, the important point being that the members shall only possess the relevant feature in common, and that irrelevant or accidental features shall cancel one another. All use of adjectives, prepositions, verbs, etc., depends on this principle. The prepositions are particularly interesting, the kinds of contexts upon which they depend being plainly different in extent and diversity of members. "Inside" and "outside", it would appear, are the least complicated in context, and consequently, as might be expected, are easily retained in cases of disturbance of the speech functions. The metaphorical aspects of the greater part of language, and the ease with which any word may be used metaphorically, further indicate the degree to which, especially for educated persons, words have gained contexts through other words. For very simple folk with small and concrete vocabularies . . . the majority of their words have naturally been acquired in direct connection with experience. Their language has throughout many of the characteristics of proper names. Hence in part their comparative freedom from confusions, but hence also the naïve or magical attitude to words. Such linguists may perhaps be said to be beneath the level at which confusion, the penalty we pay for our power of abstraction, becomes possible.

20

MAX BLACK

Clues to the Logic of Religious Language: The Significance of Metaphor. *Here Professor Black argues that metaphors always go beyond their alleged literal equivalents in having "power to inform and enlighten"; that they have thus a cognitive content of their own; that they are purveyors of insight. We need not then be too despairing of theological arguments which are metaphorically based, for example Doctrines of the Atonement, though it would be a gross blunder to treat this language as if it were literal, which it is not. Metaphors can provide us with arguments if we refuse to take too restricted and stereotyped a view of what an "argument" is.*

To draw attention to a philosopher's metaphors is to belittle him – like praising a logician for his beautiful handwriting. Addiction to metaphor is held to be illicit, on the principle that whereof one can speak only metaphorically, thereof one ought not to speak at all. Yet the nature of the offence is unclear. I should like to do something to dispel the mystery that invests the topic; but since philosophers (for all their notorious interest in language) have so neglected the subject, I must get what help I can from the literary critics. They, at least, do not accept the commandment, "Thou shalt not commit metaphor", or assume that metaphor is incompatible with serious thought.

1

The questions I should like to see answered concern the "logical grammar" of "metaphor" and words having related meanings. It would be satisfactory to have convincing answers to the questions: "How do we recognize a case of metaphor?" "Are there any criteria for the detection of metaphors?" "Can metaphors be translated into literal expressions?" "Is metaphor properly regarded as a decoration upon 'plain sense'?" "What are the relations between metaphor and simile?" "In what sense, if any, is a metaphor 'creative'?" "What is the point of using a metaphor?" (Or, more briefly, "What do we *mean* by 'metaphor'?" The questions express attempts to become clearer about some uses of the word "metaphor" – or, if one prefers the material mode, to analyze the notion of metaphor.)

The list is not a tidy one, and several of the questions overlap in fairly obvious ways. But I hope they will sufficiently illustrate the type of inquiry that is intended.

It would be helpful to be able to start from some agreed list of "clear cases" of metaphor. Since the word "metaphor" has some intelligible uses, however vague or vacillating, it must be possible to construct such a list. Presumably, it should be easier to agree whether any given item should be included than to agree about any proposed analysis of the notion of metaphor.

Perhaps the following list of examples, chosen not altogether at random, might serve:

(i) "The chairman plowed through the discussion."
(ii) "A smoke screen of witnesses."
(iii) "An argumentative melody."
(iv) "Blotting-paper voices" (Henry James).
(v) "The poor are the negroes of Europe" (Chamfort).
(vi) "Light is but the shadow of God" (Sir Thomas Browne).
(vii) "Oh dear white children, casual as birds,
Playing amid the ruined languages" (Auden).

I hope all these will be accepted as unmistakeable *instances* of metaphor, whatever judgments may ultimately be made about the meaning of "metaphor." The examples are offered as clear cases of metaphor, but, with the possible exception of the first, they would be unsuitable as "paradigms". If we wanted to teach the meaning of "metaphor" to a child, we should need simpler examples, like "The clouds are crying" or "The branches are fighting with one another". (Is it significant that one hits upon examples of personification?) But

I have tried to include some reminders of the possible complexities that even relatively straight-forward metaphors may generate.

Consider the first example – "The chairman plowed through the discussion." An obvious point to begin with is the contrast between the word "plowed" and the remaining words by which it is accompanied. This would be commonly expressed by saying that "plowed" has here a metaphorical sense, while the other words have literal senses. Although we point to the whole sentence as an instance (a "clear case") of metaphor, our attention quickly narrows to a single word, whose presence is the proximate reason for the attribution. And similar remarks can be made about the next four examples in the list, the crucial words being, respectively, "smoke screen", "argumentative", "blotting-paper", and "negroes".

(But the situation is more complicated in the last two examples of the list. In the quotation from Sir Thomas Browne, "Light" must be supposed to have a symbolic sense, and certainly to mean far more than it would in the context of a textbook on optics. Here, the metaphorical sense of the expression "the shadow of God" imposes a meaning richer than usual upon the subject of the sentence. Similar effects can be noticed in the passage from Auden – consider for instance the meaning of "white" in the first line. I shall have to neglect such complexities in this paper.)

In general, when we speak of a relatively simple metaphor, we are referring to a sentence or another expression in which *some* words are used metaphorically while the remainder are used non-metaphorically. An attempt to construct an entire sentence of words that are used metaphorically results in a proverb, an allegory, or a riddle. No preliminary analysis of metaphor will satisfactorily cover even so trite an example as "In the night all cows are black." And cases of symbolism (in the sense in which Kafka's castle is a "symbol") also need separate treatment.

2

"The chairman plowed through the discussion." In calling this sentence a case of metaphor, we are implying that at least one word (here, the word "plowed") is being used metaphorically in the sentence, and that at least one of the remaining words is being used literally. Let us call the word "plowed" the *focus* of the metaphor, and the remainder of the sentence in which that word occurs the *frame*. (Are *we* now using metaphors – and mixed ones at that?

Does it matter?) One notion that needs to be clarified is that of the "metaphorical use" of the focus of a metaphor. Among other things, it would be good to understand how the presence of one frame can result in metaphorical use of the complementary word, while the presence of a different frame for the same word fails to result in metaphor.

If the sentence about the chairman's behaviour is translated word for word into any foreign language for which this is possible, we shall of course want to say that the translated sentence is a case of the *very same* metaphor. So, to call a sentence an instance of metaphor is to say something about its *meaning*, not about its orthography, its phonetic pattern, or its grammatical form.[1] (To use a well-known distinction, "metaphor" must be classified as a term belonging to "semantics" and not to "syntax" – or to any *physical* inquiry about language.)

Suppose somebody says, "I like to plow my memories regularly." Shall we say he is using the same metaphor as in the case already discussed, or not? Our answer will depend upon the degree of similarity we are prepared to affirm on comparing the two "frames" (for we have the same "focus" each time). Differences in the two frames will produce *some* differences in the interplay[2] between focus and frame in the two cases. Whether we regard the differences as sufficiently striking to warrant calling the sentences *two* metaphors is a matter for arbitrary decision. "Metaphor" is a loose word, at best, and we must beware of attributing to it stricter rules of usage than are actually found in practice.

So far, I have been treating "metaphor" as a predicate properly applicable to certain expressions, without attention to any occasions on which the expressions are used, or to the thoughts, acts, feelings, and intentions of speakers upon such occasions. And this is surely correct for *some* expressions. We recognize that to call a man a "cesspool" is to use a metaphor, without needing to know who uses the expression, or on what occasions, or with what intention. The rules of our language determine that some expressions must count as metaphors; and a speaker can no more change this than he can legislate that "cow" shall mean the same as "sheep". But we must also recognize that the established rules of language leave wide latitude for individual variation, initiative, and creation. There are indefinitely many contexts (including nearly all the interesting ones) where the meaning of a metaphorical expression has to be reconstructed from the speaker's intentions (and other clues) because the broad rules of standard usage are too general to supply the information needed. When Churchill, in a famous phrase, called Mussolini "that *utensil*", the tone of voice, the verbal setting, the historical background, helped to make clear *what* metaphor was being used. (Yet, even here, it is hard to see how the phrase "that utensil" could ever be applied to a man except as an insult. Here, as elsewhere, the general rules of usage function as limitations upon the speaker's freedom to mean whatever he pleases.) This is an example, though still a simple one, of how recognition and interpretation of a metaphor may require attention to the *particular circumstances* of its utterance.

It is especially noteworthy that there are, in general, no standard rules for the degree of *weight* or *emphasis* to be attached to a particular use of an expression. To know what the user of a metaphor means, we need to know how "seriously" he treats the metaphorical focus. (Would he be just as content to have some rough synonym, or would only *that* word serve? Are we to take the word lightly, attending only to its most obvious implications – or should we dwell upon its less immediate associations?) In speech we can use emphasis and phrasing as clues. But in written or printed discourse, even these rudimentary aids are absent. Yet this somewhat elusive "weight" of a (suspected or detected[3]) metaphor is of great practical importance in exegesis.

To take a philosophical example: Whether the expression "logical form" should be treated in a particular frame as having a metaphorical sense will depend upon the extent to which its user is taken to be conscious of some opposed analogy between arguments and other things (vases, clouds, battles, jokes) that are also said to have "form". Still more will it depend upon whether the writer wishes the analogy to be active in the minds of his readers; and how much his own thought depends upon and is nourished by the supposed analogy. We must not expect the "rules of language" to be of much help in such inquiries. (There is accordingly a sense of "metaphor" that belongs to "pragmatics" rather than to "semantics" – and this sense may be the one most deserving of attention.)

3

Let us try the simplest possible account that can be given of the meaning of "The chairman plowed through the discussion", to see how far it will take us. A plausible commentary (for those presumably too literal-minded to understand the original) might run somewhat as follows: "A speaker who uses the sentence in question is taken to want to say *something* about a chairman and his behavior in some meeting. Instead of saying, plainly or *directly*, that the chairman dealt summarily with objections, or ruthlessly suppressed irrelevance, or something of the sort, the speaker chose to use a word ('plowed') which, strictly speaking, means something else. But an intelligent hearer can easily guess what the speaker had in mind."[4] This account treats the metaphorical expression (let us call it "*M*") as a substitute for some other literal expression ("*L*", say) which would have expressed the same meaning, had it been used instead. On this view, the meaning of *M*, in its metaphorical occurrence, is just the *literal* meaning of *L*. The metaphorical use of an expression consists, on this view, of the use of that expression in other than its proper or normal sense, in some context that allows the improper or abnormal sense to be detected and appropriately transformed. (The reasons adduced for so remarkable a performance will be discussed later.)

Any view which holds that a metaphorical expression is used in place of some equivalent *literal* expression, I shall call a *substitution view of metaphor*. (I should like this label to cover also any analysis which views the entire sentence that is the locus of the metaphor as replacing some set of literal sentences.) Until recently, one or another form of a substitution view has been accepted by most writers (usually literary critics or writers of books on rhetoric) who have had anything to say about metaphor. To take a few examples: Whately defines a metaphor as "a word substituted for another on account of the Resemblance or Analogy between their significations".[5] Nor is the entry in the Oxford Dictionary (to jump to modern times) much different from this: "Metaphor: The figure of speech in which a name or descriptive term is transferred to some object different from, but analogous to, that to which it is properly applicable; an instance of this, a metaphorical expression."[6] So strongly entrenched is the view expressed by these definitions that a recent writer who is explicitly arguing for a different and more sophisticated view of metaphor, nevertheless slips into the old fashion by defining metaphor as "saying one thing and meaning another".[7]

According to a substitution view, the focus of a metaphor, the word or expression having a distinctively metaphorical use within a literal frame, is used to communicate a meaning that might have been expressed literally. The author substitutes *M* for *L*; it is the reader's task to invert the substitution, by using the literal meaning of *M* as a clue to the intended literal meaning of *L*. Understanding a metaphor is like deciphering a code or unraveling a riddle.

If we now ask why, on this view, the writer should set his reader the task of solving a puzzle, we shall be offered two types of answer. The first is that there may, in fact, be no literal equivalent, *L*, available in the language in question. Mathematicians spoke of the "leg" of an angle because there was no brief literal expression for a bounding line; we say "cherry lips", because there is no form of words half as convenient for saying quickly what the lips are like. Metaphor plugs the gaps in the literal vocabulary (or, at least, supplies the want of convenient abbreviations). So viewed, metaphor is a species of *catachresis*, which I shall define as the use of a word in some new sense in order to remedy a gap in the vocabulary; catachresis is the putting of new senses into old words.[8] But if a catachresis serves a genuine need, the new sense introduced will quickly become part of the *literal* sense. "Orange" may originally have been applied to the color by catachresis; but the word is now applied to the color just as "properly" (and unmetaphorically) as to the fruit. "Osculating" curves do not kiss for long, and quickly revert to a more prosaic mathematical contact. And similarly for other cases. It is the fate of catachresis to disappear when it is successful.

There are, however, many metaphors where the virtues ascribed to catachresis cannot apply, because there is, or there is supposed to be, some readily available and equally compendious literal equivalent. Thus in the somewhat unfortunate example,[9] "Richard is a lion", which modern writers have discussed with boring insistence, the literal meaning is taken to be the same as that of the sentence, "Richard is brave".[10] Here, the metaphor is not supposed to enrich the vocabulary.

When catachresis cannot be invoked, the reasons for substituting an indirect, metaphorical, expression are taken to be stylistic. We are told that the metaphorical expression may (in its literal use) refer to a more concrete object than would its literal equivalent; and this is supposed to give pleasure to the reader (the pleasure of having one's thoughts diverted from Richard to the irrelevant lion). Again, the reader is taken to enjoy problem-solving – or to delight in the author's skill at half-concealing, half-revealing his meaning. Or metaphors provide a shock of "agreeable surprise" and so on. The principle behind these "explanations" seems to be: When in doubt about some peculiarity of language, attribute its existence to the pleasure it gives a reader. A principle that has the merit of working well in default of any evidence.[11]

Whatever the merits of such speculations about the reader's response, they agree in making metaphor a *decoration*. Except in cases where a metaphor is a catachresis that remedies some temporary imperfection of literal language, the purpose of metaphor is to entertain and divert. Its use, on this view, always constitutes a deviation from the "plain and strictly appropriate style" (Whately).[12] So, if philosophers have something more important to do than give pleasure to their readers, metaphor can have no serious place in philosophical discussion.

4

The view that a metaphorical expression has a meaning that is some transform of its normal literal meaning is a special case of a more general view about "figurative" language. This holds that any figure of speech involving semantic change (and not merely syntactic change, like inversion of normal word order) consists in some transformation of a *literal* meaning. The author provides, not his intended meaning, *m*, but some function thereof, $f(m)$; the reader's task is to apply the inverse function, f^{-1}, and so to obtain $f^{-1}(f(m))$, i.e., *m*, the original meaning. When different functions are used, different tropes result. Thus, in irony, the author says the *opposite* of what he means; in hyperbole, he *exaggerates* his meaning; and so on.

What, then, is the characteristic transforming function involved in metaphor? To this the answer has been made: either *analogy* or *similarity*. *M* is either similar or analogous in meaning to its literal equivalent *L*. Once the reader has detected the ground of the intended analogy or simile (with the help of the frame, or clues drawn from the wider context) he can retrace the author's path and so reach the original literal meaning (the meaning of *L*).

If a writer holds that a metaphor consists in the *presentation* of the underlying analogy or similarity, he will be taking what I shall call a *comparison view* of metaphor. When Schopenhauer called a geometrical proof a mousetrap, he was, according to such a view, *saying* (though not explicitly): "A geometrical proof is *like* a mouse-trap, since both offer a delusive reward, entice their victims by degrees, lead to disagreeable surprise, etc." This is a view of metaphor as a condensed or elliptical *simile*. It will be noticed that a "comparison view" is a special case of a "substitution view". For it holds that the metaphorical statement might be replaced by an equivalent literal *comparison*.

Whately says: "The Simile or Comparison may be considered as differing in form only from a Metaphor; the resemblance being in that case *stated*, which in the Metaphor is implied."[13] Bain says that "the metaphor is a comparison implied in the mere use of a term" and adds, "It is in the circumstance of being confined to a word, or at most to a phrase, that we are to look for the peculiarities of the metaphor – its advantages on the one hand, and its dangers and abuses on the other."[14] This view of the metaphor, as condensed simile or comparison, has been very popular.

The chief difference between a substitution view (of the sort previously considered) and the special form of it that I have called a comparison view may be illustrated by the stock example of "Richard is a lion". On the first view, the sentence means approximately the same as "Richard is brave"; on the second, approximately the same as "Richard is *like* a lion (in being brave)", the added words in brackets being understood but not explicitly stated. In the second translation, as in the first, the metaphorical statement is taken to be standing in place of some literal equivalent. But the comparison view provides a more elaborate paraphrase, inasmuch as the original statement is interpreted as being about lions as well as about Richard.[15]

The main objection against a comparison view is that it suffers from a vagueness that borders upon vacuity. We are supposed to be puzzled as to how some expression (*M*), used metaphorically, can function in place of some literal expression (*L*) that is held to be an approximate synonym; and the answer offered is that what *M* stands for (in its literal use) is *similar* to what *L* stands for. But how informative is this? There is some temptation to think of similarities as "objectively given", so that a question of the form, "Is *A* like *B* in respect of *P?*" has a definite and predetermined answer. If this were so, similes might be governed by rules as strict as those controlling the statements of physics. But likeness always admits of degrees, so that a truly "objective" question would need to take some such form as "Is *A* more like *B* than *C* on such and such a scale of degrees of *P?*" Yet, in proportion as we approach such forms, metaphorical statements lose their effectiveness and their point. We need the metaphors in just the cases when there can be no question as yet of the precision of scientific statement. Metaphorical statement is not a substitute for a formal comparison or any other kind of literal statement, but has its own distinctive capacities and achievements. Often we say, "*X* is *M*", evoking some imputed connection between *M* and an imputed *L* (or, rather, to an indefinite system, L_1, L_2, L_3, . . .) in cases where, prior to the construction of the metaphor, we would have been hard put to it to find any literal resemblance between *M* and *L*. It would be more illuminating in some of these cases to say that the metaphor creates the similarity than to say that it formulates some similarity antecedently existing.[16]

5

I turn now to consider a type of analysis which I shall call an *interaction view* of metaphor. This seems to me to be free from the main defects of substitution and comparison views and to offer some important insight into the uses and limitations of metaphor.[17]

Let us begin with the following statement: "In the simplest formulation, when we use a metaphor we have two thoughts of different things active together and supported by a single word, or phrase, whose meaning is a resultant of their interaction."[18] We may discover what is here intended by applying Richard's remark to our earlier example, "The poor are the negroes of Europe." The substitution view, at its crudest, tells us that something is being indirectly said about the poor of Europe. (But what? That they are an oppressed class, a standing reproach to the community's official ideals, that poverty is inherited and indelible?) The comparison view claims that the epigram presents some comparison between the poor and the negroes. In opposition to both, Richards says that our "thoughts" about European poor and American negroes are "active together" and "interact" to produce a meaning that is a resultant of that interaction.

I think this must mean that in the given context the focal word "negroes" obtains a new meaning, which is not quite its meaning in literal uses, nor quite the meaning which any literal substitute would have. The new context (the "frame" of the metaphor, in my terminology) imposes extension of meaning upon the focal word. And

I take Richards to be saying that for the metaphor to work the reader must remain aware of the extension of meaning – must attend to both the old and the new meanings together.[19]

But how is this extension or change of meaning brought about? At one point, Richards speaks of the "common characteristics" of the two terms (the poor and negroes) as "the ground of the metaphor" (*The Philosophy of Rhetoric*, p. 117), so that in its metaphorical use a word or expression must connote only a *selection* from the characteristics connoted in its literal uses. This, however, seems a rare lapse into the older and less sophisticated analyses he is trying to supersede.[20] He is on firmer ground when he says that the reader is forced to "connect" the two ideas (p. 125). In this "connection" resides the secret and the mystery of metaphor. To speak of the "interaction" of two thoughts "active together" (or, again, of their "interillumination" or "co-operation") is to *use* a metaphor emphasizing the dynamic aspects of a good reader's response to a nontrivial metaphor. I have no quarrel with the use of metaphors (if they are good ones) in talking about metaphor. But it may be as well to use several, lest we are misled by the adventitious charms of our favorites.

Let us try, for instance, to think of a metaphor as a filter. Consider the statement, "Man is a wolf." Here, we may say, are *two* subjects – the principal subject, Man (or: men) and the subsidiary subject, Wolf (or: wolves). Now the metaphorical sentence in question will not convey its intended meaning to a reader sufficiently ignorant about wolves. What is needed is not so much that the reader shall know the standard dictionary meaning of "wolf" – or be able to use that word in literal senses – as that he shall know what I will call the *system of associated commonplaces*. Imagine some layman required to say, without taking special thought, those things he held to be true about wolves; the set of statements resulting would approximate to what I am here calling the system of commonplaces associated with the word "wolf". I am assuming that in any given culture the responses made by different persons to the test suggested would agree rather closely and that even the occasional expert, who might have unusual knowledge of the subject, would still know "what the man in the street thinks about the matter". From the expert's standpoint, the system of commonplaces may include half-truths or downright mistakes (as when a whale is classified as a fish); but the important thing for the metaphor's effectiveness is not that the commonplaces shall be true, but that they should be readily and freely evoked. (Because this is so, a metaphor that works in one society may seem preposterous in another. Men who take wolves to be reincarnations of dead humans will give the statement "Man is a wolf" an interpretation different from the one I have been assuming.)

To put the matter in another way: Literal uses of the word "wolf" are governed by syntactical and semantical rules, violation of which produces nonsense or self-contradiction. In addition, I am suggesting, literal uses of the word normally commit the speaker to acceptance of a set of standard beliefs about wolves (current platitudes) that are the common possession of the members of some speech community. To deny any such piece of accepted commonplace (e.g. by saying that wolves are vegetarians – or easily domesticated) is to produce an effect of paradox and provoke a demand for justification. A speaker who says "wolf" is normally taken to be implying in some sense of that word that he is referring to something fierce, carnivorous, treacherous, and so on. The idea of a wolf is part of a system of ideas, not sharply delineated, and yet sufficiently definite to admit of detailed enumeration.

The effect, then, of (metaphorically) calling a man a "wolf" is to evoke the wolf-system of related commonplaces. If the man is a wolf, he preys upon other animals, is fierce, hungry, engaged in constant struggle, a scavenger, and so on. Each of these implied assertions has now to be made to fit the principal subject (the man) either in normal or in abnormal senses. If the metaphor is at all appropriate, this can be done – up to a point at least. A suitable hearer will be led by the wolf-system of implications to construct a corresponding system of implications about the principal subject. But these implications will *not* be those comprised in the commonplaces *normally* implied by literal uses of "man". The new implications must be determined by the pattern of implications associated with literal uses of the word "wolf". Any human traits that can without undue strain be talked about in "wolf-language" will be rendered prominent, and any that cannot will be pushed into the background. The wolf-metaphor suppresses some details, emphasizes others – in short, *organizes* our view of man.

Suppose I look at the night sky through a piece of heavily smoked glass on which certain lines have been left clear. Then I shall see only the stars that can be made to lie on the lines previously prepared upon the screen, and the stars I do see will be seen as organized by the screen's structure. We can think of a metaphor as such a screen and the system of "associated commonplaces" of the focal word as the network of lines upon the screen. We can say that the principal subject is "seen through" the metaphorical expression – or, if we prefer, that the principal subject is "projected upon" the field of the subsidiary subject. (In the latter analogy, the implication-system of the focal expression must be taken to determine the "law of projection".)

Or take another example. Suppose I am set the task of describing a battle in words drawn as largely as possible from the vocabulary of chess. These latter terms determine a system of implications which will proceed to control my description of the battle. The enforced choice of the chess vocabulary will lead some aspects of the battle to be emphasized, others to be neglected, and all to be organized in a way that would cause much more strain in other modes of description. The chess vocabulary filters and transforms: it not only selects, it brings forward aspects of the battle that might not be seen at all through another medium. (Stars that cannot be seen at all, except through telescopes.)

Nor must we neglect the shifts in attitude that regularly result from the use of metaphorical language. A wolf is (conventionally) a hateful and alarming object; so, to call a man a wolf is to imply that he too is hateful and alarming (and thus to support and reinforce dyslogistic attitudes). Again, the vocabulary of chess has its primary uses in a highly artificial setting, where all expression of feeling is formally excluded: to describe a battle as if it were a game of chess is accordingly to exclude, by the choice of language, all the more emotionally disturbing aspects of warfare. (Similar by-products are not rare in philosophical uses of metaphor.)

A fairly obvious objection to the foregoing sketch of the "interaction view" is that it has to hold that some of the "associated commonplaces" themselves suffer metaphorical change of meaning in the process of transfer from the subsidiary to the principal subject. And these changes, if they occur, can hardly be explained by the account given. The primary metaphor, it might be said, has been analyzed into a set of subordinate metaphors, so the account given is either circular or leads to an infinite regress.

This might be met by denying that *all* changes of meaning in the "associated commonplaces" must be counted as metaphorical shifts. Many of them are best described as extensions of meaning, because they do not involve apprehended connections between two systems of concepts. I have not undertaken to explain how such extensions or shifts occur in general, and I do not think any simple account will fit all cases. (It is easy enough to mutter "analogy", but closer examination soon shows all kinds of "grounds" for shifts of meaning with context – and even no ground at all, sometimes.)

Secondly, I would not deny that a metaphor may involve a number of subordinate metaphors among its implications. But these subordinate metaphors are, I think, usually intended to be taken less "emphatically", i.e. with less stress upon their implications. (The implications of a metaphor are like the overtones of a musical chord; to attach too much "weight" to them is like trying to make the overtones sound as loud as the main notes – and just as pointless.) In any case, primary and subordinate metaphors will normally belong to the same field of discourse, so that they mutually reinforce one and the same system of implications. Conversely, where substantially new metaphors appear as the primary metaphor is unraveled, there is serious risk of confusion of thought (compare the customary prohibition against "mixed metaphors").

But the preceding account of metaphor needs correction, if it is to be reasonably adequate. Reference to "associated commonplaces" will fit the commonest cases where the author simply plays upon the stock of common knowledge (and common misinformation) presumably shared by the reader and himself. But in a poem, or a piece of sustained prose, the writer can establish a novel pattern of implications for the literal uses of the key expressions, prior to using them as vehicles for his metaphors. (An author can do much to suppress unwanted implications of the word "contract", by explicit discussion of its intended meaning, before he proceeds to develop a contract theory of sovereignty. Or a naturalist who really knows wolves may tell us so much about them that *his* description of man as a wolf diverges quite markedly from the stock uses of that figure.) Metaphors can be supported by specially constructed systems of implications, as well as by accepted commonplaces; they can be made to measure and need not be reach-me-downs.

It was a simplification, again, to speak as if the implication-system of the metaphorical expression remains unaltered by the metaphorical statement. The nature of the intended application helps to determine the character of the system to be applied (as though the stars could partly determine the character of the observation-screen by which we looked at them). If to call a man a wolf is to put him in a special light, we must not forget that the metaphor makes the wolf seem more human than he otherwise would.

I hope such complications as these can be accommodated within the outline of an "interaction view" that I have tried to present.

6

Since I have been making so much use of example and illustration, it may be as well to state explicitly (and by way of summary) some of the chief respects in which the "interaction" view recommended differs from a "substitution" or a "comparison" view.

In the form in which I have been expounding it, the "interaction view" is committed to the following seven claims:

1. A metaphorical statement has two distinct subjects – a "principal" subject and a "subsidiary" one.[21]
2. These subjects are often best regarded as "systems of things", rather than "things".
3. The metaphor works by applying to the principal subject a system of "associated implications" characteristic of the subsidiary subject.
4. These implications usually consist of "commonplaces" about the subsidiary subject, but may, in suitable cases, consist of deviant implications established *ad hoc* by the writer.
5. The metaphor selects, emphasizes, suppresses, and organizes features of the principal subject by implying statements about it that normally apply to the subsidiary subject.
6. This involves shifts in meaning of words belonging to the same family or system as the metaphorical expression; and some of these shifts, though not all, may be metaphorical transfers. (The subordinate metaphors are, however, to be read less "emphatically".)
7. There is, in general, no simple "ground" for the necessary shifts of meaning – no blanket reason why some metaphors work and others fail.

It will be found, upon consideration, that point (1) is incompatible with the simplest forms of a "substitution view", point (7) is formally incompatible with a "comparison view"; while the remaining points elaborate reasons for regarding "comparison views" as inadequate.

But it is easy to overstate the conflicts between these three views. If we were to insist that only examples satisfying all seven of the claims listed above should be allowed to count as "genuine" metaphors, we should restrict the correct uses of the word "metaphor" to a very small number of cases. This would be to advocate a persuasive definition of "metaphor" that would tend to make all metaphors interestingly complex.[22] And such a deviation from current uses of the word "metaphor" would leave us without a convenient label for the more trivial cases. Now it is in just such trivial cases that "substitution" and "comparison" views sometimes seem nearer the mark than "interaction" views. The point might be met by classifying metaphors as instances of substitution, comparison, or interaction. Only the last kind are of importance in philosophy.

For substitution-metaphors and comparison-metaphors can be replaced by literal translations (with possible exception for the case of catachresis) – by sacrificing some of the charm, vivacity, or wit of the original, but with no loss of *cognitive* content. But "interaction-metaphors" are not expendable. Their mode of operation requires the reader to use a system of implications (a system of "commonplaces" – or a special system established for the purpose in hand) as a means for selecting, emphasizing, and organizing relations in a different field. This use of a "subsidiary subject" to foster insight into a "principal subject" is a distinctive intellectual operation (though one familiar enough through our experiences of learning anything whatever), demanding simultaneous awareness of both subjects but not reducible to any comparison between the two.

Suppose we try to state the cognitive content of an interaction-metaphor in "plain language". Up to a point, we may succeed in stating a number of the relevant relations between the two subjects (though in view of the extension of meaning accompanying the shift in the subsidiary subjects implication system, too much must not be expected of the literal paraphrase). But the set of literal statements so obtained will not have the same power to inform and enlighten as the original. For one thing, the implications, previously left for a suitable reader to educe for himself, with a nice feeling for their relative priorities and degrees of importance, are now presented explicitly as though having equal weight. The literal paraphrase inevitably says too much – and with the wrong emphasis. One of the points I most wish to stress is that the loss in such cases is a loss in cognitive content; the relevant weakness of the literal paraphrase is not that it may be tiresomely prolix or boringly explicit (or deficient in qualities of style); it fails to be a translation because it fails to give the insight that the metaphor did.

But "explication", or elaboration of the metaphor's grounds, if not regarded as an adequate cognitive substitute for the original, may be extremely valuable. A powerful metaphor will no more be harmed by such probing than a musical masterpiece by analysis of its harmonic and melodic structure. No doubt metaphors are dangerous – and perhaps especially so in philosophy. But a prohibition against their use would be a willful and harmful restriction upon our powers of inquiry.[23]

NOTES

1. Any part of speech can be used metaphorically (though the results are meagre and uninteresting in the case of conjunctions); any form of verbal expression may contain a metaphorical focus.

2. Here I am using language appropriate to the "interaction view" of metaphor that is discussed later in this paper.

3. Here, I wish these words to be read with as little "weight" as possible!

4. Notice how this type of paraphrase naturally conveys some implication of *fault* on the part of the metaphor's author. There is a strong suggestion that he ought to have made up his mind as to what he really wanted to say – the metaphor is depicted as a way of glossing over unclarity and vagueness.

5. Richard Whately, *Elements of Rhetoric* (7th rev. ed., London, 1846), p. 280.

6. Under "Figure" we find: "Any of the various 'forms' of expression, deviating from the normal arrangement or use of words, which are adopted in order to give beauty, variety, or force to a composition; e.g., Aposiopesis, Hyperbole, Metaphor, etc." If we took this strictly we might be led to say that a transfer of a word not adopted for the sake of introducing "beauty, variety, or force" must necessarily fail to be a case of metaphor. Or will "variety" automatically cover every transfer? It will be noticed that the O.E.D.'s definition is no improvement upon Whately's. Where he speaks of a "word" being substituted, the O.E.D. prefers "name or descriptive term." If this is meant to restrict metaphors to nouns (and adjectives?) it is demonstrably mistaken. But, if not, what *is* "descriptive term" supposed to mean? And why has Whately's reference to "Resemblance or Analogy" been trimmed into a reference to analogy alone?

7. Owen Barfield, "Poetic Diction and Legal Fiction," in *Essays Presented to Charles Williams* (Oxford, 1947), pp. 106–27. The definition of metaphor occurs on p. 111, where metaphor is treated as a special case of what Barfield calls "tarning." The whole essay deserves to be read.

8. The O.E.D. defines catachresis as: "Improper use of words; application of a term to a thing which it does not properly denote; abuse or perversion of a

trope or metaphor." I wish to exclude the pejorative suggestions. There is nothing perverse or abusive in stretching old words to fit new situations. Catachresis is merely a striking case of the transformation of meaning that is constantly occurring in any living language.

9. Can we imagine anybody saying this nowadays and seriously meaning anything? I find it hard to do so. But in default of an authentic context of use, any analysis is liable to be thin, obvious, and unprofitable.

10. A full discussion of this example, complete with diagrams, will be found in Gustaf Stern's *Meaning and Change of Meaning* (Göteborgs Högskolas Arsskrift, vol. 38, 1932, part 1), pp. 300 ff. Stern's account tries to show how the reader is led by the context to *select* from the connotation of "lion" the attribute (bravery) that will fit Richard the man. I take him to be defending a form of the substitution view.

11. Aristotle ascribes the use of metaphor to delight in learning; Cicero traces delight in metaphor to the enjoyment of the author's ingenuity in overpassing the immediate, or in the vivid presentation of the principal subject. For references to these and other traditional views, see E. M. Cope, *An Introduction to Aristotle's Rhetoric* (London, 1867), Book III, Appendix B, Ch. 2, "On Metaphor".

12. Thus Stern (*op. cit.*) says of all figures of speech that "they are intended to serve the expressive and purposive functions of speech better than the 'plain statement' " (p. 296). A metaphor produces an "enhancement" (*Steigerung*) of the subject, but the factors leading to its use "involve the expressive and effective (purposive) functions of speech, not the symbolic and communicative functions" (p. 290). That is to say, metaphors may evince feelings or predispose others to act and feel in various ways – but they do not typically *say* anything.

13. Whately, *loc. cit.* He proceeds to draw a distinction between "Resemblance, strictly so called, i.e., *direct* resemblance between the objects themselves in question (as when we speak of '*table*-land', or compare great waves to *mountains*)" and "Analogy, which is the resemblance of Ratios – a similarity of the relations they bear to certain other objects; as when we speak of the '*light* of reason' or of 'revelation'; or compare a wounded and captive warrior to a stranded ship."

14. Alexander Bain, *English Composition and Rhetoric* (enl. ed., London, 1887), p. 159.

15. Comparison views probably derive from Aristotle's brief statement in the *Poetics:* "Metaphor consists in giving the thing a name that belongs to something else; the transference being either from genus to species, or from species to genus, or from species to species, or on grounds of analogy" (1457b). I have no space to give Aristotle's discussion the detailed examination it deserves. An able defence of a view based on Aristotle will be found in S. J. Brown's *The World of Imagery* (London, 1927, esp. pp. 67 ff.).

16. Much more would need to be said in a thorough examination of the comparison view. It would be revealing, for instance, to consider the contrasting types of case in which a formal comparison is preferred to a metaphor. A comparison is often a prelude to an explicit statement of the grounds of resemblance whereas we do not expect a metaphor to explain itself. (Cf. the difference between *comparing* a man's face with a wolf mask by looking for points of resemblance –

and seeing the human face *as* vulpine.) But no doubt the line between *some* metaphors and *some* similes is not a sharp one.

17. The best sources are the writings of I. A. Richards, especially Chapter 5 ("Metaphor") and Chapter 6 ("Command of Metaphor") of his *The Philosophy of Rhetoric* (Oxford, 1936). Chapters 7 and 8 of his *Interpretation in Teaching* (London, 1938) cover much the same ground. W. Bedell Stanford's *Greek Metaphor* (Oxford, 1936) defends what he calls an "integration theory" (see esp. pp. 101 ff.) with much learning and skill. Unfortunately, both writers have great trouble in making clear the nature of the positions they are defending. Chapter 18 of W. Empson's *The Structure of Complex Words* (London, 1951) is a useful discussion of Richards' views on metaphor.

18. *The Philosophy of Rhetoric*, p. 93. Richards also says that metaphor is "fundamentally a borrowing between and intercourse of *thoughts*, a transaction between contexts" (p. 94). Metaphor, he says, requires two ideas "which co-operate in an inclusive meaning" (p. 119).

19. It is this, perhaps, that leads Richards to say that "talk about the identification or fusion that a metaphor effects is nearly always misleading and pernicious" (*ibid.*, p. 127).

20. Usually, Richards tries to show that similarity between the two terms is at best *part* of the basis for the interaction of meanings in a metaphor.

21. This point has often been made. E.g.: "As to metaphorical expression, that is a great excellence in style, when it is used with propriety, for it gives you two ideas for one" (Samuel Johnson, quoted by Richards, *ibid.*, p. 93).

The choice of labels for the "subjects" is troublesome. See the "note on terminology" (n. 23, below).

22. I can sympathize with Empson's contention that "The term ['metaphor'] had better correspond to what the speakers themselves feel to be a rich or suggestive or persuasive use of a word, rather than include uses like the *leg* of a table" (*The Structure of Complex Words*, p. 333). But there is the opposite danger, also, of making metaphors too important by definition, and so narrowing our view of the subject excessively.

23. (*A note on terminology*): For metaphors that fit a substitution or comparison view, the factors needing to be distinguished are: (i) some word or expression *E*, (ii) occurring in some verbal "frame" *F*, so that (iii) *F*(*E*) is the metaphorical statement in question; (iv) the meaning *m′*(*E*) which *E* has in *F*(*E*), (v) which is the same as the literal meaning, *m*(*X*), of some literal synonym, *X*. A sufficient technical vocabulary would be: "metaphorical expression" (for *E*), "metaphorical statement" (for *F*(*E*)), "metaphorical meaning" (for *m′*) and "literal meaning" (for *m*).

Where the interaction view is appropriate, the situation is more complicated. We may also need to refer to (vi) the principal subject of *F*(*E*), say *P* (roughly, what the statement is "really" about); (vii) the subsidiary subject, *S* (what *F*(*E*) would be about if read literally); (viii) the relevant system of implications, *I*, connected with *S*; and (ix) the resulting system of attributions, *A*, asserted of *P*. We must accept at least so much complexity if we agree that the meaning of *E* in its setting *F* depends upon the transformation of *I* into *A* by using language, normally applied to *S*, to apply to *P* instead.

Richards has suggested using the words "tenor" and "vehicle" for the two "*thoughts*" which, in his view, are "active together" (for "the two *ideas* that metaphor, at its simplest, gives us" – *The Philosophy of Rhetoric*, p. 96, my italics) and urges that we reserve "the word 'metaphor' for the whole double unit" (*ibid.*). But this picture of two *ideas* working upon each other is an inconvenient fiction. And it is significant that Richards himself soon lapses into speaking of "tenor" and "vehicle" as "things" (e.g. on p. 118). Richards' "vehicle" vacillates in reference between the metaphorical expression (*E*), the subsidiary subject (*S*) and the connected implication system (*I*). It is less clear what his "tenor" means: sometimes it stands for the principal subject (*P*), sometimes for the implications connected with that subject (which I have not symbolized above), sometimes, in spite of Richards' own intentions, for the *resultant* meaning (or as we might say the "full import") of *E* in its context, *F*(*E*).

There is probably no hope of getting an accepted terminology so long as writers upon the subject are still so much at variance with one another.

PART FIVE: THE LOGICAL CHARACTER OF RELIGIOUS LANGUAGE

21

R. W. HEPBURN

Does Religious Discourse delineate in a parable a way of life? *Professor Hepburn here examines the view that what is important about a religious story or parable is not its historicity but its ability to delineate "a way of life that we judge to be valuable". Such a view of religious discourse could obviously escape some of the problems of Christian belief, not least those arising around its historical element, and some of these problems are touched on in other extracts. But, says Professor Hepburn, and rightly, this view could not be said to be an wholly adequate account of the Christian position, though it can preserve some of its most valuable logical features.*

In so far as a story or parable delineates a way of life that we judge to be valuable, it is not of paramount importance whether or not the story or parable is historically true. It can do its job equally well if fictitious; sometimes better.

What job *can* it do? Mainly that of backing up a bare moral rule with an imaginatively vivid instance of its being practised or neglected. In a parable at its best we may have not only an illustration of what the rule enjoins, but also in very little space some useful pointers to difficulties likely to *impede* our obedience to it, insight into the good effects of obeying, and maybe still other sorts of in-

R. W. Hepburn, *Christianity and Paradox*, C. A. Watts & Co. Ltd. 1958, pp. 192–204.

formation about it – all in one story. The peculiar beauty or grace or loathsomeness of ways of life can be brought out and kept easily before the mind in such stories, far more effectively than by memorizing lists of maxims. They are most memorable and most imaginatively satisfying when bound together as incidents of one life-story, or as the events of one drama, poem, or novel, given their own aesthetic unity. They provide (what again the maxims fail to provide) a resting-place for meditation, and a standing test for the vitality and "spirit" of one's own moral life, not merely of its conformity to the rules.

It is tempting and plausible to go much further and claim that the Old and New Testaments *as a whole* (and other religious documents) provide a single extended "story" or "myth" or set of symbols, depicting a pattern of life and giving just the same sort of aids to keen self-knowledge, and stimulus to moral effort, as the parable proper gives.[1] The moral pattern of life is the fundamental thing: the story its vehicle.

Some of the theologians we looked at earlier come very near to saying this: in particular the language of "existential history" makes exactly the same emphasis – on what moral challenge history has at the present moment, not on the objective-factual happenings of the past. But the existentialist historian, we saw, does not stop there. He would not be easy in his mind if you told him that the biblical story was entirely fictitious, an extended parable *simply*, having the sole function of confirming a manner of living. He, and the vast majority of theologians with him, would insist that the attitudes that the biblical story evokes in its reader are responses to beliefs about certain *facts* – however curious facts they are – that God made the world, for instance, that he sent his Son, and that the man who believes in him shall not perish. . . . They would deny that these responses would be obtained equally strongly if the story were taken as fictitious parable. It would be unthinkable to them that in one real sense Christ *need not have died:* for on the view we are considering, the *story* of his death (whether true or not) would be enough to give backing to the Christlike way of life.

But the view is obviously an immensely attractive one to anybody who wants to be at once empiricist and religious. For it holds that the problems about the meaning of words like "God", "heaven", "resurrection" are solved by showing the part these words play in delineating the practical way of life. If they have a use of this kind, then they have a meaning. But the *Christian* surely cannot acquiesce in limiting the purpose of talk about God to this fortifying of morality by parable. The language of "transcendence", the thought of God as a personal being, wholly other to man, dwelling apart in majesty – this talk may well collapse into meaninglessness in the last analysis. And yet to sacrifice it seems at once to take one quite outside Christianity. (In saying that I do not feel guilty of making an arbitrary definition of what Christianity is.)[2]

In a similar vein, a writer recently suggested that a real source of bafflement about God is our tendency to conceive him as a cosmic artisan or engineer manipulating the world, just in the way we (sinfully) seek to dominate and manipulate our environment and one another. St John said, "God is love", and so he is quite literally. He belongs to the moral world, not to the world of cosmology and impersonality. His commandments are nothing but the statement of the "conditions in which we either do or do not encounter Love, the only Source of Life". Religious disciplines are ways of sensitizing the believer, making that encounter more enduring, and increasing the areas of life over which love is sovereign.[3]

Once more we note the centrality of moral judgement in this account. On morality everything else hinges. But the consequence again is to disqualify the theory as an account of *historical Christianity*. For if it rescues God from being a debased celestial mechanic, it is only to deny that "he" is any sort of being at all, and instead to transform "him" into a relation, the relation of love between persons. The metaphor of love "standing between" people suggests (but of course does not justify) the fancy of personifying that relation and calling it "God".

If I conclude, then, that an account of religion in terms of a moral way of life backed up by parable fails as a description of Christianity, I do *not* want to go on and say that we can therefore count it of no value. For I see in it one way of answering some of the religiously-minded sceptic's worries; and of answering them most satisfactorily. For this account does illuminate very clearly some of the most important formal features of any religious orientation of mind. And it goes far to suggest a way of retaining such an orientation, despite the theological breakdown.

We could describe as "religious" any set of attitudes and beliefs that satisfies three conditions. First, the believer commits himself to a pattern of ethical behaviour. This way of life is simply decided for as an ultimate moral choice: empirical facts will be relevant to his choice, but he can *derive* his decision from no facts whatever, not even from commands of God, should he believe in a God. But (second) what will distinguish religious from moral language is that religious discourse provides a tightly cohering extended parable or myth that vividly expresses the way of life chosen, and inspires the believer to implement it in practice. Third, the parable and its associated pattern of behaviour legislate not for any *fraction* of the believer's life, but for every aspect of it. It commands his supreme loyalty and determines his total imaginative vision of nature and man. Yet the believer suffers no loss of freedom through submitting himself to his faith: for the foundation upon which all is based would be his own own freely endorsed value judgements. Defined in this broad, formal way, a religious orientation of life would not necessarily include belief in a God, nor in the possibility of speculative philosophy.

In currant usage, however, the words "religious" and "religion" do not refer to form alone, but normally say something also about *content*. It cannot be emphasized too often that although I am claiming that a sceptic can, if he wishes, fashion a way of looking at life that merits to some degree the title "religious", I am not claiming that he can provide for himself adequate substitutes for prayer, say, or the peculiarly Christian antidotes for anxiety or fear, or the hopes which are warranted only on certain Christian assumptions about the destiny of the world. I shall suggest in the final part of this chapter that there are a few important kinds of religious experience (that is to say, part of the *content* of theistic belief) that the sceptic *may* find are still available to him, in as much as these do not depend upon belief about the world or its deities, but upon other things. We shall, however, look first in a little more detail at the task of giving a religious form or structure to the moral life.

There is no more characteristic theological activity than that of sifting away "unworthy" conceptions of God. God is not blemished by moral imperfections like men; he is morally perfect. We can think still more worthily of him than that, however. For he cannot be merely one perfect being among other possible perfect beings. He must be the source of all perfection: call him not simply "good" but "goodness itself". All else is unworthy of him. He is also lord of the universe, and so (as we have seen) cannot be thought of as just one item in the furniture of that universe. It must be inconceivable that he should *not* exist: he must exist necessarily. Or (moving in yet another direction), we think unworthily of him as long as we think of him as "being" at all: he is beyond being.

Christians have made all these affirmations, searching for that notion of God which excludes all unworthy limitations. For while the least suspicion of unworthiness remains, it cannot be *God* that is being spoken about or prayed to: by definition, he is the one in whom there is no unworthiness at all.

But it must seem to many people, even to would-be believers, that if those refinements must be made, they elevate God not only out of imperfection, but also and equally out of personal existence of any kind. "Goodness", like "love", cannot be seriously personified without absurdity. Conclusions can follow necessarily from premisses, but nothing can *exist* necessarily. And if God is beyond being: is this not to agree with the atheist, who says "There is no God"? If it is *not* the same, then we still await from the theologian a satisfactory account of the difference between his claim and that of the atheist.

The trend of this reasoning can be summed up in two ways. Either we say, "God, to be God, must be non-existent: atheism is the purest form of faith". Or else we can say (more wisely if less sensationally) that the "only thoroughly satisfactory object of reverence, or focus of ideals, must be imaginary".[4] I say more wisely, because to call this imaginary focus "God" outright is to take the risk of allowing the incompatible Christian claims about God as "personal", as "active", and so on, to return, despite the judgement that on logical grounds they must be excluded.

Now what bearing do these reflections have upon our "formal" account of religion as parable associated with a way of life? A very close bearing. The sceptic cannot conscientiously believe in God as the New Testament depicts him. It would seem to follow that little or nothing could be usefully salvaged by him from the concept of God. But we can see now that this is not wholly true. Our religiously minded sceptic can be seen as perpetually in quest of the most satisfactory set of parables to sum up his moral decisions. He will achieve progress, whenever he manages to replace some ambiguous, sprawling story by a terse illuminating one, or finds a more comprehensive symbol for a wide range of experiences he wishes to consider as related together in some way. His *ideal*, doubtless never to be realized, is to catch up his whole understanding of life as it is and as it should be in a single unified vision. The notion of an ideal imaginary focus is precisely what he needs in making clear to himself the nature of this task, and in pointing the direction in which his quest must go. And it is as a development of the idea of God that this notion is most readily derived.

He faces a many-sided task. It involves the scrutiny of alternative modes of living, seen as far as possible in the round, realized vividly in the imagination, and held in some powerful symbol. The field from which he will glean material is indefinitely large. It need not be confined to a single sacred book, nor indeed to explicitly theological writings. He may stock his armoury of symbols from such novels as Orwell's *Animal Farm*, and Koestler's *Darkness at Noon*; from Dostoievsky's *The Idiot*, from Bunyan and from Spenser, promiscuously; from Euripides in *The Bacchae*. Upon each encounter with these and the like myth-makers something will be taken, something rejected; the moral struggle seen more sharply through the lens of the new parable; new linkages made between old symbols – across the years, between the authors, and between the cultures. It is a task in which imagination cooperates intimately with moral judgement – discriminating, amending, adapting, in order to build up an image of the best way of life and of the best way of capturing it, in myth, parable, and symbol.

This still does not exhaust the field from which material may be taken. The richest store of all may, of course, be found in one's own personal experience of life, as retained by memory. By reflecting creatively on one's past, one may strive to draw together the strands of one's life into the total parable, bringing them into relation (the closest we can attain) with the ideal, unattainable focus.

To organize one's life in this way, would I think be admitted by some people as a genuinely religious activity, in one acceptable sense of the word. But others will be far more struck by the *difference* between it and traditional religions, and lament how bleak a prospect it extends to the unfortunate sceptic. It is a religion only of the *individual*, he will say – the working out of private myths in private ivory towers. Whereas, "true" religion essentially involves fellowship, the breaking down of barriers, the sharing of *public* worship centred on a *public* parable. Or again, he may judge that the sceptic cuts a rather pathetic figure, once one sees what solid beliefs he is really left with. In a friendless, enormous universe, he makes his little decisions and clothes them in stories of his own devising, seeking to forget his puniness, his mortality, his loneliness, like a condemned prisoner scratching feeble drawings on the walls of his cell. Third, he may say, "Call this view of life 'religious" if you like, but does it really deserve the name, if you set alongside it (something it cannot duplicate) the great Christian theme of the soul's pilgrimage or adventure into the unknown, with faith as its sole guide?"

I think it can be shown that these three indictments, although natural enough, are not altogether fair.

First, we must admit that there is certainly no guarantee that any one set of symbols, any one parable, will commend itself to a sufficiently large number of people as to constitute a shared, public religion. But since the parables are desired above all to express a *moral* pattern of life, that is, to embody a blue print for social, not solitary living, it is to be expected that people who hold to similar moral patterns will also respond sympathetically to the same parables, that they should take seriously one another's criticisms of the *adequacy* of those parables, as people engaged in a common task.

Whatever the differences among their parables and symbols, secular religious people would be united in one respect. All would be engaged in the same sifting, discriminating activity that we have tried to describe earlier. But to stress *this*, it might be objected, would be rather like making a religion out of the *search* for a religion. It might be: but would that be so paradoxical, or even so very unfamiliar? Theologians constantly declare that no analogy or image or symbol can adequately express God's nature. He is Father, but not in all respects like earthly fathers; he loves us, but with more than a human love . . . and so on. The best that can be done is to assert some analogy and then say, "But no: he is not quite like that", and then another analogy, and largely cancel it in turn. No shot is a bull's-eye, but the cluster of near-misses manages to locate the target in a rough-and-ready fashion. More seriously: the progress towards knowledge of God includes the destruction of successive symbols, the endless pruning away of misleading associations. The aim of all this labour (to the Christian) is a knowledge of a God who in some sense *is*. The sceptic, denying this, may nevertheless engage in his closely analogous search for parable – with a sense of equal dedication and of fellowship with others who undertake it along with him.

Second: the Christian's symbols and parables not only back up a set of moral decisions (the Christian ethic) but also tell him something about the world he lives in. The heavens declare God's glory: he makes the clouds his chariot and walks upon the wings of the wind. No corner of the universe lacks his presence. If we make our bed in hell, behold he is there. Personal being, intelligence, and purpose are to be encountered not only in humanity and in the works of humanity; but the entire world is replete with them. So far the Christian. Is he right in claiming that without these religious assumptions the world could be seen as little more than a vast friendless tomb or prison?

Our religiously minded sceptic would be entitled to reply that this grim vision is by no means *forced* upon sceptics. It is one out of many possible imaginative slants on the world, none of which is more authoritative than any other, so long as they all are consistent with the facts.[5] To take one very simple instance. Men certainly are minute compared in size and length of life with, say, the solar system. Yet anyone who concluded ' Men therefore are miserable creatures – tiny and pathetically short-lived" would be expressing only one (imaginatively interesting though chilly) slant, but not at all the whole truth. Someone else might properly reply, 'No; men are large creatures and long-lived: compare them with molecules and lightning flashes."

To take another example: "Nature is indifferent to all values: see her callousness in the T.B. bacillus and polio virus." This invites the reply, "But without these natural conditions, without *just* those evolutionary mechanisms, no intelligent life or purpose or awareness of beauty would have ever been possible." Neither a satanic nor a benign vision exhausts nature's ambiguity. Poets and painters are endlessly singling out alternative pictures of man's relation to nature. Some are quixotic and fanciful, the plaything of a lyric or sketch: but one lingers over others, because in some way they project on to nature a vision with which one would be well content to live, which one would choose, before any other perspective, as providing the perfect backcloth to the way of life one has opted to follow. If we set supreme value upon *men*, then the perspective will not be one in which men are dwarfed by cosmic immensity: the world will be seen as the theatre of moral drama; elements in nature as symbols of human conflicts, achievements, and disasters. We may, of course, realize from time to time that our slant is no more than one out of many other possible slants, and that it is sustained by the work of imagination. But we will be fortified by recalling that the alternative to the slant we seek to maintain (the one which backs up our moral decisions) is some *other* slant, which does this task less effectively. The alternative is not "reality" in place of "illusion"; for *every* way of looking at nature in the round involves plumping for some slant or other. There is no escaping them. Obviously then, the religiously minded sceptic will search not only for symbols that directly express his moral judgements in human terms (like the Grand Inquisitor in Dostoievsky, or Big Brother in *Nineteen Eighty-Four*), but at the same time for what we could call symbols of *context* or *setting* (like the nature poems of Kathleen Raine, or the landscapes of Graham Sutherland or Paul Nash).

In short, nature is pliant to the imagination to an extent often ignored by orthodox theologians: and sceptics are not necessarily immured within some single fearful dungeon of loneliness from which there can be no escape. On the other hand, it would be foolish to claim that an agnostic's imaginative slant, however well adapted to his judgements of value, could provide an exact equivalent to the biblical conceptions of God's presence in every part of the universe or of his love for man. To take a critical case: the Christian would deny that a man who suffered and perhaps died in complete solitariness was out of the reach of real personal encounter during his ordeal; the denial of this is part of what is meant by his talk of God's omnipresence. The unbeliever has no equivalent comfort, and would be unwise to delude himself that he had.

Third: the idea of life as "pilgrimage" is an astonishingly pervasive one among religions of widely different types. It is at home most naturally among those that believe men to be capable of reaching beatitude in the strength of their own aspiring love for God. But even those forms of Christianity which most vigorously deny men the power to "save themselves", and see salvation as God's work alone, have still clung to the pilgrimage-motif, and in fact developed it more richly than the other. If Plotinus sums up the first group with his quest of the alone to the Alone, Bunyan's Pilgrim nobly represents the second. It would be, on the face of it, quite reasonable to complain that if our secular religious orientation could not in any way embrace this notable image of pilgrimage, it would be very much poorer and less satisfying in consequence.

The sense of movement, voyaging, questing, in the Christian notion of pilgrimage, has (at least) two strands. First, there is the effort to realize the demands of Christian ethics, the "movement" from challenge to challenge, the discovery of ways of coping with a succession of testing situations (Vanity Fair, the Slough of Despond), all of which are incorporated as significant landmarks in the pilgrimage-route. Next, as a kind of counterpoint to this theme, the pilgrimage is equally a journey "from this world to that which is to come".[6] The imagery of moral progress as a journey merges with that of death as a journey to the hereafter.

Our problem is this. Suppose we have to discount this second strand altogether, can the pilgrimage-motif be retained: and even if it can, does it really collapse into a fatuous platitude, a picturesque but unilluminating way of looking at the moral life, without any real imaginative grip? It is fair to suggest that if what I have so far said about moral decision were the whole story, this conclusion would be forced on us. But, fortunately, that over-simplified account needs amending in any case.

We have spoken as if people opted for a moral code, rather as they might commission a building to construct a house from a particular architect's plan. In each case, it is implied, we know exactly what we are choosing: we can clearly visualize the finished house, and, in the moral case, we can conceive precisely what it would be like to live in that way. On this account, to realize the chosen way of life may be a strenuous task, but cannot have the spirit of an adventure into unmapped country. We know very well to what we are committing ourselves. Now, this is in fact never our position with regard to any momentous moral choice. We begin with a general and rather empty conception of what we want to achieve – say, a way of life in which love of neighbour is the dominating theme. But what precisely loving one's neighbour is going to amount to, what particular forms it should take in particular situations and with particular neighbours, we do not yet know. How far love involves the vigorous persuading of others to do what one thinks good for them, and how far it involves a near-refusal to manipulate anyone's life, cannot be answered by repeating the slogan "Love your neighbour", or by referring to a "parable" (commending love) in which this tricky question is not touched upon. *New* decisions must frequently be made which were never envisaged at an earlier stage in one's moral experience.

Furthermore, the effects of our moral decision on other people and also on ourselves will soon present us with situations very different from those in which our original commitment was made: and it will *go on* constantly changing in ways hard to foresee. That activity of constant adjustment between means and ends, reassessment of policies in the light of unexpected results, the enriching of one's conception of the "goal", the skimming away of immature, crude elements in one's original idea of it, and the effort to give all this expression in the symbols and parables of which we have spoken – that may reassure us that the ideal of pilgrimage is *not* so foreign to this conception of life as we feared. The metaphor of a changing landscape of pilgrimage, of an obscurely seen destination, a *direction* rather than a clear landmark; the determination not to sit passively under experience as it comes, but to bring it as much as possible into relation (as parable or imaginative slant) with the total vision of life; these fit our outlined secular faith quite as much as they do Christianity. We lose inevitably that strand of meaning in which the pilgrimage of this life reaches its terminus only in the life to come. And this is real loss, without question. But we may still derive from the idea of pilgrimage and over arching, controlling symbol within which all other symbols, myths and stories can find their setting.

NOTES

1. Compare R. B. Braithwaite, *An Empiricist's View of the Nature of Religious Belief* (C.U.P., 1955).
2. Here I disagree with Professor Braithwaite, who argues that an account of religious language in terms of "parable" *is* compatible with traditional Christianity.
3. John Wren-Lewis, *The Philosophical Quarterly*, July, 1955.
4. Compare, in this section, Professor J. N. Findlay's article, "Can God's Existence be Disproved?", in *New Essays in Philosophical Theology*, ed. Flew and MacIntyre, (SCM Press, 1955).
5. See Antony Flew and Ronald W. Hepburn, "Problems of Perspective", in *The Plain View* for Winter 1955.
6. The long title of *The Pilgrim's Progress*.

22

IAN T. RAMSEY

The logical structure of Religious Language: Models and Disclosures. *This extract gives an analysis of religious language which centres on the logical concept of model, these models being grounded in situations of "cosmic disclosure". Against this background the author faces the question as to how far, and on what grounds, such language can be said to be* about *anything at all, and how on this view it is possible to give good reasons for preferring one pattern of religious discourse to another. There are some concluding remarks on the bearing of such a view on the practice of preaching, and how it leads to better understandings of Christian doctrine and helps us guard against misunderstandings as well.*

In this paper[1] I hope to show how talk about God arises around, and derives from, what I shall call models. I shall then consider some of the problems raised by this view, and finally glance at some of its wider implications.

Let me start by recalling that at one time, and in the Old Testament in particular, people made free use of all kinds of pictures, images, metaphors, models[2] in their talk about God. No one has illustrated this more plainly than Eric Heaton in his book *His Servants the Prophets* where he remarks that, in the Old Testament, "Yahweh's relationship to his people is represented under the figures of a father, mother, nurse, brother, husband, friend, warrior, shepherd, farmer, metal-worker, builder, potter, fuller, physician, judge, tradesman, King, fisherman, and scribe – to mention, almost

Ian T. Ramsey, "Talking about God", *Myth and Symbol*, ed. F. W. Dillistone, SPCK 1966, pp. 76–92, 95–97.

at random, only a few of the activities of the community" (p. 71).

Let us remind ourselves of how and where these pictures, these models, occur in the Bible by taking up references which for the most part are those which Mr Heaton gives us.

First, God is talked of in terms of phrases which spread from, and presuppose a family model:

1. *Father*. There is the promise in Jer. 3.19: "Ye shall call me 'My father' and shall not turn away from following me."
2. *Mother*. In Deut. 32.18 the Hebrews are accused of forgetting "God that gave thee birth", or rather more explicitly in Isa. 66.13 God promises Jerusalem: "As one whom his mother comforteth, so will I comfort you."
3. *Husband*. Not surprisingly in Hosea – the book which, as is well known, more than any other uses the model of personal relationships in its discourse about God – we find an express preference for the picture of God as husband instead of God as an overlord, a distinction which was as novel in a secular context as in reference to God: "It shall be at that day, saith the Lord, that thou shalt call me Ishi [= My husband] and shalt call me no more Baali [= My Master]" (Hos. 2.16).
4. *Friend*. In Jer. 3.4 "the companion of my youth" is used as an appropriate phrase for God, though the verse also speaks of God as "My father". Here God is spoken of at one and the same time as father and friend, a point to which I will return later.

But God is also pictured more widely in terms of men's work and crafts and professions; and again, for the most part with the help of Mr Heaton, we may recall many verses with phrases which point back to such pictures as these twelve I will now mention.

1. *The shepherd*. God is a shepherd whose sheep are men: "Ye are my sheep, the sheep of my pasture are many . . . saith the Lord God (Ezek. 34.31).
2. *The farmer*. "I will sift the house of Israel . . . like as corn is sifted in a sieve: yet shall not the least grain fall on the earth" (Amos 9.9).
3. *The dairymaid*. Job speaks of God as one who has "poured me out as milk, and curdled me like cheese" (Job 10.10).
4. *The fuller – the laundress*. In Mal. 3.2 God is said to be "like fuller's soap", a theme further developed in Isa. 4.4 which speaks

of a time when God will have "washed away the filth of the daughters of Zion".

5. *The builder*. In Amos 7.7 we read that "the Lord stood beside (*or* upon) a wall made by a plumbline, with a plumbline in his hand".

6. *The potter*. "Behold, as the clay in the potter's hand. so are ye in mine hand O house of Israel" (Jer. 18.6) – and the verse has echoes in Isaiah where as with the "father and friend" of Jeremiah, we now have God as "father and potter": "O Lord, thou art our father: we are the clay, and thou our potter" (Isa. 64.8).

7. *The fisherman*. In Hab. 1.14,15 men are "as the fishes of the sea" and God "taketh up all of them with his angle, he catcheth them in his net, and gathereth them in his drag: therefore he rejoiceth and is glad".

8. *The tradesman*. The well-known opening verse of Isa. 55 comes readily to mind: "Ho, everyone that thirsteth, come ye to the waters, and he that hath no money; come ye, buy, and eat: yea, come, buy wine and milk without money and without price."

9. *The physician*. Jer. 30 says of Israel and Judah that their "hurt is incurable", their "wound grievous", that they have no "healing medicines". But in verse 17 we read that God will restore their health: "I will restore health into thee, and I will heal thee of thy wounds, saith the Lord."

10. *The teacher and scribe*. The well-known verse from Jer. 31: "I will put my law (my teaching) in their inward parts, and in their heart will I write it".

11. *The nurse*. "I have nursed (nourished) and brought up children, and they have rebelled against me" (Isa. 1.2).

12. *The metal worker*. In Mal. 3.2,3 God is "like a refiner's fire . . . and he shall sit as a refiner and purifier of silver".

Finally, pictures from a national setting are also used in the Old Testament to enable man to be articulate about God. We have, for example, the models of the King, the warrior, and the judge:

1. *The King*. In Jer. 10.7: "Who would not fear thee, O King of the nations . . . forasmuch as among all the wise men of the nations, and in all their royal estate there is none like unto thee", and verse 10 "The Lord is the true God . . . and an everlasting King".

2. *The warrior.* We read in Isa. 63.1 how God comes "marching in the greatness of his strength", and the theme is developed in the next few verses.
3. *The judge.* "The Lord is our judge, the Lord is our lawgiver", says Isa. 33.22, and the verse continues: "The Lord is our King; he will save us". The verse virtually combines all the national models.

Here is theological language directly related, as Mr. Heaton said, "to the world of experience": here are religious situations linked with "secular" situations; here is talk about God which has plain links with the discourse of ordinary life. Here is religious life and theological language linked with the life and talk of home and family and friends: linked with man's work and talk whether it be in the fields or in the city, whether it be the work and talk of the craftsman or that of a profession; linked with the life and talk of the nation. The same could also be said about the characterization of God as "my rock, and my fortress . . . my strong rock . . . my shield, and the horn of my salvation, my high tower" (Ps. 18.2). Here is language about God gaining its relevance by means of what I have called "models". Now, what is involved when models are used in this way? Let us answer this question by reference in turn to each of the three groups I have mentioned above.

First then, those models associated with home and friends. How do they come to be used in talk about God? Let us begin by recognizing that on occasion circumstances all "go our way", as it is often said. On these occasions, the world displays predominantly favourable features, features which give rise to a sense of dependence, but dependence on what is reliable and secure. Such features are those, for example, which characterize the changing seasons in such a way that the farmer ploughs hopefully and harvests thankfully. Or it may happen that when we are faced with some major problem as to vocation, or emigration, or the suffering of an aged relative, or marriage, there occurs a complex set of circumstances, too complex and too diversified to be the result of any one man's design, which helps us to resolve the problem as well for those around us as for ourselves. Or it may be that we are walking in remote, mountainous country, and as night comes on we are filled with all kinds of uncertainties and anxieties. But then we refresh ourselves at a mountain stream, look up to the stars as symbols of stability, and find our path illuminated by the moon. A sense of kinship with nature strikes us; the Universe is reliable after all.

But, it might be asked, how do situations like this lead to homely phrases – what I have called models – being used in discourse about God? My answer begins by reminding ourselves that there are patterns of behaviour characteristically associated with a father, mother, husband, or friend which are reminiscent of the patterns of these natural circumstances – that there are, for example, features of a friend's behaviour – his reliability and trustworthiness – whose pattern resembles in an important way the pattern of seed-time and harvest. Moreover, in the personal case it is in and through such patterns that we see certain men and women – a husband, mother, father, friend – as more than what they plainly and obviously are, namely human organisms in specialized relationships. Around such patterns occurs what we may call a "disclosure", as when we "see" twelve lines on a blackboard as a box; as when a cluster of lines called more technically an "envelope" discloses an ellipse to us; as when two images take on another dimension and become a scene with "depth", looking (as we say) "very real" in a 3-D viewer. When such a disclosure occurs around a human pattern we speak of knowing people as they "really are", of there being "deep" affection between us, of loving them "for themselves". You may recall the "pop" song: "I love you for a hundred thousand reasons" – these reasons no doubt ranging from purely verifiable features and behaviour – hair, eyes, shape, tone of voice – to more distinctively personal reasons – trustfulness against the evidence – until as the climax: "But most of all I love you 'cos you're you" – someone whose uniqueness and transcendence is disclosed in, and through, these patterns of behaviour. "Husband", "mother", "father", "friend" – these are words which while they are undoubtedly associated with certain characteristic behaviour patterns have a transcendent reference as well – and are grounded is disclosures.

Building on these reflections, my next suggestion is that the human case as a catalyst for the cosmic case, to generate a cosmic disclosure. The cosmic pattern chimes in with the human pattern; the human pattern has already led to a finite disclosure – of persons – and their matching then evokes a cosmic disclosure around natural events such as seed-time and harvest. It is as and when a cosmic disclosure is thereby evoked that we are able to speak of God – what the cosmic disclosure discloses – in terms of the models with which the finite situations have supplied us. It is on these occasions that we speak of a "sense of kinship" with the Universe, of a "friendly" valley – so friendly that, as Ps. 65 would express it, "the valley laughs and sings with us".[3]

To turn now to the second group of phrases – those which originate in models taken from man's work and crafts. Once again there must have been, at least in the case of Israel, a correspondence of patterns. There must, for example, be some pattern discernible in the behaviour of sheep which was repeated in the social behaviour of the Israelites. Alternatively, the events of the nation must be such that words like "straining" and "sifting" become appropriate, so that it becomes possible to speak of the nation going through a severe period of testing, or through trying times, or being wounded or hurt. In all this no religious phrases are begged. Even the most secular man might speak of Germany smarting from the grievous wounds of Versailles, or France being incurably hurt by the war of 1870-1. Or we might speak of the life of a nation being strained or soured, of its public representatives being no longer upright, of our lives being moulded by current events or caught in the net of circumstances.

The phrases might be used, and no doubt often are used, without any religious overtones whatever. That indeed, so far, is my point, namely that these phrases relate to patterns of events recognizable by all, believers or not. What further conditions are wanted for theological language to arise? If genuine theological language is to arise, the characteristic behaviour of what the Income Tax Schedules call a "trade, profession, or vocation", i.e. shepherd, farmer, dairymaid, fuller, builder, potter, metal-worker, fisherman, tradesman, physician, teacher must, as in our own case, disclose an activity which gives to the overt "professional" behaviour a distinctively personal and transcendent backing. We ourselves may then be used as catalysts to evoke a cosmic disclosure around the national pattern.

So once again – and this time when national events display patterns which, having their counterparts in human activity, become at the next move occasions of a cosmic disclosure – a corresponding pattern in the Universe may lead to a cosmic disclosure, reveal God, and make possible the use of an appropriate model.

The third case – the case of those models which originate in the context of national or international politics – King, warrior, judge –

is different again. Here the model carries within itself the possibility of limitless development, and so the possibility arises of evoking a cosmic disclosure by developing a pattern whose range is unlimited.[4] Let me illustrate from the case of King. Each King, as the old Bidding Prayer phrases it, is over all persons and in all causes as well ecclesiastical as temporal within his dominions supreme. So why in principle impose any limit on the concept – any restriction of power in space and time? Then, as the King-pattern is developed, at some point or other a cosmic disclosure may occur, when (as we would say) the God of all power and might, the King of the whole earth will be disclosed. The model of warrior likewise embodies in itself the possibility of limitless inclusion, through victory, until the same kind of build-up of a power pattern leads to a cosmic disclosure. Of the Judge – easily universalized by the concept of Justice he embodies – points to yet another limitless pattern which can generate a cosmic disclosure, and so become another model for God.

Now it is in terms of these models that we become theologically articulate, that we talk about God. Sometimes this discourse is well developed as it is already in some of the verses we quoted; on other occasions it is hardly developed at all though the *prima facie* possibility of considerable development is always implicit. Let us recall some examples.

The model of a father gives rise to talk about "backsliding children" who if they but turn and are faithful will inherit a pleasant land and enjoy a distinguished heritage (Jer. 3.18,19); talk of a husband leads to talk of a betrothal "in righteousness, and in judgement, and in lovingkindness, and in mercies" and in "faithfulness" (Hos. 2.19,20). The shepherd is one of the most developed models, as we may see in Ezek. 34, for example, verses 12, 13, 14. "As a shepherd seeketh out his flock in the day that he is amongst his sheep that are scattered abroad, so will I seek out my sheep . . . and I will feed them upon the mountains of Israel by the watercourses . . . I will feed them with good pasture . . . there shall they lie down in a good fold." Again the potter leads the religious man to say as of God that "when the vessel that he made of the clay was marred in the hand of the potter, he made it again another vessel" (Jer. 18.4). We have seen already from Jer. 30 how the physician, like the shepherd, model is prolific in its articulation possibilities, and the same could be said about King, or warrior, or judge. For example, God is the King who reigns for ever, gives his people the blessings of peace (Ps. 10.16; 39.11) – and (Dan. 4. 34,35) his dominion is everlasting, he doeth according to his will . . . among the inhabitants of the earth. The theme of God as judge characterizes many psalms, for example, 7. 8-11; 58.11; 135.14, to take three almost at random. God as the powerful warrior is epitomized in Ps. 68. "Let God arise, and let his enemies be scattered", a psalm which has led many a soldier from Cromwell to Montgomery to be theologically articulate – perhaps indeed too articulate, though that is to anticipate difficulties to which I shall now very soon turn.

In these ways, then, in terms of a model set in a cosmic disclosure, we talk about God, and our theology contrives to be relevant. But such articulation is no free-for-all; it develops under checks and balances. There are cautions to be exercised, and problems to be fac ed, and to these various difficulties we now turn.

In the first place, it is clear that while undoubtedly, and as we have seen, some models are much more fertile than others, giving rise much more quickly to much more discourse, every model is sooner or later inadequate. Models like father, shepherd, physician, King may be much more fertile than builder or tradesman, but even discourse about fathers, shepherds, physicians, and Kings must sooner or later be incongruous. No one is so captivated by the physician model that he is emboldened to ask whether God will benefit from the new deal to be given to consultants by the Ministry of Health. Some models may take us a long way in theological talking, but eventually even they must grind to a halt. While therefore a model gives us relevance, and there will be a high or a low degree of relevance depending on the fertility of the model, we must be alert to the solecisms it will sooner or later produce.

There will be at least two cautions which we shall always observe. First we shall not remain content with any one model. Already we have seen how God was spoken of as King and judge; as father and friend; as father and potter. So the language that is most reliable will be that discourse which is licensed by, and consistent with, the widest possible range of models. We can already see in broad outline the character of this multi-model discourse. It will speak of God as caring for, providing for, as guiding, testing, healing, and cleansing, as possessing a moral authority and calling forth a total devotion and response; and something of this same discourse might well be derived from impersonal models, for example, rock, fortress, shield. Because a model like protector or guide by being more fertile for providing discourse is more "dominant" than models such as shepherd and potter, God will be more reliably spoken of as protector and guide than as shepherd or even as both shepherd and potter. But we shall need to see the limitations of even these strands of discourse, and if we look for discourse which harmonizes these dominant strands in such a way as to exclude the limitations of each, we may well arrive at discourse about love or perhaps activity; when we shall conclude that God is spoken of most reliably as "Love" or perhaps as just "the living God". The important point to recognize is that such characterizations of God as these are utterly valueless and positively misleading unless they are suitably contextualized in a multi-model discourse. It is a point which Professor Flew overlooked – or, worse, parodied – in his criticisms of talk about God's love in the Falsification controversy,[5] and it is a point which few of his critics explicitly recognized. So the first caution to be observed in talking about God is: use as many models as possible, and from these develop the most consistent discourse possible. Never suppose the supply of models has been exhausted.

The second caution we shall need to observe is this. If we are to talk reliably about God we must be alert to the need to fit our discourse at all points to patterns of events in the world around us. The discourse is, as we have seen, derived from models, by no matter how complex a route, and there will always be the possibility – nay more, the necessity – of relating our discourse to events of the world around us. We must always give our language the kind of empirical fit which is exemplified in our earlier illustrations of seedtime and harvest, the moor-land walk, national events, or a monarchical constitution. Talk about God will not be related to the world around us as a scientific hypothesis is related to it. But meaning and relevance is no prerogative of scientific assertions.

These reflections and cautions have already raised a number of points to whose fuller discussion I now turn.

One problem on which we have already touched may be developed as follows: if we speak of God in terms of models such as King and friend and potter and shield, can we express preferences between these models and give reasons for our preferences? Can we speak of one model, for example, King being better than another, for example, shield; of this model, for example, King being less good than that of, say, father; or of some particular model, for example, criminal being quite inadequate? These questions lead us naturally to another problem. To use the concept of model, it might be said, presupposes some independent access to what is modelled, presupposes an original with which the model may be compared. Must not this whole talk of models therefore presuppose some knowledge of God which is quite independent of models and symbols, and against which the success (or failure) of a particular symbol or model can be measured? Indeed, without such an independent access to God, can we ever avoid a sheer relativism? It might be granted by the critic that models may be useful as sermon illustrations, and, in words reminiscent of Locke, may commend theology to those who "have not leisure for learning and logic". Said Locke: "When the hand is used to the plough and the spade, the head is seldom elevated to sublime notions, or exercised in mysterious reasonings. 'Tis well if men of that rank (to say nothing of the other sex) can comprehend plain propositions, and a short reasoning about things familiar to their minds, and nearly allied to their daily experience."[6] Are models, then, along these lines no more than visual aids for those who cannot rise to the transparent view provided by theological concepts? Models may be of psychological and even sociological importance, but (it is alleged) they are of no epistemological or ontological significance. Indeed (it is said) they either beg or by-pass epistemological or ontological questions.[7]

We have here particular versions of two problems which are quite central to contemporary discussions of religious language, the problems respectively of preferences and of reference. The *reference* problem may be formulated as follows: how, with this account of models and disclosures, can we be sure we are talking about God, and not merely about ourselves or, as it is sometimes expressed, about our own "experience"? The problem of *preferences* is: if, as is the case, we have a vast variety of models for God, on what grounds do we grade models, and express a reasonable preference for one model rather than another? We will consider each of these two problems in turn.

The Problem of Reference

Let us first recall that on my view, belief in God arises from what I have called cosmic disclosures, situations where the Universe "comes alive", where a "dead", "dull", "flat" existence takes on "depth" or another "dimension". Such situations can occur on countless occasions of the most varied kind – by a fireside, or on a country walk; on a wind-swept moor, or in the crowds at Charing Cross; while reading the Bible, or attending Mass – there is no situation which cannot in principle give rise to a cosmic disclosure, and some we have examined in greater detail above. Now because of the cosmic character of such a disclosure, because of its all-embracing range, because in it the whole Universe confronts us,[8] I think we are entitled to speak of there being a single individuation expressing itself in each and all of these disclosures. In other words, from any and every cosmic disclosure we can claim to believe in one *x* (where *x* for the moment remains to be elucidated) precisely because we talk of there being "one world".

Now, as will be evident from what has been already said, not even a cosmic disclosure brings with it a privileged interpretation, any more than does any other situation or "experience" (if the word "experience" be allowed). Indeed the principle of choice between different explications is a question I shall face presently when we look at the problem of preferences. Nevertheless, I would claim that it is quite clear that cosmic disclosures are ontologically privileged in so far as they disclose that which confronts us as a basic "given", that which is set over against ourselves in every situation of this kind, that which individuates the Universe.

It is, I hope, evident that on this view when we appeal to "cosmic disclosures" we are not just talking about ourselves, nor merely of our own "experience", we are not just appealing to our own private way of looking at the world. If that were so, then the appeal to cosmic disclosures would be a scarcely-veiled form of atheism, which is what Professor Ninian Smart supposes to be the case.[9] On the contrary, a cosmic disclosure reveals something of whose existence we are aware precisely because we are aware of *being* confronted. Indeed we speak of a disclosure precisely when we acknowledge such a confrontation, something declaring itself to us, something relatively active when we are relatively passive. In a cosmic disclosure the whole Universe is individuated and particularized in this way.

I realize, of course, as I hinted above, that I have not yet given any reasons for speaking of what a cosmic disclosure discloses of *God;* I have given no reasons for talking of the objective reference of a cosmic disclosure in terms of God. But those reasons cannot be given without considering the problem of preferences to which I now turn.

The Problem of Preferences

The cosmic disclosures from which, on my view, belief in God arises are all characterized by some model. This will, I trust, be clear from what I have already said above. But speaking more generally, we may distinguish at least two possibilities. The model may, by development in various ways, have generated the cosmic disclosure. All our earlier examples illustrate that first possibility. But, taking a broader view, we may remark that some cosmic disclosures "just happen". This is the case of what used to be called "religious experience" – when a model would be self-selected – being some kind of focal point – with regard to each particular situation of this type. In other words, a cosmic disclosure will in the one way or in the other supply a model as that which alone enables us to be articulate about what has disclosed itself to us. A cosmic disclosure will supply a model either because it has been generated by the use of the model,[10] or because the situation itself high-lights a particular feature within it. Models are in this way and to this degree, but only in this way and to this degree, self-authenticating. If there is no model, there is no sensible articulation, and no test possible of the claim to have had a cosmic disclosure. Some mystical experiences seem to be in this curious epistemological position, and to be in this way ontologically problematical as well as verbally baffling.

It is at this point that I will take up an earlier footnote[11] and confess that while my use of the word "model" has obvious affinities with a popular use of the word which (as I remarked in the footnote) lies behind the second objection which gave rise to this discussion, nevertheless my use of the word "model" is a somewhat technical one. A theological model is a way of understanding what has been objectively disclosed in a cosmic disclosure; like all models it is never a perfect replica; but it is further and most importantly unlike ordinary "picturing models" (for example, the boy's model train) in that its objective reference is never given independently of the model. It is indeed what I have called a "disclosure model", a type of model not without its parallels in science and elsewhere. If the reader wishes for a more adequate discussion of the general question of the status of a theological model, I would respectfully refer him to my *Models and Mystery* where the topic receives a somewhat fuller treatment. For our present purpose, my point is merely that it is most important not to be misled by features of modelling which do not carry over into the theological cases. We must not assimilate theological models to models which picture their originals. But, it will now be asked, what then in a cosmic disclosure are the models of? How can we claim them to be models of God?

At this point let us recall what was said on the problem of reference. Since there is only *one* reference for *all* disclosure illustrations, it is this which, in ways better or worse, *every* model contrives to talk about. For this purpose, any particular model supplied by a particular cosmic disclosure will have to be incorporated with every other possible model, and this means that its articulation possibilities will have to be earned as it rubs its shoulders with other models. A model will thus establish itself in two ways:

1. By justifiying itself as far as it can alongside other models. Each model enables us to talk in a certain way of what a cosmic disclosure discloses – this we have seen by reference, for example, to the models of father, husband, shepherd, potter, physician, and King. As we have remarked above, we develop discourse from each model only with a constant eye on other models; at various points these other models will supply stop cards to inhibit further discourse in that particular direction. Talk about God thus develops by a mingling of discourse from different models. Now, the more a model can exist successfully in competition with other models, the more justifiably does it provide discourse about what the cosmic disclosure discloses. One model, for example, protector is better than another, for example, laundress, if its discourse is more widely ranging. A model like person is better, than, say shepherd or potter because it can say all that these other models can say and more besides; in this way it can absorb the discourse from two or more models. Summarizing, we might say that this first set of criteria which enables us to express preferences between models is explicitly related to their relative dominance in the discourse.

2. But there are other criteria of preference between models, and these arise from the way the multi-model discourse "fits" the Universe. There is obviously the logical possibility that there could be theological discourse arising from a dominant model which in that way was definitive, which nevertheless failed on this second test. The model of "love" will certainly have to meet the challenge of evil and suffering in the Universe and in this way to grapple with the "problem of evil";[12] but even more importantly there will have to be specific situations which can be legitimately "interpreted by love" if the model of love has any initial justification at all. There must

be a pattern of empirical circumstances which fit "loving" discourse when used of God. Such a fit is pragmatic in the widest sense; but it is not given by experimental vertification in a strict scientific sense. This was the point I tried to make and illustrate in the three groups of examples above. The kind of empirical fit which provides a second set of criteria for preferences between models is much more like the kind of fit which detectives look for between certain new clues and a "theory" of the crime with which they are provisionally working.

But this brings us back to our crucial question. Suppose we have developed discourse as comprehensively, consistently, coherently as possible, making the most economical and coherent development of as many models as possible, and granting that this discourse talks of that "other" which the cosmic disclosure has disclosed to us, can we legitimately say that this is discourse about *God*? Under what conditions do we rightly speak of models being models for God?

Let me answer that question by taking first an illustration I have used elsewhere. Suppose we draw a series of regular polygons with an ever-increasing number of sides, and further draw them such that their vertices are always equidistant from a fixed point. What shall we produce? The plain, down-to-earth man will say: "A lot of polygons" – and he is obviously and undoubtedly correct. But is that the whole story? For my present purpose I hope not. At some point or other, something else, I suggest, may strike us, something else – besides the polygons – is "seen"; something else is "disclosed". We *might* say "a circle". But suppose we had never heard about circles and yet that the disclosure had occurred. Suppose that in these circumstances we then used the symbol x to talk of what was then disclosed, of that to which polygon talk led when it was developed in this way. If now we wanted to speak of x – to contextualize x – talk of polygons would be a good approximation; indeed, it would be the only *reasonable* approximation – because polygon talk has led us to this which had been disclosed. It would, for example, be unreasonable to talk of x in terms of Democracy. Further, the larger its number of sides, the better approximation to x would a polygon be. So that if someone said: "I'd love an x-like swimming pool" we should know that, *reasonably*, he would be more satisfied with a pool of 1008 sides than with one of three sides. In this way, we should talk of what is disclosed by means of approximations we have traversed *en route*, and there would be the possibility of reasonable preferences. Finally, if after all this someone discovered one day a treatise on circles, it might soon become evident that there were close similarities between circle-discourse and *x*-discourse, and on that basis there might be a reasonable recommendation to read "*x*" as "circle".

Now in the same way, we might choose to call what a cosmic disclosure discloses as "*x*" and we have already seen that there could be good grounds for belief in "one *x*". Further, we should then talk about *x* in terms of any model which the various routes to a cosmic disclosure had provided; and we should talk the more reasonably about *x* in terms of this or any model, the longer it had been cautiously developed under checks and balances, which amounts to saying the greater the number of models which had been incorporated into our discourse. Any one model would enable us to be articulate about *x*, in some way or another, but if we wanted to talk as adequately as possible about *x* we should build out the most consistent, comprehensive, coherent, and simple discourse from as many models as possible. Now, if we did this, my contention is that we should see a language emerging which fitted closer and closer to the language which a believer uses about God, and because of this increasing fit, the further we had gone, the more reasonably should we then conclude "For *x*, read God", and the more reasonably should we talk of the models being models of God, and the cosmic disclosure disclosing God.

It is in such ways as these that I should grapple with the various epistemological and ontological problems which are raised by an appeal to disclosures; that I should defend my claim that cosmic disclosures have an inalienable objective reference and my claim that the word "God" can be legitimately used to specify this reference. Further, it is along these lines that I should argue that when the word "God" is so used, we speak of God in terms of discourse derived from models, between which an expression of preferences is possible; and that the word "God" thus derives its meaning in use as and when it is contextualized in multi-model discourse, which is subject both to logical criteria and the criterion of "empirical fit".

This, in outline, is the way in which I would justify my claim that the models occurring in cosmic disclosures are models of the one God, who reveals himself in any and every cosmic disclosure.

. . . Theologians have far too often supposed, and mistakenly, that the most generalized doctrines were most free from all contamination (as it would have been judged) with metaphor, or as I would say, models. But none of us must ever despise the models whence our theological discourse is hewn, for without these we have no way to the cosmic disclosure and no way back to relevance. Without its models, theology will always run the risk of being no more than word-spinning. There is a theological sophistication which, as Mr Heaton remarks is "pitiful self-deception". He continues: "Metaphor – *mere* metaphor – is all we have to help us understand God, no matter how discreetly we try to disguise the fact by thinning out a selection of images into pseudo-philosophical 'doctrines'. The 'fatherhood' of God, the 'Kingship' of God, the 'love' of God, the 'wrath' of God and the rest remain metaphorical because they were and still are attached at some point to human experience. They would be incomprehensible (and therefore useless) if they were not." Only when we remember that will our preaching "become at once more personal, more imaginative and more intelligible". He concludes: "At the moment, it really does seem that we are all desperately afraid of leaving the well-trodden path of theological jargon and of claiming that measure of imaginative freedom which all the great preachers from Amos to St Paul assumed – not as a right, but as a pastoral necessity."

Presented with some theological phrase, then, of whose meaning (if meaning it has) we are doubtful or even inclined to deny, my recipe for understanding it is:

(*a*) Do not be content to take the phrase in isolation, but search for its appropriate context, verbal and non-verbal.
(*b*) At this point try to pick out the model(s) from which the context is derived; these should help us to discover that "basis in fact" for the theological assertion – its bearing on the world around us.
(*c*) At the same time no model will ever be a picturing model; if that occurred the language might seem to be relevant but it could not be *theological*. See, then, how any particular model has been qualified to generate that cosmic disclosure in which I am bound to think that the ultimate ground of all theological assertions will be found.

Theology must always have some fit with the world around us – that is true and a point which it is important to emphasize. Further, this "fit" arises in virtue of the language to which the different models collectively give rise. But those models originate in a cosmic disclosure, and here is the basis for all talk about God.

This I would say is even true of doctrines such as those of the future life, of creation, and of angels. Which means that in all theological assertions the logical stress is always on God. In this sense there is something that we may call a logical imbalance about theological assertions, and this is what the qualifiers help to exhibit. Theological assertions are not flat or uniform as we might say "The cat is on the mat" is flat and uniform. If we speak of God catching men in his net, and gathering them in his drag, do not let us have such an interest in fishing that we revel in developing discourse of the net and drag, and forget that it is not necessarily theology at all. If this seems an incredible mistake, think of those who have lavished time and thought on the details of the Last Assize or the temperature of hell in a way which denied the very character of the God of whom they were talking.

Talk about God, and theological assertions in general, then, point us in two directions: in the one direction to that cosmic disclosure where God reveals himself; and in the other direction to some particular models into whose discourse they fit, discourse which relates to patterns in the world around us. Talk about God must combine understanding and mystery; it must relate to models and disclosures. Meanwhile, the believer is committed to an endless exploration of countless models, in this way constantly improving his understanding of the one God who confronts him in any and every cosmic disclosure.

Christian Doctrine: Some Clues to its Logic. *By a brief reference to a theme from classical doctrinal controversy, this extract shows the kind of bearing which logical empiricism might have on our understanding of patristic debate. It might help us to reach a more reliable formulation of Christian claims, and to decide how far and at what point the controversies were sheer muddle.*

Doctrines are not rightly understood as descriptions of God; they provide rules for, guides to, the best ways of theological talking that we can devise. Christian Doctrines are the most reliable guide we can

Ian T. Ramsey, "Logical Empiricism and Patristics," *studia Patristica V*, ed. F. L. Cross, Akadamie-Verlag, Berlin 1962, pp. 541–46.

produce to the best ways of talking about what God has done in Christ. Doctrines are not photographs of God delivered unambiguously through the conciliar post-bag; they are essays in language, man's endeavours to grapple as consistently and reliably as possible with a mystery about which (*pace* Wittgenstein) he cannot be silent. They are rules for significant stuttering.

Let me illustrate the bearing of contemporary empiricism on patristics by reference to just one doctrine – the *communicatio idiomatum* often described as the principle of the interchange of the properties (ἀντίδοσις τῶν ἰδιωμάτων) – though for contemporary empiricists the title: interchange of names (ἀντίδοσις τῶν ὀνομάτων) obviously promises better things. We are all familiar with expositions of the doctrine in terms such as these: While the human and divine natures in Christ were separate, the attributes of either can be freely interchanged and predicted of the one person of the Saviour, because of the union of the natures in that one person. It was as we are told, anticipated in Tertullian,[13] used by Origen[14] and Augustine,[15] and came to full fruition in Athanasius,[16] being put to good account by Cyril of Alexandria[17] and Leo[18] and restated in the creed of Chalcedon.[19] On the other hand, it puzzled and offended Apollinarius who disliked the degree of separation which the principle seemed to involve and felt compelled to make by contrast such paradoxical assertions as: "God was born", "God was crucified", "God died" so as to spot-light the one nature.[20] It also puzzled Eutyches[21] who, in this respect like Apollinarius could not see how, with one person, there could be other than one nature.

Now, so long as we regard language as homogeneous and descriptive of what are supposed to be broadly similar states of affairs, even if in different worlds, it is difficult to avoid the kind of misgivings voiced by Apollinarius and Eutyches respectively. Nor did orthodoxy help its cause in attempting to explain the principle by analogies from descriptively given phenomena. It was of no help whatever to perpetuate the description-myth by taking wine and water as an account of *perichoresis*.[22] We return to the point later.

Orthodoxy takes something of a turn for the better with Augustine, who considers the union of the natures as having some analogy in ourselves[23] as does Gregory of Nyssa in Oratio Catechetica 10.11. But Gregory goes no further than to say "Let one accept only what is fitting in the likeness, but reject what is incongruous". Cp. Augustine Epist. 137, 3, 11. At the same time both Gregory and Augustine emphasise the point that we can hardly expect to have explanations of christological union, when we cannot even find explanations "of the manner in which the soul is united to the body as to constitute the one person of a man" (Augustine Epist. 137, 11). The logical problem which the doctrine sets out to solve is how to explicate the status of the word "person" when we speak of two "natures" united in one "person". Contemporary empiricism approaching such a doctrine as that of *communicatio idiomatum* would argue that here is a doctrine which gets into hopeless difficulties when it is developed on the assumption that all language is homogeneously descriptive. Let me then set out the problem in its stark simplicity and see the significance of the important and novel logical suggestions which it makes.

The basic problem is that of having two sorts of language about Jesus. On the one hand: he was hungry, he was tired, he had compassion, he wept. On the other hand: by him were all things made, he is eternal, glorified, he will judge the world. Do not let us say: here are two separate "natures". Or rather: do not take such an assertion as if it were descriptive, giving the elements of a quasi-scientific Christological analysis. Take it as a picturesque way of saying: here are two logically different languages; how can they be united?

A problem then immediately arises because two logically different languages cannot readily be mixed without committing the logical blunder of type-trespass,[24] without generating nonsense such as the following: "Muscle = √tendon" (mixing the languagesof physiology and mathematics); "The State is a Wage-earner" (mixing language about a class and language about its members).

And the solution? Two logically different languages can, however, be united (the principle suggests) by language of a different logical order altogether. "Person" must therefore have a logical behaviour different both from terms descriptive of public behaviour – "weeping", "being hungry" and "tired", and from (so-called) "divine" phrases, e.g. "glorified", "eternal". It must indeed be a highly peculiar word. If now we wish to have illustrations of this logical point, the water and wine image is plainly hopeless. Why? Because "water" and "wine", and (say) "soft drink" or "beverage" for the mixture, all these are logical kinsmen – same-type words belonging to descriptive language. Here is a picture utterly devoid of merit. To parallel "Person" and "I" is better, for "I" is a word which interlocks with a vast variety of language. We say of "I" – "I'm a neurotic", "I'm a wage-earner", "I'm a child of God", "I've a soul", "I've a body". We can perhaps see a fresh point in the hints that Gregory of Nyssa and Augustine were making. At the same time it would seem that if "person" includes both the strands mentioned above, then any assertions about the "one person" will be understood by reference to an act of worship, something which implies "what's seen" and more than "what's seen", something which is genuinely mysterious, something whose focus is Jesus Christ. In this sense I think that Nestorius' remark,[25] "Separo naturas, sed conjungo reverentiam" (Nature's distinguished; but "unity" and "reverence" go together) can be accepted without too strained an interpretation. In other words, Nestorius was right to see that the only grounding for such a word as "person" was a situation of reverence and worship. We are reminded that Christological doctrine only arises because a worshipful situation arises around the acknowledged humanity of Jesus.

The *communicatio idiomatum* then is only valuable as a doctrinal slogan. It points up the peculiar and distinctive logical status which the word "person" must have if we are to solve the Christological problem, a status of which "person" as we ordinarily use the word only gives us a broad hint. As I hinted earlier the *communicatio idiomatum* comes dangerously near to being the logical howler it would be if it did not pre-suppose the word "person" with a highly complex logic. In other words, the *communicatio idiomatum* principle is merely a corollary of this concept of "person" and only on that account and in that context escapes being a major blunder.

Meanwhile, let no one weep for the ontology that is lost, or the descriptive view of language it was invented to satisfy. Let our approach to doctrine be dominated by an eye for that odd, variegated language which Christian doctrine must display if it is to be appropriate to its topic. Nor is this a suggestion which comes from the side of philosophy alone. Many years ago Dr Bethune-Baker added a footnote to the chapter on Arianism in his *Early History of Christian Doctrine*, to which I have called attention elsewhere: "All attempts to explain the nature and relations of the Deity must largely depend on metaphor, and no one metaphor can exhaust these relations. . . . From one point of view Sonship is a true description of the inner relations of the Godhead: from another point of view the title Logos describes them best. Each metaphor must be limited by the other."[26] We may be logically nervous over "description" and describe", but to take that footnote seriously would involve a re-writing of patristic theology from quite a new and valuable standpoint.

NOTES

1. The paper incorporates, in a revised form, most of the paper given to the Modern Churchmen's Conference in August 1964 and subsequently printed in *The Modern Churchman*, Vol. VIII, No. 1 (New Series), October 1964; but it has been enlarged by the addition of a new section dealing with various difficulties raised by the views which are set out in what is now the earlier part of the paper.

2. My preference is for the word "model" because, by virtue of its wider use in contemporary philosophical discussion, it carries with it natural logical overtones and takes us at once into a logical context. By contrast with "model", "image" seems to me to have too strong a psychological ancestry, and to beg or to by-pass too many epistemological and ontological questions. For the close relation between model and metaphor see my *Models and Mystery*, Ch. III. I choose "model", then, because it is least likely to prejudice discussion and most likely to direct our attention to logical, epistemological, and ontological issues.

3. I have of course tried to set out the exercise in its logical order; but it may well be that in appropriate circumstances we immediately talk of the world being "friendly" and "co-operative".

4. See, for example, my *Religious Language*, esp. Ch. II.

5. See for example, *New Essays in Philosophical Theology*, ed. A. G. N. Flew and A. MacIntyre (SCM Press), p. 99.

6. *The Reasonableness of Christianity*, ed. I. T. Ramsey, para. 252, p. 76.

7. The reader will already notice, by recalling note 2 above, that part of this objection arises from confusing a model with an image, from thinking of all models as "picturing models", as not only in a popular sense "pictures" but related to their originals as photographs are to that which they picture. For a further discussion, see below, p. 88, and my *Models and Mystery*.

8. Witness such expressions appropriate to cosmic disclosures as "Here I stand, I can no other" (a Luther *contra mundum*), or "You're the *whole world* to me".

9. See, for example, *Theology* LXVIII, No. 535, January 1965, pp. 33–5 with which might be taken *Theology* LXVIII, No. 536, February 1965, pp. 109–11, and *Theology* LXVIII, No. 541, July 1965, pp. 351–2.

10. See the three groups of examples above.

11. Footnote 7 above.

12. That of course was Professor Flew's point in the discussion to which we have referred above.

13. Adv. Prax. 27, "We see the double status, the two not confused but conjoined in one person, God and man". 29, "And the peculiar properties of each substance are preserved intact, so that in him the spirit conducted its own affairs, that is the deeds of power and work and signs . . . and the flesh underwent its sufferings". Cp. De Carne Christi 5. Adv. Marcionem II 27.

14. De Principiis II 63. "All through the Scriptures, not only are human predicates applied to the divine nature, but the human nature is adorned by appellations of divine dignity".

15. De Trinitate I 13, 28.

16. Or. c. Ar. III 31–33, cf. IV 6.7.

17. Cyril ad Nest. II 1, 72 ff. "Since it was the body which had become his own that suffered these things, he himself is said to have suffered on our behalf"; and "inasmuch as it was his own body which by the grace of God tasted death on behalf of everyone, he himself is said to have suffered that death."

18. Tome of Leo, esp. 4.5, "Each nature keeps its own characteristics without diminution . . . one and the same person is truly Son of God and truly Son of Man".

19. Hahn §146, Denzinger §148.

20. See J. F. Bethune-Baker, Introduction to the Early History of Christian Doctrine, 1933, p. 246. Also H. A. Wolfson, loc. cit. Ch. XVI, Sec. IV (a) and J. Draeseke, Apollinarios von Laodicea, Leipzig, 1892 (TU 7), p. 345, 1.27. H. Lietzmann, Apollinarios von Laodicea, Tübingen, 1904, p. 257, 1.15 as quoted by Wolfson on p. 434.

21. See H. A. Wolfson, loc. cit. 444–45; Conc. Const. Sessio VII (Mansi VI.744) quoted H. Bettenson, Docs. Chr. Church, p. 69.

22. Cp. H. A. Wolfson, pp. 418–28 esp. "The attempt on the part of the Fathers to explain the interchange of properties by their perichoresis into one another really means an attempt to explain it by the analogy of the Stoic 'mixture'" (p. 420).

23. De Civ. Dei XIII 24.

24. See Bertrand Russell and A. N. Whitehead, *Principia Mathematica*, Introduction, Ch. II. Bertrand Russell, *Introduction to Mathematical Philosophy*, pp. 53, 135, 185, 188. Gilbert Ryle, "Categories" (Ch. IV of *Logic and Language*, Series II, ed. A. G. N. Flew), and extract 15 above.

25. See J. F. Bethune-Baker, loc. cit. p. 262; Bazaar of Heracleides (G. R. Driver and L. Hodgson) p. 312. Cp. Migne, Patrologia Graeca 77, 193.

26. Loc. cit. p. 160. Cp. my comments in *Religious Language* pp. 183–84.

23

DONALD D. EVANS

An Application to Theology of Logical Insights associated with J. L. Austin. *In this highly original and important work, Professor D. D. Evans is concerned to bring the insights of logical empiricism, and especially those of J. L. Austin, to bear on our understanding of Christian doctrine. This particular passage also introduces us to the very fertile notion of "onlooks".*

. . . If I were to ask you, "What is your attitude to death, or to your present illness, or to your work, or to sex?", your replies would not naturally be preceded by the phrase, "In my opinion". Rather, you would say something like:

"I look on death as the mockery of human hopes (or as the gateway to a higher form of life)."

"I look on my suffering as a wise discipline, imposed by God (or as an opportunity for self-discipline, or as something trivial compared with my growing inner wisdom, or as an annoying interference with my work)."

"I look on my work as a way of making money, no more (or as my one reason for living, or as my calling from God)."

"I look on sex as a sordid animal urge (or as an expression of a profoundly spiritual relation)."

I have coined the word "onlook" as a substantive for what it is to "look on *x* as *y*". It is necessary to coin a word, for no existing word is quite appropriate. The word "view" would be misleading, since it is so close to "opinion", especially in its plural form, "my views

Donald D. Evans, *The Logic of Self-Involvement*, SCM Press 1963, pp. 125–35 249–52. Republished 1969 by Herder & Herder, New York, and used by permission.

tion of a status, function or role to *x* in my own mind, though I may have no official authority to do so in a public way. Thus the Verdictive element sometimes is a sort of private, unofficial Exercitive. Sometimes the conceptual framework is non-literal and highly imaginative: for example, death as a "mockery". Sometimes *x* is placed in a future structural context rather than a present one: for example, Smith as a "future district manager". The onlook sometimes expresses a world-view: for example, "I look on matter as the ultimate reality" or "I look on desire as the source of all evil".

An onlook is not merely speculative, subjective or fanciful; in such cases we would not say, "I look on *x* as *y*", but "I picture *x* as *y*" (for example, atoms as billiard balls), "I *see x* as *y*" (for example, the trick drawing as a rabbit, and then as a duck), or "I *imagine x is y*" (for example, the clouds are warriors). Onlooks are practical, putatively-objective and serious. They are appraised in such terms as profound / superficial, reasonable / unreasonable, true-to-reality / mistaken, adequate / inadequate, coherent / inconsistent.

The formulation of an onlook resembles the forming of an opinion in that it involves a decision that certain words are most appropriate in the matter being considered. The words in onlooks are sometimes not meant literally, – for example, looking on God as a "shepherd" or the State as a "machine" – but they are chosen in all seriousness. The decision that a certain word applies is rather like the forming of a verdict, for example, that a car accident was a case of "negligence". At any rate, the formulation of an onlook is more like the deliberative process leading to a Verdictive performative than it is like applying the word "cat" to a cat (where everyone would agree that it is a cat). The onlook-decision that a word applies is not made arbitrarily; reasons, and sometimes evidence, provide a basis. Indeed, for onlooks as well as for expressions of opinion and various Verdictives, only one of the alternatives may appear to be at all reasonable. Often, of course, it is difficult to abstract and state the reasons or evidence, which are embedded in an individual's total life-experience, an experience which has already been permeated and shaped by various interpretative onlooks.

The combination of Commissive and Verdictive aspects in an expression of onlook is important. In saying, "I look on *x* as *y*", I commit myself to a policy of behaviour and thought and I register my decision that *x* is appropriately described as *y*; my utterance combines an undertaking with a judgment. One cannot abstract what is undertaken (for example, in relation to my suffering) from my view of it (for example, as God's discipline); or rather, if one does abstract some action which is interpreted in terms other than the onlook (for example, refraining from groans), this is at best only a part of what is undertaken. One undertakes to do certain things, viewing them or interpreting them in a certain way. Indeed, the commitment to public behaviour is sometimes much less definite than the commitment to *thought* concerning one's behaviour and concerning others. This is specially evident in some religious onlooks, for example, "I look on each man as a brother for whom Christ died".

In this section we have considered some of the logical features which onlooks have in common. In the next section we shall note some of the important differences among onlooks. Before we do so, however, I should clarify one important matter: the relation between the formulae, "look on *x* as *y*" and "see *x* as *y*". We found that we could not replace "see the drawing as rabbit" by "look on the drawing as a rabbit"; a similar non-equivalence would occur in other cases of simple Gestalt perceptions, where "see *x* as *y*" is logically parallel to "hear *x* as *y*". But there are many cases where we *can* replace "see *x* as *y*" by "look on *x* as *y*"; indeed, it is true of most of my examples of onlooks that, if they had been expressed in terms of "see *x* as *y*", they could have been changed into "look on *x* as *y*" with only a minimal change of meaning:

"I see death as the mockery of human hopes."
"I look on death as the mockery of human hopes."
"I see life as a game."
"I look on life as a game."
"I see myself as a prodigal son seeking divine forgiveness."
"I look on myself as a prodigal son seeking divine forgiveness."
"I see Adenauer as the architect of the new Germany."
"I look on Adenauer as the architect of the new Germany."

Hence onlooks are not restricted to the formula, "look on *x* as *y*", though they are typically and reliably indicated by it. Other formulae which *may* indicate an onlook are, "see *x* as *y*", "regard *x* as *y*", and "think of *x* as *y*".

2.2 *Classification of onlooks*

Some onlooks are quite *literal* in their meaning:

"I look on Smith as a future district manager."
"I look on Brown as the cause of all our trouble."

When it is an established fact that "*x* is *y*", we do not say, "I look on *x* as *y*"; we would not say, "I look on Macmillan as Prime Minister" or "I look on cars as a means of transport". But Smith is not yet a district manager, and Brown's responsibility has not yet been demonstrated. For a literal factual onlook, *x* is not yet *y*, or *x* is not yet known to be *y*; but the procedure for verifying the content of the onlook, "*x* is *y*", is straightforward.

Sometimes, however, an onlook is literal although the speaker and others would agree that "*x* is *y*". For example, if I say, "I look on Jones as my friend", I imply that I think that he *is* my friend. My utterance contains a value-word, "friend", however; the content, "*x* is *y*", is not a statement of fact but a Verdictive (and Commissive) utterance. Hence I can in this case say, "I look on *x* as *y*" and mean it literally, without implying that "*x* is not *y*". This can happen in another sort of case, which is illustrated by the following:

"I look on Smith as a means by which I may gain access to the President."
"I look on my suffering as an opportunity for self-discipline."

Here too, it would not be odd to say, and to mean literally, "Smith *is* a means . . ." or "My suffering *is* an opportunity . . .". Such an utterance, however, would not be a flat Constative; it would be an abbreviated form of the expression of onlook, in which I undertake to make *x become y*. Whether or not "*x* is *y*" is true (or becomes true) depends on whether or not I act in accordance with "I look on *x* as *y*".

Many onlooks, however, are non-literal. When I "look on Henry as a brother", it is not that Henry happens not to be my brother *yet* though he will be some day; and it is not that he is not yet *known* to be my brother, though I suspect that he is. If I say, "I look on Henry as a brother", I imply that Henry is not (strictly or literally) my brother at all. I am comparing Henry with someone who is, or who might be, my brother. Similarly I compare students with parasites, the State with an organism, the vicar with a shepherd. The formula, "I look on *x* as *y*" is applicable in such cases, not because *x* is not yet *y*, or because *x* is not yet known to be *y*, but because *x* is not strictly or literally *y* at all.

Some non-literal comparisons, however, are not open to being expressed in an onlook-formula at all:

"Her cheeks are roses."
"The sun is a sower of light."
"Feelings are the eyes of the heart."

Such metaphors tend to be called "*mere* metaphors", for there is no obvious appropriate attitude to roses, sowers or eyes. If I accept such a metaphor, I do not commit myself to any particular pattern of behaviour or thought. Other metaphors, nevertheless, do have an important attitudinal significance – as we have seen.[1]

When we use the formula "look on *x* as *y*", we assume that there is an appropriate way of thinking and behaving in relation to *y*, so that we are committing ourselves to a similar way of behaving and thinking in relation to *x*. Consider these examples:

"I look on death as the gateway to a spiritual form of life."
"I look on alcoholism as a disease."
"I look on all Tories as vermin."
"I look on my life as a game."
"I look on the vicar as my shepherd."
"I look on God as our father."

It is of course possible that someone may dread a spiritual form of life, or regard disease with moral disapproval, or love vermin, or play all games in deadly earnest, or distrust shepherds, or despise fathers; but if he does, it would be eccentric and misleading to express one of these onlooks. An onlook depends for its communicable meaning on the fact that there is an obviously-appropriate way of behaving or thinking in relation to *y*: the speaker commits himself (though not Indefeasibly) to a similar attitude towards *x*. But there is no sharp dividing-line between onlook-comparisons and metaphors. For example, is "The spider is an artist" an eligible candidate for the formula "look on *x* as *y*"? And some literal onlooks may be ambiguous because we do not know what the speaker regards as the appopriate way of dealing with *y*: for example, a South African says, "I look on Verwoerd as the champion of white supremacy in Africa."

But let us set aside both mere-metaphors on the one hand and literal onlooks on the other, and focus our attention on two main kinds of non-literal onlooks. Consider these two examples:

(I) "I look on all Tories as vermin."
(II) "I look on students as parasites."

In (I), the only similarity between Tories and vermin which the speaker is suggesting is that the feelings and behaviour appropriate in relation to vermin are in some way like those appropriate in relation to Tories; the speaker may have reasons for alleging this similarity of appropriate response, but he does not indicate them. In (II), the speaker alleges a similarity of appropriate response, but his words suggest also an independent similarity as the basis of this: as parasites feed on useful, self-sustaining organisms, so students. . . . Consider some other examples, which illustrate the difference between (I) and (II):

(I) "I look on Henry as a brother."
"I look on Smith as a tool."
"I look on the vicar as my shepherd."
(II) "I look on music as a language."
"I look on alcoholism as a disease."
"I look on Adenauer as the architect of the new Germany."

In the (I)-examples, the similarity which is implied between *x* and *y* is mainly in terms of appropriate attitude: *x* is *such that* the attitude appropriate to *y* is similar to the attitude appropriate to *x*. Henry may or may not have brother-like qualities, Smith may or may not have tool-like qualities, the vicar may or may not have shepherd-like qualities. All we can gather from what the speaker says is that there is something or other about Henry, Smith and the vicar which makes a particular attitude appropriate. Indeed, one may say, "I look on Henry as a brother, but he is *not*", and so on.

The speaker in the (II)-examples suggests a similarity which is independent of any similarity of appropriate attitude. The meaning of "I look on *x* as *y*" can here be readily analysed by abstracting a content (for example, "Alcoholism is a disease") and then adding autobiographical and Commissive elements. Such an analysis is scarcely feasible for the (I)-examples, since the comparison of *x* and *y* involves a reference to the speaker's attitudes. Note also that, for the (II)-examples, it would be odd to add, "but it (he) is not".

I propose that we call the (I)-examples "parabolic onlooks", and the (II)-examples "analogical onlooks". I do not claim that all non-literal onlooks obviously belong to one or other of these classes. Some analogical onlooks are virtually literal, for example, "I look on alcoholism as a disease". And many non-literal onlooks combine analogical and parabolic features: for example, "I look on the State as an organism" suggests various similarities between the State and an organism which can be only *partially* explained without reference to a recommended way of behaving in relation to the State.

The examples of parabolic onlooks which have been given are not in any way bizarre or elusive. We may interpret them as "x is *such that* the attitude appropriate to y is similar to the attitude approxiate to x"; but that "such that" can be filled in if required. The speaker has not said how x is similar to y, but he can do so on request; for example, "I look on Henry as a brother because he has behaved in a brotherly way towards me". The similarity, however, might be much less straightforward:

(*a*) "Henry reminds me of my brother Jim. I can't say what the similarity is, but he does."

(*b*) "My friend John tells me that Henry has in fact behaved in a very brotherly way towards me. John says that he is in a position to know, though he can't explain it to me; and I trust John's word."

These two answers bring us closer to a logical parallel with some parabolic onlooks in religion, where "I look on God as y", but, (*a*) I cannot specify the similarity between God and y, or (*b*) I trust the testimony of someone else (for example, Jesus) that God *is* like y. In either case I can believe that "God is like y" and act accordingly. This is not a matter of acting *as if* I believed that God is like y; for example, it is not a matter of acting as if I believed that God is like a father. Rather, I actually do believe that God is like a father; but what I mean by this is to be explained in terms of human attitudes: I believe that God is *such that* the attitude appropriate to Him is similar to that which is appropriate towards a human father. In the words of Edwyn Bevan:[2]

> The Theist or Christian does not merely say: "Act as if there were a God who is a loving Father, and you will find certain desirable results follow" (that is Pragmatism): he says, "Act as if there were God who is a loving Father, and you will, in so doing, be making the right response to that which God really is. God is really of such a character that, if any of us could know Him as He is (which we cannot do) and then had to describe in human language to men upon earth what we saw, he would have to say: 'What I see is undescribable, but if you think of God as a loving Father, I cannot put the reality to you in a better way than that: that is the nearest you can get.' "

God *is* like a father, but the nature of the likeness is obscure, and I believe in it mainly because I accept the authoritative words of Jesus. In Part II we shall see that biblical talk about God as Creator involves similar parabolic onlooks.

But let us consider a secular example which is logically similar to religious parabolic onlooks. A father says to his small son: "That bare wire is very hot". The son is too young to understand about electricity and shocks, but he knows what a hot thing is, and he knows that it is foolish to touch it, that it causes sudden pain, etc. Hence what the father says is true for practical purposes; the word "hot" serves to inculcate the appropriate attitude. The father accommodates his language to the boy's understanding. Later on, the boy will be able to understand language that is literally true. Similarly God accommodates His revelation to human language and understanding, and later on, after death, we will be able to understand in literal terms.

Now let us consider an example which carries us over the bridge from secular-moral to religious language:

> I look on every human being as a person. By "person" I do not merely mean "human being". What I mean is this: In every person there is something which claims my concern, reverence, personal involvment and acknowledgement of value—my "*agapē*", to use the New Testament word. This attitued does not depend on his particular, observable qualities. A person is a being *such that* "*agapē*" is the appropriate attitude. A person has something extra which makes this attitude appropriate, but I cannto specify this "something extra" except in terms of "*agapē*".

Not everyone, of course, is willing to talk in this way.[3] Some philosophers may think that it is a crude mistake if one fills in the "such that" by a metaphysical entity. What is important to notice here, however, is how such an onlook differs from analogical onlooks, for example, from "I look on alcoholism as a disease". Here the meaning of the onlook's content can be ascertained, and the legitimacy of the onlook can be debated, without reference to attitudes. But in the "person"-onlook, the comparison is an indirect one, involving a reference to attitudes each human being has particular characteristics to which we respond with various attitudes; but to one attitude ("*agapē*") there is no correlative particular-characteristic; that to which this attitude is a correlative response is the man's "person" or "soul". In ordinary parabolic onlooks there is a straightforward way of comparing *x* and *y*, which the speaker merely does not mention, though he could easily do so. But some religious or quasi-religious parabolic onlooks allow no such direct comparison at all; the comparison between *x* and *y* inherently involves a reference to attitudes; and the onlook is used to suggest some metaphysical entity in relationship with me. Such parabolic onlooks may be called "metaphysical".

In this second extract Professor Evans brings his particular development of Austinian analysis to help elucidate the logic of Creation. He shows that the Creation narratives in the Bible, as well as philosophical doctrines of Creation, should all be seen as being expressed in language which, in different ways, is self-involving.

I have shown that "causal" language concerning Creation can be interpreted as an expression of various parabolic onlooks. Appropriate onlook-attitudes are indicated by various interrelated images: potter, builder, victor, magic word, breath of life, self-revealer, and directive purpose. To accept each parable is to adopt an outlook-attitude; the language is self-involving. Also, a non-superficial understanding of each parable requires a life lived in accordance with the onlook; the language is rapportive. (One may accept each parable as a lone individual, but in the biblical context the acceptance is likely to involve a self-identification with a group: "We look on ourselves as pots, formed by a potter".)

At the beginning of this chapter I said that, even if a *human* action is performative (Exercitive, Verdictive or Commissive), impressive-expressive and profound in rationale, it has a causal "core" which we can abstract. If we say, simply, "Jones moves his arm" or "Jones makes pots", our language is neither self-involving nor rapportive. What then is the causal "core" of the divine action which is called "Creation"? In this chapter, I have argued that when the causal element in Creation is abstracted from the elements which are obviously performative, impressive-expressive or profound in rationale, we can only talk about it in parables, in language which is both self-involving and rapportive. Does this mean that Creation is not really an action at all?

No. It does mean, however, that Creation differs from human actions in two important ways. In the first place, human actions are related to particular observables as these are distinguished from other observables: *This* arm would not have moved, *this* pot would still be clay, if Jones had not acted. World-Creation, however, has to do with *any* and *all* observables. If we ask, "What difference would it make if there were no such action?" the answer is, "There would be no events and no entities; there would be nothing at all (except God)". If we ask, further, "What human action is analogous to this action of 'sustaining' everything in existence?" the answer is, "No human action is genuinely analogous; human actions provide only images for parables, and these parables indicate appropriate onlook-attitudes to God."

The first way in which world-Creation differs from human actions is thus its (parabolical) all-inclusiveness. The second way is closely connected with the first. A human action is related to an event or an entity which can be (or could have been) reported *neutrally* – regardless of one's onlooks or other attitudes. A human action may also include elements which cannot be observed and reported neutrally, but there must be this "core". World-Creation, however, has no such "core" which can be observed and reported neutrally – except *everything* (the result of the action); and this "core" does not serve to distinguish the action. World-Creation is distinguished only in terms of onlook-attitudes; world-Creation is an action *such that* various onlook-attitudes are appropriate, various metaphysical parabolic onlooks. Onlooks are not mere metaphors. The expression of an onlook commits me to a way of behaving and thinking, a mode of life. Moreover, such an onlook is not a case of "Let's pretend". I do not merely *act as if* I believed that there is a God who is like a potter (or a victor, etc.) I act in accordance with a positive belief that God *is* like a potter; but I cannot describe this likeness except by referring to human attitudes. The *reality* of God, or of God's action, is not being denied; but what is *meant* by "God the Creator" cannot be abstracted from human attitudes. Indeed, if "reality" is not merely a question of sheer existence but of *importance* to men, then surely the "reality" of God is being strenuously affirmed by anyone who expresses the various parabolic onlooks concerning God the Creator.

In the biblical context there are various parabolic onlooks concerning God the Creator. Some are expressed in "causal" language which *becomes* self-involving when it is used as part of a parable: I look on God as a potter who forms me, a victor over chaos, a man breathing life into me, and so on. Other parabolic onlooks are expressed in language which already *is* self-involving when it is used as part of a parable: I look on myself as God's servant and steward, I look on my own existence as a gift, I look on nature's beneficial regularities as God's pledge, and I look on nature's impressive features as expressions of God's glory. All biblical language concerning God as Creator is parabolic; but this does not detract from the "reality" of the Creator or His action. It does mean that the power, authority and glory of the Creator are recognized or discerned only in so far as we respond to them, and that we respond to them by taking up a group of onlook-attitudes which together form part of a whole religious way of life.

What does this account of Creation indicate concerning other Christian affirmations of faith? I cannot give an adequate answer to this question here, but I shall close this chapter by forestalling one possible misinterpretation: No minimizing of the factual element is *inherent* in my philosophical analysis. Even if the only "matter of fact" which is directly connected with the idea of Creation is the sheer existence of anything and everything, many Christian affirmations (concerning atonement, providence or miracles) may have an inherent connection with particular matters of fact. My analysis does not rule out the possibility of such a connection. On the contrary, it proves a logical framework which may be very useful to theologians who discuss the connection or lack of connection.

NOTES

1. Thomist accounts of metaphor as "analogy of improper proportionality" tend to stress "dynamic likeness" at the expense of the *attitudinal* significance. I shall argue that the latter is primary when metaphors are applied to God. For a Thomist account, see James F. Anderson, *The Bond of Being*, Herder, St Louis, 1949, ch. XIV.

2. *Symbolism and Belief*, London, 1938, pp. 335–36.

3. For a favourable presentation and discussion of this sort of talk, see A. Farrer, *The Freedom of the Will*, London, 1958, pp. 305–8, and *Faith and Logic* (ed. B. Mitchell), London, 1957, pp. 15–21.

24

E. E. EVANS-PRITCHARD

The logical peculiarities of Religious Discourse: An example from a non-Christian religion. *In this extract Professor Evans-Pritchard elucidates some of the features of religious language by taking examples from a different religion altogether, that of the Nuer tribe. The examples show the use made of metaphor and poetry, how paradox arises in this brand of religious discourse, and there is in particular a discussion of language about the Spirit. Broadly speaking, the language can be seen as an attempt to talk about God in terms of correlated signs of his divine activity, and the extract can be profitably read alongside those from Maimonides.*

Nuer do not claim to see God, nor do they think that anyone can know what he is like in himself. When they speak about his nature they do so by adjectives which refer to attributes, such as "great" and "good", or in metaphors taken from the world around them, likening his invisibility and ubiquity to wind and air, his greatness to the universe he has created, and his grandeur to an ox with widespread horns. They are no more than metaphors for Nuer, who do not say that any of these things is God, but only that he is like (*cere*) them. They express in these poetic images as best they can what they think must be some of his attributes.

Nevertheless, certain things are said, or may be said, "to be" God – rain, lightning, and various other natural – in the Nuer way of speech, created – things which are of common interest. There is here an ambiguity, or an obscurity, to be elucidated, for Nuer

E. E. Evans-Pritchard, *Nuer Religion*, 1956, pp. 123–26, 131–32, 139–43.

are not now saying that God or Spirit is like this or that, but that this or that "is" God or Spirit. Elucidation here does not, however, present great difficulties.

God being conceived of as in the sky, those celestial phenomena which are of particular significance for Nuer, rain and lightning, are said, in a sense we have to determine, to be him. There is no noun denoting either phenomenon and they can only be spoken of by verbs indicating a function of the sky, as "*ce nhial deam*", "the sky rained", and "*ce nhial mar*", "the sky thundered". Also pestilences, murrains, death, and indeed almost any natural phenomenon significant for men are commonly regarded by Nuer as manifestations from above, activities of divine being. Even the earthly totems are conceived of as a relationship deriving from some singular intervention of Spirit from above in human affairs. It is chiefly by these signs that Nuer have knowledge of God. It might be held, therefore, that the Nuer conception of God is a conceptualization of events which, on account of their strangeness or variability as well as on account of their potentiality for fortune or misfortune, are said to be his activities or his activities in one or other of his hypostases or refractions. Support for such a view might be found in the way Nuer sometimes speak of one or other of these effects. They may say of rain or lightning or pestilence "*e kwoth*", "it is God", and in storms they pray to God to come to earth gently and not in fury – to come gently, it will be noted, not to make the rain come gently.

I do not discuss this ontological question here beyond saying that were we to suppose that such phenomena are in themselves regarded as God we would misunderstand and misrepresent Nuer religious thought, which is pre-eminently dualistic. It is true that for them there is no abstract duality of natural and supernatural, but there is such a duality between *kwoth*, Spirit, which is immaterial rather than supernatural, and *cak*, creation, the material world known to the senses. Rain and lightning and pestilences and murrains belong to this created world and are referred to by Nuer as *nyin kwoth*, instruments of God.

Nevertheless, they and other effects of significance for men are οιοσημία, signs or manifestations of divine activity; and since Nuer apprehend divine activity in these signs, in God's revelation of himself to them in material forms, the signs are, in a lower medium, what they signify, so that Nuer may say of them "*e kwoth*", "it is God". Rain and pestilence come from God and are therefore manifestations of him, and in this sense rain and pestilence are God, in the sense that he reveals himself in their falling. But though one can say of rain or pestilence that it is God one cannot say of God that he is rain or pestilence. This would make no sense for a number of reasons. In the first place, the situation could scarcely arise, God not being an observable object, in which Nuer would require or desire to say about him that he is anything. In the second place, the worth *kwoth* does not here refer to a particular refraction of Spirit, a spirit, but to Spirit in its oneness, God, and he could not be in any way identified with any one of his manifestations to the exclusion of all the others. A third, and the most cogent, reason is that rain is water which falls from the sky and pestilence is a bodily condition and they are therefore in their nature material things and not Spirit. Indeed, as a rule, rain is only thought of in connexion with Spirit, and is therefore only said to be Spirit, when it does not fall in due season or falls too much or too violently with storm and lightning – when, that is, the rain has some special significance for human affairs. This gives us a clue to what is meant when Nuer say of something that it is God or that it is a spirit of the air, as thunder may be said to be the spirit *wiu* or a prophet of the spirit *deng* may be said to be *deng* – especially as Nuer readily expand such statements by adding that thunder, rain, and pestilence are all instruments (*nyin*) of God or that they are sent by (*jak*) God, and that the spirit *deng* has filled (*gwang*) the prophet through whom it speaks. In the statement here that something is Spirit or a spirit the particle *e*, which we translate "is", cannot therefore have the meaning of identity in a substantial sense. Indeed, it is because Spirit is conceived of in itself, as the creator and the one, and quite apart from any of its material manifestations, that phenomena can be said to be sent by it or to be its instruments. When Nuer say of rain or lightning that it is God they are making an elliptical statement. What is understood is not that the thing in itself is Spirit but that it is what we would call a medium or manifestation or sign of divine activity in relation to men and of significance for them. What precisely is posited by the hearer of any such elliptical statement depends on the nature of the situation by reference to which it is made. A vulture is not thought of as being in itself Spirit; it is a bird. But if it perches on the crown of a byre or hut Nuer may say "*e kwoth*", "it is Spirit", meaning that its doing so is a spiritual signal presaging disaster. A lion is not thought of as being in itself Spirit; it is a beast. But it may, on account of some event which brings it into a peculiar relation to man, such as being born, as Nuer think sometimes happens, as twin to a human child, be regarded as a revelation of Spirit for a particular family and lineage. Likewise, diseases, or rather their symptoms, are not thought of as being in themselves Spirit, but their appearance in individuals may be regarded as manifestations of Spirit for those individuals. Spirit acts, and thereby reveals itself, through these creatures.

It seems odd, if not absurd, to a European when he is told that a twin is a bird as though it were an obvious fact, for Nuer are not saying that a twin is like a bird but that he is a bird. There seems to be a complete contradiction in the statement; and it was precisely on statements of this kind recorded by observers of primitive peoples that Lévy-Bruhl based his theory of the prelogical mentality of these peoples, its chief characteristic being, in his view, that it permits such evident contradictions – that a thing can be what it is and at the same time something altogether different. But, in fact, no contradiction is involved in the statement, which, on the contrary, appears quite sensible, and even true, to one who presents the idea to himself in the Nuer language and within their system of religious thought. He does not then take their statements about twins any more literally than they make and understand them themselves. They are not saying that a twin has a beak, feathers, and so forth. Nor in their everyday relations with twins do Nuer speak of them as birds or act towards them as though they were birds. They treat them as what they are, men and women. But in addition to being men and women they are of a twin-birth, and a twin-birth is a special revelation of Spirit; and Nuer express this special character of twins in the "twins are birds" formula because twins and birds, though for different reasons, are both associated with Spirit and this makes twins, like birds, "people of the above" and "children of God", and hence a bird a suitable symbol in which to express the special relationship in which a twin stands to God. When, therefore, Nuer say that a twin is a bird they are not speaking of either as it appears in the flesh. They are speaking of the *anima* of the twin, what they call his *tie*, a concept which includes both what we call the personality and the soul; and they are speaking of the association birds have with Spirit through their ability to enter the realm to which Spirit is likened in metaphor and where Nuer think it chiefly is, or may be. The formula does not express a dyadic relationship between twins and birds but a triadic relationship between twins, birds, and God. In respect to God twins and birds have a similar character.

. . . When Nuer say of something "*e kwoth*", "it is Spirit", or give it a name of which it can be further said "that is Spirit", the "is" does not in all instances have the same connotation. It may be an elliptical statement, signifying that the thing referred to is a manifestation of Spirit in the sense of God revealing himself in instruments or effects. Or it may be a symbolical statement, signifying that what in itself is not Spirit but represents Spirit to certain persons is for these persons Spirit in such contexts as direct attention to the symbolic character of an object to the exclusion of whatever other qualities it may possess. Or it may be a statement signifying something closer to identity of the thing spoken of with what it is said to be, Spirit. The statements never, however, signify complete identity of anything with Spirit, because Nuer think of Spirit as something more than any of its modes, signs, effects, representations, and so forth, and also as something of a different nature from the created things which they are. They are not able to define what it is, but when it acts within the phenomenal world they say it has come from above, where it is conceived to be and whence it is thought to descend. Consequently Spirit in any form can be detached in the mind from the things said to be it, even if they cannot always be so easily detached from the idea of Spirit.

I can take the analysis no farther; but if it is inconclusive it at least shows, if it is correct, how wide of the mark have been anthropological attempts to explain the kind of statements we have been considering. Anthropological explanations display two main errors. The first, best exemplified in the writings of Lévy-Bruhl, is that when a people say that something is something else which is different they are contravening the Law of Contradiction and substituting for it a law of their own prelogical way of thinking, that of mystical participation. I hope at least to have shown that Nuer do not assert identity between the two things. They may say that one is the other and in certain situations act towards it as though it were that other, or something like it, but they are aware, no doubt with varying degrees of awareness, and readily say, though with varying degrees of clarity and emphasis, that the two things are different. Moreover, it will have been noted that in the seemingly equivocal statements we have considered, with perhaps one exception, the terms cannot be reversed. The exception is the statement that twins are birds, because it can also be said that birds are twins. That a hatch of birds are twins is a statement, to which we also can give assent, which does not derive logically from the statement that twins are birds but from a perception independent of that proposition; so it does not concern our problem. Rain may be said to be God but God cannot be said to be rain; a cucumber may be called an ox but an ox cannot be called a cucumber; and the crocodile may be said to be Spirit but Spirit cannot be said to be the crocodile. Consequently these are not statements of identity. They are statements not that something is other than it is but that in a certain sense and in particular contexts something has some extra quality which does not belong to it in its own nature; and this quality is not contrary to, or incompatible with, its nature but something added to it which does not alter what it was but makes it something more, in respect to this quality, than it was. Consequently, no contradiction, it seems to me, is involved in the statements.

Whether the predicate refers to a conception or to a visible object the addition makes the subject equivalent to it in respect to the quality which both now have in common in such contexts as focus the attention on that quality alone. The things referred to are not the same as each other but they are the same in that one respect, and the equivalence, denoted by the copula, is not one of substance but of quality. Consequently we cannot speak here, as Lévy-Bruhl does, of mystical participation, or at any rate not in his sense of the words, because the two things are not thought to be linked by a mystical bond but simply by a symbolic nexus. Therefore, what is done to birds is not thought to affect twins, and if a totem is harmed the spirit of that totem may be offended but it is not harmed by the harm done to the totemic creature.

That the relation between the thing said to be something else and that something else it is said to be is an ideal one is indeed obvious, but anthropological explanations of modes of primitive thought as wide apart as those of Tylor, Max Müller, and Lévy-Bruhl, are based on the assuption that though for us the relation is an ideal one primitive peoples mistake it for a real one; and those anthropologists who sponsor psychological explanations often make the same assumption. This is the second error. If my interpretation is correct, Nuer know very well when they say that a crocodile is Spirit that it is only Spirit in the sense that Spirit is represented to some people by that symbol just as they know very well that a cucumber is only an ox in the sense that they treat it as one in sacrifice. That they do not mistake ideal relations for real ones is shown by many examples in this book: the identification of a sacrificial spear with that of the ancestor (p. 240), the identification of man with ox in sacrifice (p. 262), the identification of a man's herd with that of the ancestor of his clan (p. 258), the identification of sickness and sin in a sacrificial context (pp. 191–2), and the identification of the left hand with death and evil (pp. 233–6). It is shown also in the symbolism of many of their rites, where their purpose is expressed in mimicry (pp. 231–2).

I think that one reason why it was not readily perceived that statements that something is something else should not be taken as matter-of-fact statements is that it was not recognized that they are made in relation to a third term not mentioned in them but understood. They are statements, as far as the Nuer are concerned, not that A is B, but that A and B have something in common in relation to C. This is evident when we give some thought to the matter. A cucumber is equivalent to an ox in respect to God who accepts it in the place of an ox. A crocodile is equivalent to Spirit only when conceived of as a representation of God to a lineage. Consequently, though Nuer do not mistake ideal relations for real ones, an ideal equivalence is none the less true for them, because within their system of religious thought things are not just what they appear to be but as they are conceived of in relation to God.

This implies experience on an imaginative level of thought where the mind moves in figures, symbols, metaphors, analogies, and many an elaboration of poetic fancy and language; and another reason why there has been misunderstanding is that the poetic sense of primitive peoples have not been sufficiently allowed for, so that it has not been appreciated that what they say is often to be understood in that sense and not in any ordinary sense. This is certainly the case with the Nuer, as we see in this chapter and in many places elsewhere in this book, for example, in their hymns. In all their poems and songs also they play on words and images to such an extent that no European can translate them without commentary from Nuer, and even Nuer themselves cannot always say what meaning they had for their authors. It is the same with their cattle-

and dance-names, which are chosen both for euphony and to express analogies. How Nuer delight in playing with words is also seen in the fun they have in making up tongue-twisters, sentences which are difficult to pronounce without a mistake, and slips of the tongue, usually slips in the presence of mothers-in-law, which turn quite ordinary remarks into obscenities. Lacking plastic and visual arts, the imagination of this sensitive people finds its sole expression in ideas, images, and words.

In this and the last chapter I have attempted to lay bare some features of the Nuer conception of Spirit. We are not asking what Spirit is but what is the Nuer conception of *kwoth*, which we translate "Spirit". Since it is a conception that we are inquiring into, our inquiry is an exploration of ideas. In the course of it we have found that whilst Nuer conceive of Spirit as creator and father in the heavens they also think of it in many different representations (what I have called refractions of Spirit) in relation to social groups, categories, and persons. The conception of Spirit has, we found, a social dimension (we can also say, since the statement can be reversed, that the social structure has a spiritual dimension). We found also that Spirit, in the Nuer conception of it, is experienced in signs, media, and symbols through which it is manifested to the senses. Fundamentally, however, this is not a relation of Spirit to things but a relation of Spirit to persons through things, so that, here again, we are ultimately concerned with the relation of God and man . . .

SELECT TOPICS